W9-CHY-937

OFF THE BEATEN PATH™ SERIES

Ohio

SEVENTH EDITION

Off the Beaten Path™

by George and Carol Zimmermann

The Globe Pequot Press

Old Saybrook, Connecticut

Copyright © 1983, 1985, 1988, 1991, 1993, 1996, 1998 by George and Carol Zimmermann

All rights reserved. No part of this book may be reproduced or transmitted in any form by any means, electronic or mechanical, including photocopying and recording, or by any information storage and retrieval system, except as may be expressly permitted by the 1976 Copyright Act or by the publisher. Requests for permission should be made in writing to The Globe Pequot Press, P.O. Box 833, Old Saybrook, Connecticut 06475.

Off the Beaten Path is a trademark of The Globe Pequot Press.

Cover photo by Images © PhotoDisc, Inc.
Cover and text design by Laura Augustine
Maps created by Equator Graphics © The Globe Pequot Press
Illustrations on pages 172 and 190 by Carole Drong. All other illustrations by Keith Knore.

Library of Congress Cataloging-in-Publication Data

Zimmermann, George, 1952-Zimmermann, Carol, 1954
     Ohio : off the beaten path / George and Carol Zimmermann; illustrated by Keith Knore. —
7th ed.
     p. cm. —(Off the beaten path series)
  Includes index.
  ISBN 0-7627-0273-7
  1. Ohio—Guidebooks. I. Zimmermann, Carol, 1954- II. Title. III. Series.
  F489.3.Z55   1998
  917.7104´43—dc21   98-35828
                                              CIP

Manufactured in the United States of America
Seventh Edition/First Printing

To Brian, America's best son.

NORTHWEST OHIO

Toledo

NORTHEAST OHIO

Cleveland

Akron

Lima

Mansfield

Canton

WEST CENTRAL OHIO

EAST CENTRAL OHIO

Newark

Columbus

Dayton

Lancaster

SOUTHWEST OHIO

SOUTHEAST OHIO

Cincinnati

Contents

Acknowledgments

Our thanks to the Ohio Department of Natural Resources and the Ohio Historical Society for providing supplemental information and materials about many of the places described in this book. Their cooperation made researching *Ohio: Off the Beaten Path*™ a productive and enjoyable endeavor.

Introduction

Ohio is an excellent state to explore—it has breathtaking natural beauty, a rich historical heritage, countless fine restaurants, and varied and unique overnight lodging. *Ohio: Off the Beaten Path*™ exposes the reader to Ohio's best—from rolling pastoral farmland to rugged wooded cliffs and gorges, from restored canal towns and gristmills to country inns and working historical farms. After years of researching and traveling the state, we can only conclude that Ohio offers a wealth of opportunities for recreation, for appreciating the history that shaped its present and future, and for pleasurable excursions to suit any tastes or interests.

Most of the destinations described in this book, be they historical, culinary, or recreational, are located away from interstate highways and major metropolitan areas—an indication of our preference for scenic roads and picturesque towns and villages (traveling by interstate highway just does not provide the enjoyment of winding through forests and cresting hills on a narrow, two-lane country road). To take full advantage of *Ohio: Off the Beaten Path*™, you will need an Ohio highway map. The Ohio Division of Travel and Tourism will mail you a map at no charge if you call 1–800–BUCKEYE. That toll-free number can also provide another valuable service—confirmation of specific information on thousands of sites and attractions around the state. Although every effort has been made to ensure that addresses, phone numbers, rates, hours, and seasons of the places described in this book are accurate at the time of publication, establishments do change owners or hours of operation, relocate, and even close. For this reason, we advise taking advantage of the state's toll-free service to verify important information before making that two- or three-hour drive. Another excellent resource is the Division of Travel and Tourism's web site, www.ohiotourism.com, which includes links to hundreds of other Ohio tourism web sites.

Whether spending a week, a weekend, or just an afternoon traveling to a new destination, you will probably find as we did that Ohio's friendly people and splendid countryside make any trip that much more rewarding. And if you have yet to experience the state's historic and recreational opportunities, we believe you will be impressed and amazed by all Ohio has to offer.

Prices at the restaurants in *Ohio: Off the Beaten Path*™ are typical for the region. At most of those included in this book, you'll find lunch selections from $5.00 to $12.00 and dinner entrees from $8.00 to $20.00. For more specific pricing information, call ahead to the restaurant of your choice.

The prices and rates listed in this guidebook were confirmed at press time. We recommend, however, that you call establishments before traveling to obtain current information.

Cuyahoga Valley

Tranquil, stream-fed Chippewa Lake provides the setting for an outstanding country dining establishment, the **Oaks Lodge.** Eight acres of tall trees surround this rambling former estate, which rests a stone's throw from the water. Railroad industrialist J. F. Townsend remodeled this former farmhouse in 1914, using it to entertain such captains of industry as J. Pierpont Morgan. Townsend dubbed the place Five Oaks for the semicircle of oak trees that graced the front of the home at the time.

Don Casper and Al Hitchins purchased the property in 1961 and earned a reputation for an innovative menu and an impressive kitchen. Each of the four dining areas has its own distinct character, and the large windows allow a view of the large patio—a perfect spot for a cocktail or after-dinner drink—and the gazebo at water's edge.

Dinner at the Oaks Lodge includes dishes such as rack of lamb, roast prime rib (Friday and Saturday only), several cuts of steak, and veal gesina, which is veal sautéed in wine, butter, and mushrooms. Seafood fans can choose from Alaskan king crab legs, fresh pickerel, shrimp tempura, and the broiled shore dinner—a combination of orange roughy, scampi, tomatoes, mushrooms, peppers, and onions served on a skewer. A favorite with many regulars here is the broiled scampi in parsley and garlic butter served in individual chafing dishes.

A fine dinner salad distinguishes a quality restaurant from an ordinary one, and an Oaks Lodge salad comes brimming with carrots, cucumbers, and tomatoes. For your choice of potato, try the unusual potatoes Anna—pan-fried spuds smothered in onions and peppers. The lodge's luxurious desserts include Grand Marnier chocolate mousse, chocolate cheesecake, and an assortment of parfaits. From the fresh flowers and stylish decor (the lodge has won several awards for interior design) to the culinary expertise, the Oaks Lodge rates high marks.

The Oaks Lodge is on Medina County Road 19 on the Lake at Chippewa; (800) 922-5736, (216) 769-2601. Open Monday through Saturday,

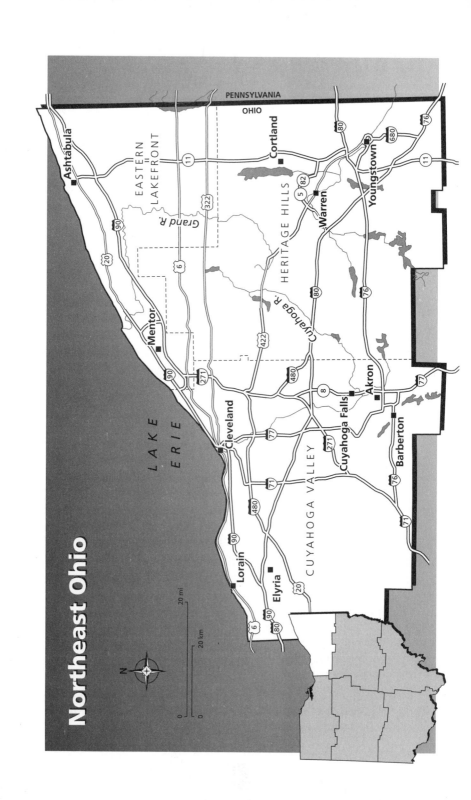

5:00–10:00 P.M.; Sunday, 3:00–9:00 P.M. American Express, MasterCard, and Visa are accepted.

Medina County is also the location of a unique annual occurrence—Ohio's equivalent of the swallows returning to Capistrano. Each year on March 15, seventy-five turkey vultures come home to roost in trees by the cliffs and caverns of Whipp's Ledges near Hinckley. With clocklike regularity, the buzzards have returned to this summer home for the past 150 years. Hinckley townspeople mark the occasion with celebrations on the first Sunday after March 15, when a "buzzard breakfast" is served.

The architect was Arthur Oviatt; the owner, Arthur Lovett Garford. The result: one of the finest residences in northeast Ohio, now the *Hickories Museum.*

Construction on this massive nineteen-room stone-and-shingle home began in 1894, lasted two and a half years, and cost Garford $100,000. On the three-and-one-half-acre lot stand many of the original shagbark hickory trees from which came the name Hickories.

Within its walls are Tiffany-style windows, six fireplaces, twelve built-in seats, and approximately sixty carved faces. Features of the grand staircase are pier mirrors, a Gothic chapel, and a bull moose head given to Mr. Garford by Teddy Roosevelt. An opulent Victorian bathroom as well as a recently restored master bedroom and guest room can be seen on the second floor.

Garford was a young banker when he hopped on a newfangled high-wheeled vehicle, the bicycle. A rough ride on the bike's hard seat launched a new career for A. L.—he invented a padded bicycle seat, which made him a millionaire. His interests would grow to include such diverse items as golf balls, telephone parts, lighting fixtures, and steel; he also became involved in car and truck manufacturing, mining, and publishing.

The Hickories Museum is at 509 Washington Avenue, Elyria; (440) 322–3341. Open March through December, Tuesday through Friday, 11:00 A.M.–4:00 P.M. Admission: $3.50 for adults, $1.00 for children.

Founded in 1917, the **Allen Memorial Art Museum** at Oberlin College is ranked as one of the finest college or university collections in the nation. Cass Gilbert designed the original building; he also designed four other buildings for Oberlin College between 1907 and 1931. The museum's contemporary addition opened in 1977.

The museum's collection consists of some 14,000 objects ranging from ancient Egypt to contemporary America. Collection highlights include strength in Dutch and Flemish paintings of the seventeenth century, European art of the late nineteenth and twentieth centuries, and contemporary American art. Of particular note are the Mary A. Ainsworth collection of Japanese woodblock prints, the Charles Martin Hall collection of Islamic carpets, the Joseph and Enid Bissett collection of modern European paintings, and a comprehensive collection of Old Master prints, including Rembrandt and Durer. In addition to the galleries, a number of sculptures can be found on the museum's well-manicured grounds.

The Allen Memorial Art Museum is at 87 North Main Street, Oberlin; (440) 775–8665. Open Tuesday through Saturday, 10:00 A.M.–5:00 P.M.; Sunday, 1:00–5:00 P.M. No admission charge.

Take the high road or take the low road, but those wishing for a wee bit of Scotland in Ohio should take to the road in late June to celebrate the Ohio Scottish Game Weekend, in Oberlin. Visitors can enjoy the colorful Scottish games and the traditional dress in the parade of clan tartans. In addition there is a competition among the pipe and drum corps. The event is held in late June in Oberlin. Call (440) 442–2147 for information.

If you hanker for shopping as it was in the good old days, before there were huge malls and frozen yogurt, then drop in at *Durkee's General Store* in Grafton. Here you'll find oiled oak floors, a large red coffee grinder, a pot-bellied stove, and an open cracker barrel. Proprietor Dave Bescan, a descendant of Horace Durkee, who established this enterprise back in 1889, mixes history and commerce at this family-run business. Looking for bib overalls, a sausage grinder, or corncob-smoked bacon slabs? Dave's got them, along with apple peelers, washboards, Civil War hardtack, cowbells, lye soap, rock candy, oil lamps, and hundreds of other unique items.

Grafton is also the site of an annual tobacco-spitting contest. Contestants are judged for both distance and accuracy, with brass spittoons awarded to the winners.

Durkee's General Store is at 919 Main Street, Grafton; (440) 926–3488. Open Monday through Saturday, 10:00 A.M.–5:30 P.M.

One of the top ten car collections, according to *Car Collector* magazine, is the *Crawford Auto Aviation Museum* in Cleveland. The collection tells the history of technological as well as stylistic changes and developments in the auto industry. With some 200 cars in the collection, the vehicles range from the famous to the obscure, from a Model T to a modern Jaguar. For example, the visitor can admire a rare 1897 Panhard et Lavassor, which was the first automobile to enclose the passenger area and protect the occupants from the elements. The car enthusiast can also view the 1982 Indy car driven by Ohio's own Bobby Rahal.

Since car manufacturing is now centered on a few, dominant companies, many people may not know just how many small automotive manufacturers existed in the early 1900s. The Crawford Auto Aviation Museum highlights the remarkable number of carmakers, which were located in the Cleveland area. Between 1898 and 1931 more than eighty makes of cars were produced here, including the Winton Bullet. Alexander Winton was the leading automotive pioneer in Cleveland, selling his first car in 1898. The Winton Bullet held the land speed record in 1902 and is on display in the museum.

Along with the car collection, the museum also features bikes, motorcycles, and aircraft. The centerpiece of the aviation collection is a 1912

Curtiss Hydroaeroplane, which was once piloted by Cleveland aviator Al Engel. Along with the permanent collection, the museum also hosts special exhibits and shows related to cars and aircraft.

This museum is part of a larger complex, the Western Reserve Historical Society's University Circle. This campuslike setting also houses a History Museum in a turn-of-the-century mansion. A visitor to this museum can go on a mansion tour and view a costume collection, exhibits on the settlement of the Cleveland area, and various special displays. Also in the complex is the renowned Cleveland Museum of Art. The University Circle library is one of the best genealogical resources in the nation.

The Crawford Auto Aviation Museum is located at 10825 East Boulevard, Cleveland; (216) 721-5722. Open Monday through Saturday, 10:00 A.M.–5:00 P.M.; Sunday, noon–5:00 P.M. Admission: adults $6.50; children (6 to 12) $4.50.

Perhaps the most famous exhibit at the *Health Museum of Cleveland* is Juno, the "Transparent Talking Woman." This plastic replica of the human body, with all organs in place and visible, has been entertaining and educating for more than four decades. This popular exhibit is named for the goddess Juno, who is recognized as the embodiment of virtue and protectress of women.

Your next stop might be the Giant Tooth, a model of a real lower-left, first molar enlarged 384 times to an impressive height of 18 feet and weight of more than two tons. Or see the model of the Bates Baby, the largest baby born in the state of Ohio, weighing in at twenty-three and three-quarters pounds at birth.

In the Theater of Hearing, you'll learn the story of sound, and you can test how well you hear, how you sound to others, and whether you are tone deaf. If you're traveling with children, you'll probably spend the most time in the Family Discovery Center, with its many hands-on exhibits geared for youngsters. Other museum exhibits highlight topics such as aging, breast examination, vision, and human sexuality.

The Health Museum of Cleveland is at 8911 Euclid Avenue, Cleveland; (216) 231-5050. Open Monday through Friday, 9:00 A.M.–5:00 P.M.; Saturday, 10:00 A.M.–5:00 P.M.; Sunday, noon–5:00 P.M. Admission: adults, $4.50; children, $3.00.

If you haven't had your fill of health and science, head down Euclid Avenue to the *Dittrick Museum of Medical History*. This museum presents the medical history of Cleveland and the Western Reserve. Exhibits trace advances in diagnostic technology from the stethoscope to the Xray machine. Visitors inspect an array of early surgical instruments, bloodletting tools, and the museum's collection of microscopes. Also featured are two complete and furnished doctors' offices, one from 1880 and the other from 1930.

The Dittrick Museum of Medical History is at 11000 Euclid Avenue, Cleveland; (216) 368–3648. Open Monday through Friday, 10:00 A.M.–5:00 P.M. No admission charge.

Most critics have and will continue to debate the location of the "birthplace" of rock and roll, but there's no debate that Cleveland has now provided a home for rock with the opening of the *Rock and Roll Hall of Fame and Museum.* The spectacular $92-million facility overlooks Lake Erie. Designed by renowned architect I. M. Pei, the 50,000-square-foot building consists of bold geometric forms and dramatic spaces anchored by a 162-foot tower.

Rock fans of all ages will discover memorabilia from all phases of rock and roll, from its birth in the fifties, its explosion in the sixties, and its evolution to the present. Among the highlights of this most extensive collection are John Lennon's Sgt. Pepper uniform and the Rickenbacker guitar he used at the Shea Stadium concert, the black leather stage outfit Elvis wore during his 1968 "comeback" TV special, Tina Turner's "Acid Queen" costume from the movie *Tommy,* Jim Morrison's Cub Scout uniform, and Jimi Hendrix's handwritten lyrics to "Purple Haze." The original recording equipment from Sam Phillips's Memphis Recording Service is on display, along with Janis Joplin's psychedelic Porsche convertible.

Music plays throughout the museum, except in the actual top-floor Hall of Fame. Film and video presentations trace the history of rock and offer snapshots of its various incarnations and tangents. If you are or ever have been a fan of rock and roll, this is a must see.

The Rock and Roll Hall of Fame and Museum is at One Key Plaza, Cleveland; (888) 764–ROCK, (216) 781–7625. Open daily, 10:00 A.M–5:30 P.M. (until 9:00 P.M. on Wednesday). Admission: adults, $14.95; children (ages 4 to 11), $11.50. Entrance is by timed tickets.

The original homes of the Shakers, a religious colony founded in 1822,

Talk about "necessity being the mother of invention"! The mayor of North Olmsted was given one week's notice that the railway connecting his community with Cleveland was calling it quits. Mayor Charles Seltzer had until midnight February 28, 1931, to find a way to get 150 of his constituents to work.

His solution: that North Olmsted start a municipal bus line, the first in Ohio. City Council concurred, and they all scrambled to purchase two used buses and two sets of license plates and hire two drivers. At 5:00 A.M. March 1, two freshly painted red and white coaches hit the road, changing Ohio transportation history.

has been lost to time. However, the unique and eloquently simple furniture that this sect produced has been preserved and is exhibited at the *Shaker Historical Museum*. The hand-made furniture along with other objects from the Shaker community are displayed in a Tudor mansion that was built on the site of the largest of the original Shaker residences. The museum overlooks Shaker Lake in Shaker Heights, which was once called the North Union Colony.

The Shaker community had branches throughout the northeastern United States. It was a religion that stressed a simple lifestyle and the virtues of social justice, equality, and freedom. In the mid-1800s, more than 200 people lived and worked in the North Union Colony. Before mass production of furniture put them out of business, Shaker furniture was in demand because of its high quality and simple, functional form. Replicas and miniatures of some of the Shaker pieces are available in the gift shop.

The Shaker Historical Museum is located at 16740 South Park Boulevard, Shaker Heights; (216) 921-1201. Open: Tuesday through Friday and Sunday, 2:00–5:00 P.M. No admission charge.

The Western Reserve region of Ohio was "reserved" for settlers moving west from Connecticut after the American Revolution. One of those settlers, Jonathan Hale, relocated his family in 1810, establishing a farm in the rolling acreage of what is today northern Summit County. The Hale

Twins Day Festival

Y ou'll be seeing double, but that's to be expected if you visit Twinsburg for the annual Twins Day Festival. What better place than Twinsburg to host a national gathering of those special siblings that we call twins?

Matched sets of brothers and sisters come from all over the nation to gather for this celebration of duality. Infants and oldsters and in-betweeners all attend. Some are so close in looks and dress down to the hat, the socks, or the tie tack that you have to wonder how even their mothers and fathers tell them apart!

Triplets, quadruplets, and beyond are also welcome. To add to the fun of celebrating these look-a-likes, there's a parade, a fireworks display, arts and crafts, food, of course, and even a golf tournament (with identical twins on the course, keeping the scoring straight could be a challenge).

The Twins Day Festival is held the first weekend in August, Twinsburg. For more information call (330) 425-3625 (or get your twin to call).

Barberton All Fired Up

property remained in the family until the death of Miss Clara Belle Ritchie, great-granddaughter of Jonathan, in 1956. She willed the farm to the Western Reserve Historical Society, stipulating that it be opened to the public so that as many people as possible could "be informed as to the history and culture of the Western Reserve."

The history and culture of the region are faithfully preserved at the working *Hale Farm and Village.* Guides in period clothing explain the significance and origins of the furnishings and artifacts displayed in the Hale farmhouse, a 150-year-old, three-story brick structure. Some of the items exhibited were transported to Ohio from Connecticut with the Hale family. The guides also demonstrate pioneer cooking and skills such as setting the proper tension on a rope spring bed. Outside, a small antique sawmill powered by a marvelous 1923 portable steam engine cuts timber into boards for use in the village.

Ohio Columbus Barber was a premier matchmaker, but not one involved in pairing couples for romance. No, Barber and his company, Diamond Match Company, made fire-starting matches, a quarter-billion a day during the company's heyday.

Barber came from a family of matchmakers: his father made them, too, and peddled them. The younger Barber founded Diamond Match in 1880, and his success resulted in the creation of a new town, Barberton, which he conceived and promoted. He was known during his day as the "Match King."

Thirteen buildings dating from the early 1800s make up the Western Reserve Village. United States Senator Benjamin F. Wade worked in the law office, built in 1820. And the large fireplace and rough-hewn floors and beams in the one-room schoolhouse typify the rustic construction techniques of the early nineteenth century. Craftspeople demonstrate spinning and weaving in the Stow House, and a potter, glassblower, candle maker, and blacksmith work at their trades. Other demonstrations include hearth cooking, broom making, brick making, and cheese making. Perhaps the most intriguing building is the Meetinghouse, which was built as a Baptist church in Streetsboro, Ohio, in 1851. Sliding aside some boards behind the pulpit reveals a 4-foot-deep, 1,000-gallon tank used at one time for total-immersion baptisms.

Hale Farm and Village is in the 32,000-acre Cuyahoga Valley National Recreation Area at 2686 Oak Hill Road, in Bath; (800) 589–9703, (330) 666–3711. Open late May through October, Tuesday through Saturday, 10:00 A.M.–5:00 P.M.; Sundays and holidays, noon–5:00 P.M. Admission: adults, $9.00, children ages 6 to 12, $5.50.

The *Cuyahoga Valley National Recreation Area* follows the Cuyahoga River for 22 miles between Akron and Cleveland. The park offers numerous hiking, nature, and bicycle trails, scenic overlooks, and picnic areas.

Top Annual Events

Springfest, Youngstown,
early May; (330) 740–7116

Blossom Time, Chargin Falls,
May; (440) 247–1004

Civil War Encampment,
Burton, May; (440) 834–4012

Port Fest, Lorain, June; (440) 204–2267
or (440) 245–8477 ext. 1060

Clifton Arts and Musicfest,
Cleveland, June; (216) 228–4383

Strawberry Festival and Craft Bazaar,
Jefferson, June; (440) 293–4421
or (352) 343–8256

Ohio Scottish Games Weekend,
Oberlin, June; (440) 442–2147

Home Days Festival, Garfield Heights,
July 4th weekend; (216) 475–1100

Freedom Festival, Eastlake,
July 4th weekend; (440) 951–1416

Shakespeare at Stan Hywet, Akron,
July; (330) 836–5533

Log Cabin and Crafts Show,
Austintown, July; (330) 792–1129

Summit County Fair, Akron, late
July–early August; (330) 633–6200

Civil War Reenactment,
Bath, August; (800) 589–9703

Twins Day Festival,
Twinsburg, August; (330) 425–3652

Ring of Fire, Lakeview,
September; (937) 843–5392

Pioneer Days Festival, Vermilion,
September; (440) 458–5121

Apple Festival, Hartford,
September; (330) 772–3961

Spirit Walk, Medina,
September; (330) 723–2201

Civil War Encampment,
Mesopotamia, September;
(440) 693–4249

Johnny Appleseed Festival, Brunswick,
September; (330) 225–5577

Woollybear Festival, Vermilion,
October; (330) 264–5518

Ice Festival, Medina,
mid-February; (800) 463–3462

Geauga County Maple Festival,
Chardon, April; (440) 286–3007
or (440) 285–9050

Winter sports in the park include sledding, ice skating, and cross-country skiing. Two complete ski centers, Brandywine in Sagamore Hills and Boston Mills in nearby Peninsula (both at 800–875–4241, 330–467–2242), serve downhill skiers with complete ski shops, lifts, instruction, and equipment rentals.

Nestled in 800 acres of rolling hills between Akron and Cleveland is one of America's premier outdoor cultural and entertainment complexes, *Blossom Music Center.* The summer home (and a major source of revenue) for the renowned Cleveland Orchestra, Blossom also attracts audiences for performances that range from opera to ballet, from jazz to rock and roll.

The nation's top artists take the stage in the innovative pavilion, a fan-shaped open-air structure seating 5,281. Its enormous roof rises 94 feet above the stage level (it's the largest shingled area in the country), creating a sound chamber requiring little or no electronic amplification for those seated in the pavilion.

Four acres of lawn on the gentle hillside provide outdoor seating for another 13,500 patrons. A unique computerized sound system has a delay feature that transmits the sound from speakers at precisely the moment the sound from the stage reaches the lawn audience, creating near perfect listening conditions.

Artists perform almost every evening during the June through September season. A full-service restaurant is open on all concert nights. For information and a schedule of coming attractions, call or write Blossom Music Center, 1145 West Steels Corners Road, Cuyahoga Falls 44223. April through September phone the center at (330) 920–8040.

What do Thomas Edison, Alexander Graham Bell, and Wilbur and Orville Wright have in common? Two things: They were all great American inventors, and they are 4 of the 120 inventors who have been inducted into the National Inventors Hall of Fame at *Inventure Place.*

Inventure Place, which opened in 1995, is dedicated to the creative process. Inside this 77,000-square-foot interactive science center, you can conduct a symphony with rubber bands and a laser, build your own sound system, strum a laser harp, fire an air cannon, make a movie, transform a toaster into a work of art, animate your own cartoon, pilot a helicopter, construct a computer, or demolish a dishwasher. The quality and creativity of the exhibits win over young and old alike.

Inventure Place is at 221 South Broadway, Akron; (800) 968–4332, (330) 762–4463. Open Monday through Saturday, 9:00 A.M.–5:00 P.M.; Sunday, noon–5:00 P.M. Admission: adults, $7.50; children and students, $6.00.

The *Akron Art Museum* consists of more than 3,000 paintings, photographs, and works on paper. The collection is known for its strength in three areas: American Impressionist and Tonalist paintings from the turn of the century, painting and sculpture since 1960, and photography. A unique collection contains the work of self-taught Ohio artists.

BFGoodrich executive Edwin C. Shaw amassed a collection of American post–Civil War paintings and prints between 1916 and 1923 and is responsible for the museum's depth in this area. Financial upheaval during the Depression forced Shaw to try to sell much of the collection, but a lack of interest in American art at the time kept that from happening. Shaw, one of the museum's founders, bequeathed thirty-nine works to the Akron Art Institute (as the museum was called before 1980) by

Settling Akron

The building of the Ohio & Erie Canal spurred the settlement of Akron, named from the Greek word akros, *meaning "summit" or "high place." Early gristmills were built in the area because of the available water power.*

Two entrepreneurs also contributed to the city's development. In 1863, Ferdinand Schumacher constructed the Empire Barley Mill, which supplied cereal to the Union Army and launched the American cereal industry. His enterprise later became known as Quaker Oats.

In 1870, New Yorker Dr. Benjamin Franklin Goodyear moved to Akron and rounded up investors for his company, which produced fire hoses and other rubber products. With the arrival of the auto industry and the demand for rubber tires, the rest of the story is well-known, with Akron becoming the rubber capital of the world.

artists such as William Merritt Chase, Thomas Dewing, Frederick Childe Hassam, Frederick Frieseke, and Dwight W. Tyron.

Since the late 1960s, the museum has concentrated on modern and contemporary art, and in the 1970s it officially limited its collections and exhibitions to work produced from 1850 to the present. An endowment allows the museum to add to its collections of painting and sculpture since 1960, as did proceeds from works that did not meet the museum's 1850 demarcation and were sold off.

The Akron Art Museum is at 70 East Market Street, Akron; (330) 376–9185. Open Tuesday through Friday, 11:00 A.M.–5:00 P.M.; Saturday, 10:00 A.M.–5:00 P.M.; Sunday, noon–5:00 P.M. No admission charge.

Constructed at a cost of $2 million, Frank A. and Gertrude Seiberling's **Stan Hywet Hall** in Akron took four years to build and was completed in 1915. Frank Seiberling founded the Goodyear and Seiberling rubber companies, and this lavish sixty-five-room mansion gives testimony to the personal wealth amassed by industrialists in that era.

Considered to be one of the finest examples of American Tudor Revival architecture, Stan Hywet is patterned after three Tudor estates in England, with elements of each incorporated in the design of the structure. As is typical of Tudor buildings, windows, doors, chimneys, and roof peaks are asymmetrical and appear randomly placed. The name Stan Hywet means "stone quarry" in Anglo-Saxon, a reference to the quarry once located on the original 3,000-acre estate that supplied much of the stone used in the hall's construction.

Molded plaster ceilings and hand-carved oak walls, both commonly used in English Tudor residences, can be found throughout the Seiberling home. The Seiberlings went to considerable trouble to make Stan Hywet as faithful as possible to the Tudor stylethey concealed telephones behind wall coverings and installed twenty-three working fire-

Stan Hywet/Shakespeare

places, even though the building is equipped with central heating. They also built in a rope elevator for hauling firewood from the basement to the upper floors.

Formal balls and other social functions were held in the large music room, which has three massive crystal chandeliers, sixteen wall sconces, and a second-floor balcony for a small orchestra. The formal dining room seats forty, and a mural above the oak walls depicts the story of Chaucer's *Canterbury Tales*. Rare American chestnut, a type of wood that's no longer available because of devastating blight, lines the walls of the billiard room.

The Seiberlings removed the walls, floor, and ceiling from a room in an English manor house scheduled for demolition and installed these materials in the second-floor master bedroom. Also in their bedroom is an original Tudor canopy bed, circa 1575. Throughout the tour, guides point out many of the outstanding pieces in the Seiberlings' priceless collection of antiques. The two urns in the fountain room, for example, date from before the birth of Christ.

The owners of the impressive Stan Hywet Hall were well known for their love of music and the performing arts. That love continues as the estate hosts Shakespeare at Stan Hywet each July.

Outdoor performances are held in the early evenings on the grounds of the great hall. Generally the performances are held on two consecutive weekends in July. The grand mansion and grounds also are the setting for other special activities, including art shows and teas on the terrace featuring period music and entertainment. For information on Shakespeare and other special events at Stan Hywet call (330) 836–5533.

Manicured gardens, woodlands crisscrossed with paths and trails, and splendid shrubbery surround Stan Hywet Hall. Clear stream water pours over a stone waterfall in a cool pond in the tall trees just behind the Seiberling mansion.

Stan Hywet Hall is at 714 North Portage Path, in Akron; (330) 836–5533. Open January through March, Tuesday through Saturday, 10:00 A.M.–4:00 P.M. and Sunday, 1:00–4:00 P.M.; April through December, daily, 9:00 A.M.–6:00 P.M. Admission: adults, $8.00; children (ages 6 to 12), $4.00.

From Stan Hywet Hall, take Portage Path south for a drive past many fine old Akron homes and estates. If you continue south to the intersection of Copley Road and South Portage Path, you will find two museums.

The mansion of Colonel Simon Perkins was constructed adjacent to the historic Portage Path at Akron between the years 1835 and 1837. The home is an example of the Greek Revival style, which had great influence on architecture during the early settlement of the Western

Reserve. Built of native sandstone on the brow of a hill, the **Perkins Mansion,** with its two-story portico, overlooks the city of Akron. Through the years, it has become recognized as one of the most imposing homes of northern Ohio.

Colonel Perkins was born to General and Mrs. Simon Perkins at Warren, Ohio, in 1805. His father organized the Western Reserve Bank in 1813, and, in connection with Paul Williams, founded the village of Akron in 1825.

Colonel Perkins, who served in the Ohio legislature and was an active promoter of the Cleveland, Zanesville & Cincinnati Railroad, purchased 115 acres of land on this site in 1832 for $1,300. Perkins and his wife, sister of the future governor of Ohio, David Tod, resided in Warren before moving to Akron in 1835. While the mansion was under construction, they lived in a small frame house, now known as the **John Brown Home.**

Surrounded by more than ten acres of beautiful grounds, the mansion today contains some of its original furnishings, as well as items connected with the early history of Summit County. Situated on the grounds are the original carriage house, a combination summer kitchen and laundry built in 1890, the original well—dug through 40 feet of sandstone—and a garage.

Across the street is the John Brown Home, so named to commemorate the two-year residency of that abolitionist leader from 1844 to 1846. At the time, Brown was associated with Colonel Simon Perkins in the sheep and wool business. The original frame structure, to which several additions have been made, is believed to have been built around 1830. Inside is an exhibit that explains the importance of the canal to the development of Akron, as well as a replica of a canalboat captain's cabin.

Both museums are operated by the Summit County Historical Society. They are open daily, 1:00–5:00 P.M.; (330) 535–1120. Admission (to both museums): adults $5.00; children (ages 6 to 16) and senior citizens, $4.00.

Just up the street from the museums, Jeanne Pinnick offers bed-and-breakfast accommodations in her 1918 **Portage House.** This three-story Tudor home provides a pleasant stop in a quiet, parklike setting for weary travelers.

Jeanne and her daughter, Carol, live on the third floor; the second-floor bedrooms are available for guests. Downstairs, the large living room is a quiet place to relax or read the evening paper.

Depending on the number of guests in the house, Jeanne serves a full breakfast either at an island in the center of the kitchen or in the formal dining room. Friendly people like the Pinnicks and modest prices are why bed-and-breakfasts are increasingly popular throughout Ohio.

The Portage House is at 601 Copley Road, Akron (330) 535–1952. Rates: $36 to $44 per night. Personal checks accepted.

For another view of Akron, cruise scenic Portage Lake on the *Portage Princess Tour Boat.* Captain John Roessner narrates tours of this beautiful glacial lake, lined by thousands of picturesque homes. In addition to the daily public cruises, lunch and dinner cruises also are available.

The Portage Princess Tour Boat is at 300 West Turkeyfoot Lake Road, Akron; (330) 499–6891. Cruises depart mid-May through mid-October, Saturday and Sunday, at 1:00 and 2:00 P.M. Rates: adults, $6.00; seniors and children, $5.00.

Heritage Hills

Founded with an initial gift from Jerry Silverman and Shannon Rodgers, the **Kent State University Museum** opened its doors in 1985. Silverman and Rodgers, New York dress manufacturers, donated 4,000 costumes and accessories, almost 1,000 pieces of decorative art, and a 5,000-volume reference library. Today, the collection consists of almost 10,000 costumes and dresses.

Highlights of the collection include the black velvet evening cape, trimmed with a band of crystals, worn by Joan Crawford in Truman Capote's *Black and White Ball.* Another favorite is the eighteenth-century English silk dress, in a style typical of the Spitafields silk weaving district in London. There's a magnificent uniform of the Chinese Imperial Palace Guard worn at the end of the Manchu dynasty around 1900 and a fancy blue silk ball gown from the French couture house of Balenciaga, circa 1958.

A second gift to the museum was the Tarter/Miller collection of some 200,000 pieces of collectible glass. A distinctive part of this collection is the Vaseline glass, so called because of its unusual yellow-green color. Made with 2 percent uranium, Vaseline glass is transparent and fluorescent under ultraviolet light.

The Kent State University Museum is in Rockwell Hall on the Kent State University campus, Kent; (330) 672–3450. Open Wednesday, Friday, and Saturday, 10:00 A.M.–4:45 P.M.; Thursday, 10:00 A.M.–8:45 P.M.; Sunday, noon–4:45 P.M. Admission: adults, $3.00; seniors, $2.00.

Many visitors to Portage County are attracted by Sea World of Ohio, home of Shamu, Dolphin Cove, the Shark Encounter, the Penguin Encounter, and the "Baywatch" Adventure water-ski show; and Geauga Lake, a 240-acre amusement park with more than one hundred rides and shows, both in Aurora. However, Garrettsville has a unique point of interest far less well known—*Garretts Mill.*

A number of Ohio gristmills provide demonstrations and information on the role of the miller in pioneer towns and villages, but Garretts Mill actually performs the function it has had since 1804—grinding grains from local farms into flour and meal.

John Garrett built this water-powered mill on the banks of rushing Silver Creek. A forty-one-bucket wheel drives the grinding stones, and a system of flights (a vertical cup conveyor mechanism) transports the grain and flour to and from the various floors of the mill. Power for Garretts Mill has not always been provided by waterwheel—in 1913 the mill was "modernized" with the installation of water turbines. A local family purchased the mill in 1970 and in 1976 reconverted it to waterwheel power.

The latest incarnation of Garretts Mill may surprise you—fine dining. Executive chef Tony Alessi and his wife, Candy, have transformed it into a culinary adventure. Their original plan was to install a meat and seafood shop, but the more time they spent in the space, the more convinced they became that the building would be perfect for a restaurant. Today, visitors to the historic structure dine on the likes of veal Oscar, angel hair pasta, and chicken divan in what is known as Alessi's Restaurant at Garretts Mill.

Alessi's Restaurant at Garretts Mill is 1 block east of the intersection of Routes 82 and 88 at 8148 Main Street, Garrettsville; (330) 527-5849. Open daily for lunch and dinner.

Just minutes from "downtown" Garrettsville, nestled on a wooded hillside, is a delightful B&B, *Blueberry Hill Bed and Breakfast.* Built in the 1870s, this beautiful Victorian home reflects innkeeper Deborah Darling's passion for music, theater, and art, including works by Warhol and Erte. As you walk the grounds you discover Darling's Arabian mare Dancing Spirit and her faithful sidekick, a goat named Noah, frolicking in the meadow. The adjoining woods are perfect for hiking and jogging.

Blueberry Hill accommodates guests in three second-floor guest rooms, two with shared bath and one with a private bath and two-person Jacuzzi. The fireplace adds warmth to the house in winter; the deck and pool are summertime favorites. A continental breakfast of homemade breads, muffins, Danish, fresh fruit, coffee, tea, and juice starts each morning.

Garretts Mill

Blueberry Hill Bed and Breakfast is at 11085 North Street, Garrettsville; (330) 527–5068. Rates: $50 to $120 per night.

The history of the Mahoning Valley is the history of the iron and steel industries. Deposits of black coal suitable for blast furnaces were discovered near Youngstown in 1845, and by the 1850s the Valley was one of the nation's centers of iron production. As technology advanced, the Valley switched to steel production; the Ohio Steel Company, the area's first steel company, was organized in 1892.

Steel mill jobs attracted immigrants from eastern and southern Europe, as well as African-Americans from the South. Working conditions for these laborers were appalling: typically twelve-hour days, six or even seven days a week, in an environment of heavy machinery, poisonous gases, and open vats of molten steel. These conditions eventually led to the formation of the United Steelworkers of America in 1936.

Youngstown's steel production and employment soared during the middle of the twentieth century, peaking in 1973. But just four years later, "Black Monday" hit the area on September 19, 1977, with the closing of Youngstown's Sheet and Tube's Campbell Works. Global changes in the steel market, labor-management disputes, and a depletion of high-grade ores all contributed to the death of the Valley's steel industry.

The ups and downs of this pivotal industry are presented at the **Youngstown Historical Center of Industry and Labor.** The Museum's permanent exhibit, "By the Sweat of Their Brow: Forging the Steel Valley," uses videos, artifacts, photographs, and reconstructed scenes to tell the story of steel in the Valley.

The Youngstown Historical Center of Industry and Labor is at 151 West Wood Street, Youngstown; (800) 262–6137, (330) 743–5934. Open Wednesday through Saturday, 9:00 A.M.–5:00 P.M.; Sunday, noon–5:00 P.M. Admission: adults, $5.00; children(ages 6 to 12), $1.25.

In a city best known for steel and other heavy industry, Youngstown's *Butler Institute of American Art* houses an outstanding permanent collection of more than 10,000 works. From the earliest Limner painters of the colonial period through contemporary masters, the Butler Institute features representative works by Benjamin West, John Singleton Copley, Winslow Homer, Thomas Eakins, Martin Johnson Heade, and Mary Cassatt.

Specialty collections include western art by the likes of Albert Bierstadt, Frederic Remington, and Victor Higgins and an expansive group of marine paintings featuring the works of Fitzhugh Lane, Edward Moran, William Bradford, and Alfred Bricher. The Lester F. Donnell Gallery of American Sports Art features paintings, sculpture, drawings, and prints of all things sporting, including works by George Bellows, John Steuart Curry, Red Grooms, Robert Riggs, and Roy Lichtenstein.

Founded in 1919 by industrialist Joseph G. Butler, Jr., the Butler Institute is housed in a classic building, the first structure built in the United States to specifically house a collection of American art. Additions to this historic edifice in the 1930s and 1960s preceded the impressive West Wing addition in 1987. This postmodern structure, awash in marble and partially lit by soaring skylights, brings to eighteen the number of galleries at the Butler Institute.

The Butler Institute of American Art is at 524 Wick Avenue, Youngstown; (330) 743–1107. Open Tuesday and Thursday through Saturday, 11:00 A.M.–4:00 P.M.; Wednesday, 11:00 A.M.–8:00 P.M.; Sunday, noon–4:00 P.M. No admission charge.

Just down the road from the Butler Institute is another Youngstown treasure, the former home of Wilford and Olive Arms, "Greystones," now the *Arms Museum.* The three main rooms on the first floor of this elegant mansion preserve the Arms's way of life, their family portraits, furniture, china, glassware, silver, linens, Oriental rugs, and objets d'art still in place.

On the lower level, a large exhibition room depicts pioneer life in the region, with a collection of farm and household tools, implements and utensils, antique toys, Native American relics, and an impressive gun collection. Second-floor exhibits explore the more recent history of the Mahoning Valley through photographs, costumes, and artifacts.

Period gowns adorn mannequins throughout the museum, and the table setting in the dining room changes periodically to rotate the display of china, crystal, and silver. Special exhibits here include toys and dolls, costumes and accessories, political memorabilia, and works of art.

The Arms Museum is at 648 Wick Avenue, Youngstown; (330) 743-2589. Open Tuesday through Friday, 1:00–4:00 P.M.; Saturday and Sunday, 1:30–5:00 P.M. Admission: adults, $2.00; children (up to 18), 50 cents.

One of Ohio's greatest city parks offers visitors 2,530 acres of streams, lakes, gardens, woods, meadows, and wildlife. It's Youngstown's *Mill Creek Park*, and it features 21 miles of roads and 15 miles of foot trails through truly spectacular scenery. Hiking, picnicking, and boating are popular pastimes on Lake Newport and Lake Glacier.

The central feature of the park is picturesque Mill Creek. Many pioneer industries developed along the creek, and relics still remain to be discovered by visitors. Lanterman's Mill operates today as it did in the early 1800s grinding corn, wheat, and buckwheat via power driven from a 14-foot oak waterwheel. The mill had ceased operation in 1888, only to reopen a century later. A covered bridge stands just south of the mill and is one of the scenic highlights of the park.

Downstream from the mill is the start of the Gorge Trail. Mill Creek borders one side of this 2-mile trail; a massive wall of sandstone forms the other boundary. The trail takes hikers past a stunning waterfall.

More than 50,000 flowering bulbs announce the arrival of spring each year at the Fellows Riverside Garden. As summer arrives a spectacle of colorful annuals takes over. The wooded setting of the shade garden is a showcase for ornamental plants that thrive in low light. Other park highlights include a golf course, tennis courts, miniature golf, an ice skating rink, ballfields, and basketball courts.

Mill Creek Park is at 810 Glenwood Avenue, Youngstown; (330) 702-3000. Open daylight hours.

Built in the 1840s by Alden J. Nash and originally called the Nash Hotel, the *Welshfield Inn* served as an Underground Railway station for slaves escaping from the South to Canada. Stagecoaches traveling between Cleveland and Pittsburgh also frequently stopped here for food and overnight accommodations.

Although lodging is no longer offered here, the tradition of serving old-fashioned country cooking has been maintained by the owners, the

Steffee family. The large dining room with a fireplace contains an eclectic mix of bentwood chairs and wooden tables; browns, greens, and other earth tones predominate, and fresh flowers dress up each table. One of the smaller dining rooms, called Peddlers Parlor, has Early American decor with antiques, Quaker lace tablecloths, and seasonal flowers. On the front porch, lawn furniture creates a friendly, informal atmosphere under the tall columns. Also under the porch roof is a huge wooden sled named Snowbird capable of carrying twenty to thirty people.

Lunches at the Welshfield Inn include entrees such as chicken à la king on a biscuit, beef tenderloin tips with mushrooms on toast, french-fried scallops, and grilled ham with a pineapple slice. Fresh vegetables are served with each luncheon selection.

Following the same pattern of straightforward dishes at reasonable prices, dinner entrees include broiled flounder, prime rib, baked ham with raisin sauce, and country fried chicken. Homemade desserts are a specialty at the inn, with a wide selection of fresh fruit pies and cream pies available. The Steffees' future plans include adding overnight accommodations, as well as patio dining and a pub.

The Welshfield Inn is on Route 422, Welshfield; (440) 834–4164. Open for lunch Tuesday through Saturday, 11:30 A.M.–2:30 P.M.; for dinner Tuesday through Thursday, 4:30–9:00 P.M.; Friday and Saturday, 4:30–10:00 P.M.; Sunday, noon–8:00 P.M. Closed late December and all of January, plus July 1–15. MasterCard, Visa, and American Express are accepted.

Approximately 16,000 Amish live in Geauga County, making it one of the largest Amish communities in the country. Wearing the traditional dark, solid-colored clothing and rejecting modern conveniences such as electricity and automobiles, the "plain people" strive for a simple farming life. Merchants in Middlefield, Ohio, provide hitching posts for their Amish customers, and the Dutch Country Kitchen Restaurant serves Amish-style meals in an unpretentious concrete-block building.

Many of the Amish operate dairy farms, and they bring their milk to the **Middlefield Cheese House** to be manufactured into Swiss cheese. The cheese plant, founded as a cooperative in 1956 by twenty-five area farmers, is one of the largest producers of quality Swiss in the United States, with an output of more than twenty million pounds annually.

Visitors are invited to view a film, *Faith and Teamwork*, which carefully describes each step in the cheese-making process. Then a tour of the

Worth Seeing

Great Lakes Science Center, Cleveland

Cleveland Museum of Art

Cleveland MetroPark Zoo

Cleveland Children's Museum

The "Flats" entertainment and dining district, Cleveland

Cheese House museum features Old World carvings from Switzerland, antique cheese-making equipment, Amish artifacts, and historical photos. Be sure to stop in the Cheese Chalet Shop, where fresh sausages, homemade breads and pastries, Geauga County maple syrup, plus a wide selection of fine cheeses are available for purchase. A light lunch of soup, sandwiches, muffins, pie, and ice cream is served.

Middlefield Cheese House is on Route 608, just north of downtown Middlefield; (440) 632–5228. Open Monday through Saturday, 7:00 A.M.–5:30 P.M. No admission charge.

Spend the night in Victorian splendor at Judy and David McDowell's **Walker-Johnson Inn.** This turn-of-the-century masterpiece offers four second-floor guest rooms furnished with period antiques.

Enjoy a leisurely tea or lemonade on the spacious patio or pretty gazebo. Weather permitting, your breakfast of fresh-squeezed juices, fresh fruit, homemade muffins and breads, plus breakfast entree will be served outdoors as well, overlooking the beautiful perennial gardens. On cold evenings, you can curl up next to the parlor's crackling fireplace. In season, the inn is expertly decorated for a Victorian Christmas.

The Walker-Johnson Inn is at 15038 South State Road (Route 608), Middlefield; (440) 632–5662. Rates: $70 to $95 per night. VISA and MasterCard are accepted.

If you have ever envied an eagle or gull soaring in a gentle breeze, try a glider ride in one of the **Cleveland Soaring Society's** two-seat gliders. The club is based at the Geauga County Airport, and a trained glider pilot will let you experience the thrill of soaring from the front seat of one of the pair of trainers.

The $40 to $100 demo rides last from twenty to fifty minutes and are offered on Wednesday afternoons and all day on weekends. No reservations are required, but since demo rides must compete with the club's forty members for the use of the aircraft, early morning or late afternoon is probably the best time.

The Cleveland Soaring Society is based at the Geauga County Airport, on Route 608, 1/2 mile south of Middlefield; (440) 632–1188, 531–7900.

Mid-February through mid-April is a special time in Geauga County— maple syrup season. Those first February thaws start the sap flowing, and farmers throughout the county use special taps and buckets to drain the sap from their sugar maple trees. Once collected it is boiled and evaporated, with thirty to sixty gallons of sap needed to make one gallon of maple syrup. Smoke rising from area sugarhouses means syrup production is underway.

The **Burton Sugar Camp** is the only municipally owned sugar camp in the country. In a ten-acre park in the center of Burton, sap from the park's 1,500 sugar maples is boiled into syrup in a rustic log cabin. The cabin is open daily from late February through April, and maple syrup products are sold on weekends from May through the middle of December.

Across the street from the cabin is the Maple House Bakery and Gift Shop, which sells homemade breads, Geauga County maple syrup, honey, and preserves. A favorite here is the old-fashioned ice cream, particularly (you guessed it) the maple and maple nut flavors.

At the south end of Burton's town square is **Century Village**—fifteen restored buildings that provide a glimpse of the Western Reserve in the 1800s. The Blacksmith Shop, built in 1822, has an impressive complement of smithy tools and equipment. For a look at upper-middle-class life in the region, the Boughton House is furnished with pieces typical of the 1840s. The B&O Railroad built the Aultman station after the Civil War, and next to it sits a twenty-ton B&O caboose. Guides from the Geauga County Historical Society conduct one-and-a-half-hour tours of the village.

Century Village is on the town square in Burton; (440) 834–4012, 834–4852 (country store). Open May through October, Tuesday through Saturday, 9:00 A.M.–noon, 1:30–5:00 P.M. Admission: adults, $5.00; children (ages 6 to 12), $3.00.

The annual Geauga County Maple Festival, held on the first weekend after Easter, takes place in Chardon, 10 miles north of Burton. Parades, maple syrup contests, a quilt and afghan show, and competitions in pancake flipping and eating, wood chopping, rooster crowing, and beard shaving with an ax are just some of the activities at this yearly celebration.

The king of maple products in Geauga County has to be Paul Richards, of **Richards Maple Products;** his family has been in the business since 1910. Paul purchases tens of thousands of gallons of syrup annually from area farmers, syrup that he transforms into pure maple spread (similar to honey butter), maple sugar, maple cream (a fudgelike concoction available with or without black walnuts), maple candy, and, of course, three grades of maple syrup. All of these are produced without the use of preservatives.

Richards Maple Products also sells a wide selection of gift boxes containing endless combinations of their various products. Catalogs of gift box selections are available by mail.

Richards Maple Products is at 545 Water Street (Route 6, west of the central business district), Chardon 44024; (440) 286–4160. Open Monday, Tuesday, Thursday, Friday, and Saturday, 9:00 A.M.–5:00 P.M.; Sunday, noon–5:00 P.M.

From late November to the middle of March, skiers hit the powder at the *Alpine Valley Ski Area.* This complete ski resort has six slopes and a backwoods trail, high-powered lighting towers for night skiing, and a 10,000-square-foot rental shop with 1,400 pairs of skis. Their P.S.I.A. ski school offers both private and group lessons. After a strenuous day on the slopes, a blazing fire in the lodge's fireplace lures skiers there to unwind. The lodge offers a great view of the slopes, as well as a full-service cafeteria, a pizza shop, and a pub called Chaser's.

The Alpine Valley Ski Area is on Route 322, 4 miles east of Chesterland; (440) 285–2211, 729–9775 (ski reports).

We have Charles M. Hall to thank for a world full of aluminum siding and aluminum everything else. Born in Thompson on December 6, 1863, Hall's family moved to Oberlin. Along with a country full of scientists, he had been trying to find a cheap way to make aluminum; Hall did his experiments in an old woodshed while still in high school.

Hall attended Oberlin College, where he continued to experiment. Eight months after graduating, the twenty-two year old discovered the process he and the others had been seeking. After a patent dispute with a French scientist claiming the same invention, Hall secured capital from Andrew Mellon and built what became the American Aluminum Company. Hall died in 1914, leaving a substantial bequest to Oberlin College.

Eastern Lakefront

olden Arboretum, one of the world's largest aboreta, encompasses 3,100 acres of wooded trails, ponds full of ducks and geese, fields, and deep ravines. Dedicated to increasing knowledge of the plant world, Holden has five primary nature trails, which take visitors past the maple collection, renowned for its beauty when the leaves change color in the fall; the conifer collection of pines, firs, spruces, and junipers; and the wildflower garden, where a showcase of Ohio's flora can be enjoyed.

The lilac and rhododendron gardens and crabapple and shrub collections are other examples of the many and varied exhibits in this vast

First Mormon Temple

The first Mormon Temple in the United States wasn't in Utah; it was built in Kirtland Hills, Ohio. Erected in 1833 by Prophet Joseph Smith and his followers (including Brigham Young), the temple commands a spectacular hilltop location. The establishment of this temple brought many newcomers to town, some in reverence and others in contempt. Financial problems, including the failure of the church bank, forced Smith and Young to flee Ohio. Smith was killed by a mob in Illinois, while Young led the faithful to Utah, where he founded Salt Lake City.

nature preserve. Occasional "Getting-to-Know-Holden" nature walks and frequent lectures are offered at the arboretum, as are memberships in the Holden Arboretum Association. Membership entitles you to free admission to the grounds, cross-country skiing privileges, and discounts on courses, lectures, and gift shop purchases. Bird-watching and wildflower walks are popular at Holden, and the arboretum has summertime nature discovery sessions as well as special programs for children on subjects such as animal communication.

The Holden Arboretum is at 9500 Sperry Road, Kirtland; (440) 946–4400. Open Tuesday through Sunday, 10:00 A.M.–5:00 P.M. Admission: adults, $4.00; children (ages 6 to 15), $2.00.

Picture, if you will, a giant tomato plant with vines as thick as your waist, fruit 6 feet across, and leaves up to 12 feet long. The stuff of science fiction? No, *science*, not *science fiction*. These are features of the creative Great Tomato Works at **Lake Farmpark.** The farmpark is an outdoor museum where city folks can learn about and learn to appreciate agriculture—the source of our food supply. The number of farmers among us has declined from more than 90 percent in 1800 to less than 3 percent today. Relatively few Americans have ever met a farmer, let alone understand what he or she does.

Try your hand milking a cow or just enjoy the 235 acres of fields and forests. Two miles of easy walking roads cross the property, and wagon and sleigh tours are also offered. You'll discover more than fifty breeds of livestock including cattle, sheep, goats, pigs, and poultry, plus orchards, gardens, and vineyards. You'll leave knowing the difference between strip cropping and contour plowing, and perhaps having seen planting, cultivating, or harvesting of fields of hay, oats, rye, wheat, corn, and barley. And no trip to the farm would be complete without a supply of antique and modern tractors.

Lake Farmpark is at 8800 Chardon Road (US 6), Kirtland; (800) 366–3276, (440) 256–2122. Open daily 9:00 A.M.–5:00 P.M. (Closed Monday, January through March.) Admission: adults (ages 12 and up), $5.00; children, $3.50.

The Debevcs have made wine for family and friends for three generations, but it wasn't until 1970 that Tony Sr. and Tony Jr. decided to convert some of their farm acreage into a commercial vineyard. *Chalet Debonne Vineyards* produced its first bottle for sale in 1972, and near-constant expansion has taken place ever since. With nearly a half million dollars invested in the latest winery equipment, the Debevcs hired Tony Carlucci, believed to be the first California winemaker to take up residence at an Ohio winery.

Guests at Chalet Debonne sample the twenty-two varieties of Debevc wine—ten white wines, six reds, and four blush wines—in a Swiss-style A-frame chalet with a large fireplace, burgundy tablecloths, and weathered barn board siding on the inside walls. Visitors may also sit under the grapevines on the patio during warm weather, and snacks such as cheese and sausage and homemade bread are served. Polka bands perform on Wednesday and Friday evenings and Saturday afternoons.

Tours of the winery take place hourly, or as needed, with members of the Debevc family explaining the various steps in wine making, from grape crushing and filtering to aging and bottling. Chalet Debonne holds 100,000 gallons of wine in various stages of fermentation in the cellar and bottled for sale.

Chalet Debonne Vineyards is off State Route 528 and Griswold Road at 7743 Doty Road, Madison; (800) 424–9463, (440) 466–3485. Open Tuesday through Saturday, noon–8:00 P.M. (open until 11:00 P.M. on Wednesday and Friday). Reduced hours in January.

Acres of vineyards can be seen throughout eastern Lake County, and five minutes from Chalet Debonne is another winery, *Grand River Vineyard.* After driving past the rows of grapevines, you reach a modern building at the edge of a cool forest. Unlike other wineries, Grand River continually changes the wines it produces, so customers have the opportunity to taste new variations and blends on each visit to this pleasant facility.

Grand River Vineyard is at 5750 Madison Road (Route 528), Madison; (440) 298–9838. Open Monday, Wednesday, and Thursday, 1:00–8:00 P.M.; Friday and Saturday, 1:00–6:00 P.M.

A restaurant at the Lake-Ashtabula county line rests on the site of one of the early log buildings in the Western Reserve. Originally known as the Webster House, the cabin was built in 1798 and measured only 12 by 15 feet, yet it was a popular stop for settlers heading west in covered wagons on the trail from Pittsburgh.

In later years, the name was changed to the New England House, and finally to its present name, the **Old Tavern.** Innkeepers expanded the tavern several times during the 1800s, and the four massive pillars were added to the front of the building in 1820.

Decorated in an Early American motif, the Old Tavern continues the tradition of serving generous portions of hearty country cooking. Dinner entrees include chicken marsala, veal Parmesan, and beef stroganoff. For seafood lovers, the Old Tavern offers grilled salmon, baked orange roughy, and stuffed broiled scampi served on the half shell. Dinner entrees are served with a salad, biscuits and jelly, choice of potato, and delicious corn fritters—warm corn bread and kernels formed into a ball and topped with maple syrup and powdered sugar. The fresh desserts are all prepared on the premises. The lemon delight torte and the bread pudding with vanilla rum sauce are very popular. Enjoy an after-dinner cocktail in the Coach House Pub.

The Old Tavern is just inside the Lake County line on Route 84, Unionville; (800) 7TAVERN, (440) 428–2091. Open Tuesday through Thursday, 11:30 A.M.–8:00 P.M.; Friday and Saturday, 11:30 A.M.–9:00 P.M.; Sunday, 9:00 A.M.–2:00 P.M. MasterCard and Visa are accepted.

Restoration is underway in the **Ashtabula Harbor** area, and twenty-six buildings have already been listed on the National Register of Historic Places. Ashtabula's heyday as a port has long since passed, but a new breed of merchants has created a charming shopping district in the hundred-year-old structures on Bridge Street, just up the hill from an unusual lift bridge. During Ashtabula's years as a thriving shipping center, it was said to have more saloons than any other port in the world except one—Singapore.

Amid the antiques and gift shops is a pleasant and reasonably priced place to dine, **Hulbert's Restaurant.** Ceiling fans slowly spin near the high tin ceiling, and exposed-brick interior walls create a turn-of-the-century atmosphere. The dining tables and chairs are an eclectic mix of antiques and contemporary pieces, and the effect is very pleasing. The tables in the O'Leary room are vintage sewing-machine cabinets. Fresh flowers dress up each table, and a large brick archway connects the two dining areas, which were once separate buildings. Wall space at Hulbert's is used to display artwork, often featuring harbor scenes and other local points of interest; some is available for purchase.

Hulbert's lunch menu offers a wide variety of sandwiches, including the hot, open-faced Drake sandwich (made famous at Chicago's Drake Hotel), which consists of ham, turkey, and sliced tomatoes, topped with melted Swiss and cheddar cheeses. Other luncheon selections range from soups and salads to quiche and the unusual cheese-stuffed flounder.

At the dinner hour, choose from two dozen entree selections—steaks, seafood, chicken and mushroom Alfredo, liver and grilled onions, and more. For a tasty appetizer, try the crisp chicken wings, served hot, medium, or mild with two zesty sauces.

Baking is a special tradition at Hulbert's—homemade pies tempt diners every day here. Warm bread pudding with bourbon sauce, fresh cinnamon rolls, and eggs Benedict are

Hulbert's Restaurant

featured for Sunday breakfast. Chocoholics of the world, try the "death by chocolate cake"—deep chocolate cake surrounded with chocolate butter cream, then topped with chocolate glaze and chocolate bits. This one is a real diet buster!

Hulbert's Restaurant is at 1033 Bridge Street, Ashtabula; (440) 964-2594. Open Monday through Thursday, 11:00 A.M.–8:00 P.M.; Friday and Saturday, 11:00 A.M.–9:00 P.M.; Sunday, 8:00 A.M.–8:00 P.M.

PLACES TO STAY IN NORTHEAST OHIO

AKRON
Akron Hilton Inn at
Quaker Square
135 South Broadway
(330) 253-5970

Portage House
601 Copley Road
(330) 535-1952

GARRETTSVILLE
Blueberry Hill Bed
and Breakfast
11085 North Street
(330) 527-5068

MIDDLEFIELD
Walker–Johnson Inn
Bed and Breakfast
15038 South State Avenue
(440) 632-5662

PAINESVILLE
Quail Hollow Resort
and Country Club
11080 Concord-
Hambden Road
(216) 350-3504

PLACES TO EAT
IN NORTHEAST OHIO

AKRON
Lou & Hy's Deli
and Restaurant
1949 West Market
(330) 836-9159

ASHTABULA
Hulbert's Restaurant
1033 Bridge Street
(440) 964-2594

CLEVELAND
Watermark
1250 Old River Road
(216) 241-1600

GARRETTSVILLE
Alessi's Restaurant
8148 Main Street
(330) 527-5849

LAKE AT CHIPPEWA
Oaks Lodge
On Medina County Road 19
(800) 922-2601
or (330) 769-2601

UNIONVILLE
Old Tavern
Just inside the Lake County
Line on Route 84
(800) 7-TAVERN
or (216) 428-2091

WELSHFIELD
Welshfield Inn
Route 422
(440) 834-4164

Helpful Web Sites

Ohio Division of Travel and Tourism:
www.ohiotourism.com

Cleveland Convention and Visitors Bureau:
www.travelcleveland.com

Cleveland Plain Dealer:
www.cleveland.com

Youngstown Convention and Visitors Bureau:
www.youngstowncvb.com

Legacy Trail

Stunning natural beauty and re-created pioneer history blend in a state park in the foothills of the Appalachians, **Beaver Creek State Park.** Wide, swift Little Beaver Creek rushes through deep gorges and past pine and fir forests, the locks of the old Sandy and Beaver Canal, and a restored pioneer village.

Private entrepreneurs constructed the canal between 1834 and 1848, connecting the Ohio River with the Ohio and Erie Canal. Though they spent $3 million on the project by its completion, the canal carried paying traffic only until 1852, when competition from the railroad doomed the canal era in this part of the state. Ironically, the directors of the Sandy and Beaver kept the Pennsylvania Railroad out of the county to avoid competition between the railroad and their canal—a move that had dire consequences for the canal towns in Columbiana County after the Sandy and Beaver failed.

Fifteen miles of hiking trails and numerous bridle trails follow Little Beaver Creek and wind through the woods up the steep foothills. Canoe rentals nearby provide the equipment for those who wish to take on the challenging creek, and primitive camping areas are scattered throughout the 3,000-acre park. The creek offers anglers a variety of fish, including smallmouth and rock bass.

Gaston's Mill, built by Samuel Conkle in 1830, dominates the park's reconstructed pioneer village. Originally powered by a large waterwheel, the mill operated until 1920, though in later years it used steam and gas engines to drive the massive grinding stones. When restored, it was converted back to waterwheel power, and on summer weekends visitors observe the mill at work and may purchase stone-ground corn, wheat, and buckwheat flour. A pioneer church, schoolhouse, cabin, and blacksmith shop, all filled with antiques from Ohio's early settlement era, surround the historic mill.

Beaver Creek State Park is off Route 7, 15 miles east of Lisbon; (330) 385–3091. Open year-round.

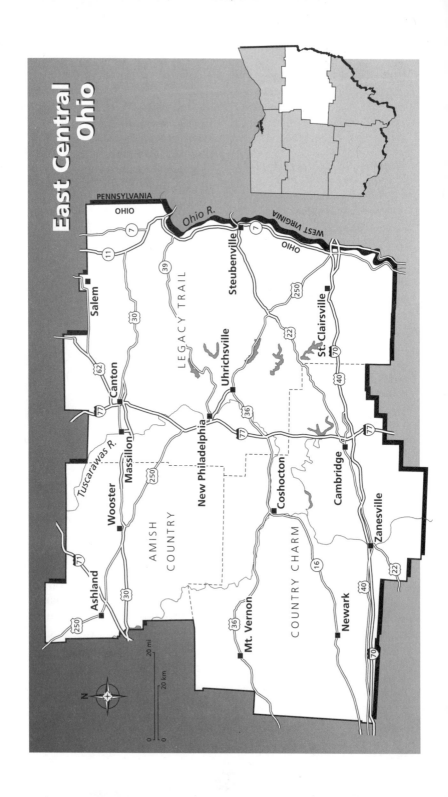

Rural Columbiana County seems an unlikely spot for a quality continental restaurant, but **Lock 24** is precisely that. The Pugh family restored a barn built in the 1830s, and the rustic beams of the original structure are plainly visible in the entry, lounge, and main dining area. Before-and-after photos document the comprehensive restoration of this attractive restaurant, which takes its name from the canal lock behind the building near the middle fork of Little Beaver Creek. A cheerful glassed-in sun porch, decorated with ceiling fans, Tiffany lamps, and both boxed and hanging plants, provides the perfect setting for a meal in the country.

Lock 24's luncheon menu features soups and salads, including a salad Niçoise, which is a mix of light tuna and fresh steamed vegetables tossed in vinaigrette dressing and garnished with ripe olives and hard-boiled egg. Or feast on the Ultimate Salad—white asparagus spears, hearts of palm, watercress, cucumbers, and ripe olives, served with Lock 24's special dressing. Other lunch offerings include omelets, hot and cold sandwiches, seafood and pasta, beef and potato cake, broiled catch of the day, and the intriguing chicken renaissance—chicken, egg noodles, mushrooms, and chives in a sherry sauce, all breaded and baked.

Unlike many country dining establishments with standard American fare, Lock 24 prides itself on serving sophisticated dinner entrees such as steak au poivre (a strip steak coated with black pepper in a brandied cream sauce), shrimp Dijon, chicken Grand Marnier, and boeuf au fromage (sliced tenderloin lightly breaded, pan fried in butter, then broiled with Roquefort and Parmesan cheeses). The menu features a variety of other innovative dishes, including the delightful sea scallops and Gulf shrimp, which are marinated in olive oil, dry vermouth, and shallots

Beaver Creek Ghost

*V*isitors to Beaver Creek State Park will want to bring a camera to get some pictures of the restored mill and locks, but be prepared to miss at least one of those shots if one of the park's ghosts is in residence. At Beaver Creek one of the men who was a lock keeper is said to continue to work shifts along the water's edge. If you visit "Jake's Lock," you may become part of his legend. In life, he sometimes worked the day shift; sometimes at night. At night he would light a lantern and keep watch for boats needing his services to transverse the lock. But one night, it is said, a bolt of lightening shot from the sky and hit poor Jake, killing him and propelling his body into the lock.

Visitors say that to this day they occasionally see the light from Jake's lantern bobbing along the side of the canal or even under the water where Jake fell that night. If you try to take a picture near the lock, the legend says that your camera may malfunction if Jake is working his shift. Be careful that that flash doesn't remind Jake of the fateful flash of lighting!

One of the 1830s locks is nicknamed, "Gretchen's Lock." Tales say that Gretchen was the daughter of Gill Hans, an engineer who came from Holland to build the lock. His daughter never adjusted to the move to America and eventually grew sick and died in 1838.

Her family made plans to return to Holland to bury their daughter. Until they could the coffin was temporarily placed in the stone sides of the lock. The arrangements were made and the family set sail with the coffin containing the remains of their homesick daughter.

But as fate would have it, their ship was sunk in a storm in the Atlantic. Legend says the girl named Gretchen has not found her rest, and instead she walks the lock that was her last, unhappy home.

Kilns Aplenty

and then broiled and served in a distinctive tomato–white butter sauce.

A Lock 24 dinner salad comes loaded with radishes, carrots, cucumbers, and tomato, and the homemade breads, particularly the carrot and pumpkin muffins, are outstanding. Banana bread pudding, New York–style cheesecake, poached pear with custard rum sauce and double fudge chocolate sauce, and crème caramel are but a sampling of the exotic dessert creations served here.

In addition to the excellent kitchen, Lock 24 offers travelers two shops for browsing. The Lock Loft Gallery features the work of eighty-five artists—everything from paintings to a wide selection of crafts. Raspberry Soup is a complete gift shop.

Lock 24 is on Route 154, 1 mile east of Route 11, near Elkton; (330) 424–3710. Open Tuesday through Friday, 11:30 A.M.–10:00 P.M.; Saturday, 11:30 A.M.–3:00 P.M., 5:00 P.M.–10:00 P.M. Visa, MasterCard, and American Express are accepted. Reservations are recommended.

As early as 1806, small kilns were fired in East Liverpool to take advantage of the unique clay and produce the popular "yellow ware" pottery. James Bennett, a potter from England, walked into town in 1839 determined to build a pottery empire. Profits from his effort the first year were $250, a huge sum in those days and just the beginning of a dramatic expansion for East Liverpool's pottery industry. By the end of the century, more than one-third of all the kilns operating in the United States were in East Liverpool—239 of them.

Perched on a hilltop overlooking 8,000 acres of rolling hills and water is a great getaway destination, ***Atwood Lake Resort.*** This complete resort complex features a rustic yet modern lodge with 100 guest rooms and 17 four-bedroom cottages in a quiet lakefront woods.

Atwood Lake is 1,540 acres of boating, swimming, and fishing, with sailboat and powerboat rentals available. Golfers will enjoy the 6,007-yard, par-70 course, which features challenging doglegs, rolling fairways, and gorgeous greens, as well as the lighted 9 hole par 3. Other amenities include five lighted tennis courts, bike rentals, hiking trails, and indoor and outdoor swimming pools.

Atwood Lake Resort is at 2650 Lodge Road, Dellroy; (800) 735–3596. Lodge rates: $85 to $125 per night, double occupancy; cottage rates, from $95 per night to $775 per week, depending on season. Visa, MasterCard, and American Express accepted.

A charming and gracious old home built just after the Civil War now houses the ***Candleglow Bed & Breakfast.*** The 1868 Victorian-style manor is surrounded by spruce trees and by the natural wonders of the

Muskingum County Conservancy District. Biking and hiking trails are nearby, as are an 18-hole championship golf course and cross-country skiing areas.

The three guest rooms keep the spirit of the late 1800s but are spacious and equipped with modern comforts such as private baths and air-conditioning. Each is differently named and appointed. The Rose Room has a king-sized, canopy bed and a claw-foot tub in the bath. Guests in the Lavender Room can relax with a whirlpool bath or shower before falling asleep in a four-poster, queen-size bed. The Green Room has a French flair and features a king-size bed and a whirlpool bath.

The Candleglow Bed & Breakfast is located at 4247 Roswell Road SW, Dellroy; (330) 735–2407. Rates: $90 per night.

Cibo's Restaurant serves authentic Italian cooking in a very unusual setting—an old movie theater. The Mohawk Theater, built in the early 1940s, presented feature films for the people of Waynesburg for decades. But since 1971 it has been spaghetti the pasta, not spaghetti the westerns, that attracts crowds at 134 West Lisbon Street.

At first, dining was limited to the Mohawk's old lobby, but now the entire theater has been remodeled and converted to a multilevel eating area, complete with ceiling fans and oak dividers. Italian favorites such as antipasto, pasta fagioli (beans), spezzato (wedding) soup, and homemade chicken noodles constitute the list of appetizers. The reasonably priced entrees include spaghetti, rigatoni, cavatelli, lasagna, ravioli, and cannelloni, and for those who have trouble choosing from that list, a combination plate offers a sample of all the above. Cibo's offers American dishes as well—steaks and chicken, plus family-style combinations of spaghetti, ravioli, chicken, lasagna, and steak. Pizza and sandwiches are also served.

Cibo's is at 134 West Lisbon Street, Waynesburg; (330) 866–3838. Open Thursday and Sunday, 11:00 A.M.–8:00 P.M.; Friday and Saturday, 11:00 A.M.–9:00 P.M. Personal checks are accepted.

William McKinley was elected the twenty-fifth president of the United States in 1896. Five years later he was gunned down at the Pan-American Exposition in Buffalo, New York. He died in office on September 14, 1901. The story of this Ohio native's life and public career is preserved at *The McKinley Museum,* a multifaceted complex that also includes the McKinley National Memorial; a museum of history, science, and industry; a children's scientific museum; and a planetarium.

Perhaps the most dramatic section of this vast museum is the Street of Shops. Visitors stroll down a nineteenth-century boulevard that is complete with a pioneer home; a general store; an early print shop; dentist's, physician's, and lawyer's offices; and a photography studio.

The McKinley's science hall offers first-class exhibits of science and nature. Collections include antique automobiles from the early 1900s and more than 1,000 model trains. The Hoover-Price Planetarium, also here, offers daily programs year-round.

The newest addition to this impressive complex is Discover World, an interactive scientific program geared for children and the young at heart. At the entrance to Discover World, you're greeted by the spine-tingling roar of a life-sized Allosaurus, with jaws that open and legs that move, thanks to the magic of robotics. Ingenious inverted periscopes let you check out the plant and animal life in a series of ponds, while a living beehive shows what being "busy as a bee" really means. Once aboard Space Station Earth, you find yourself in a scientific laboratory, where you can activate demonstrations on lasers and light waves, water in motion, and air under pressure. Young meteorologists enjoy getting in front of the video camera to announce the forecast.

President William McKinley wore a red carnation in his lapel every day for twenty-nine years. After McKinley's assassination in 1901, Ohio legislators searched for a fitting tribute to the fallen president. In his honor, they made the red carnation Ohio's state flower in 1904. Their resolution read: "for its beauty, its fragrance and its fitness, let it be adopted as the state flower of Ohio; and let the action of its adoption be to the memory of William McKinley."

Not contented with a single state flower, Ohio lawmakers declared the trillium grandiflorum the state wildflower in 1987. They noted that the large-flowered or white trillium is found in all eighty-eight Ohio counties and is easy to identify.

The McKinley Museum is at 800 McKinley Monument Drive, NW, Canton; (330) 455-7043. Summer hours: Monday through Saturday, 9:00 A.M.–6:00 P.M.; Sunday, noon–6:00 P.M. The rest of the year: Monday through Saturday, 9:00 A.M.–5:00 P.M.; Sunday, noon–5:00 P.M. Admission: adults, $6.00; children (ages 3 to 18), $4.00.

Canton was once home to the Canton Bulldogs, an early-day powerhouse in professional football. Today Canton, where the National Football League began in 1920, is the home of the national shrine of professional football, the *Pro Football Hall of Fame.* This five-building complex delights every pigskin addict, with action films, displays, and gridiron history. Expanded in 1995, the highlight of the Hall is the GameDay Theater, where visitors are treated to a unique rotating theater.

The extravaganza begins with a locker-room segment, featuring actual pregame preparations few "outsiders" ever see. The theater then rotates 180 degrees into the stadium, where NFL football is presented for the first time in Cinemascope on a screen almost two stories high.

A 7-foot bronze rendition of Jim Thorpe greets visitors to this comprehensive museum. Exhibits trace the history of the sport from the first game in 1892 to the latest teams. In the Pro Football Photo Art Gallery, you'll find the best of professional sports photography. The Black Man in Pro Football display tells the story of African-Americans in the NFL. A favorite here is the new hall of heroes, where the best of the best are honored. Each year a new class is enshrined, to join the ranks of pro football legends. After your tour, stop by the museum store for those can't-be-passed-up football souvenirs.

The Pro Football Hall of Fame is at 2121 George Halas Drive, NW, Canton; (330) 456–8207, 456–7762. Open daily 9:00 A.M.–5:00 P.M. (closing at 8:00 P.M. during the summer). Admission: adults, $9.00; children (6 to 14), $4.00.

For those who appreciate the rumble seats, wooden-spoke wheels, and V-16 engines of antique automobiles, a stop at the *Canton Classic Car Museum* is a must. The museum, housed in one of Ohio's earliest and most successful Ford-Lincoln dealerships (1914–29), comprises dozens of meticulously restored vehicles, from a bright red 1921 Pierce Arrow tow truck to a 1938 Cadillac convertible with a 452-cubic-inch, 185-horsepower engine.

Six Packard automobiles, from model years between 1920 and 1946, trace the evolution of that distinctive make. For elegant driving, the museum contains a pair of Rolls-Royces—a red and white 1929 Phantom I convertible and a 1938 Phantom III with open driver's compartment. The museum also has a rare Marmon Sixteen, which, according to an advertisement used at a 1931 automobile show, "looks and performs like no other car—16 cylinders, 200 horsepower and under $5,000."

The two-seat 1929 Kissel White Eagle Speedster (available with rumble seat) conjures up images of goggles, blowing scarves, and deserted country roads. The very rare 1914 Benham is the only survivor of the nineteen cars produced by the short-lived automaker, which folded after only one year in business. Celebrity cars include Amelia Earhart's 1916 Pierce Arrow, Queen Elizabeth's 1939 Canadian tour car, and a movie car from *Those Daring Young Men in Their Jaunty Jalopies.*

In addition to the fine old cars, vintage gas and steam engines and other automotive paraphernalia are on display. In the restoration shop, future classics await rejuvenation.

Canton Classic Car Museum

The Canton Classic Car Museum is at 555 Market Avenue South, Canton; (330) 455–3603. Open daily, 10:00 A.M.–5:00 P.M. Admission: adults, $3.00; children, $1.00.

Daniel and Mary Hoover arrived in 1850 on their eighty-two-acre farm, where Daniel founded a leather tannery. At the turn of the century, Daniel's son, W. H. Hoover, realized that the coming age of automobiles would drastically reduce the demand for leather goods such as harnesses and saddles. So W. H. Hoover searched for a new product for the Hoover Company and bought the rights to inventor Murray Spangler's upright vacuum cleaner. In 1908 Hoover offered the public the first commercially viable upright vacuum cleaner, the Hoover Suction Sweeper Model O.

In less than a decade, the Hoover Company blossomed into an international concern. With its world headquarters in North Canton, the company has established the *Hoover Historical Center* on the family's original Stark County farmstead.

A six-minute video presentation details the history of the company, and guided tours begin in the tannery, where many leather-working tools and artifacts from the late 1800s are displayed. The two-story white farmhouse contains what has to be the world's most complete collection of antique vacuums, ranging from the 1869 Whirlwind Cleaner, the first vacuum cleaner offered for sale, to modern Hoover units.

The Kotten Suction Cleaner, built in 1910, required the operator to stand and rock on the bellows to create suction—it sold for $25. The 1905 Skinner electric vacuum was advertised as a portable but weighed more than a hundred pounds! Murray Spangler's original 1907 upright stands next to the Hoover Model O, which launched this multinational corporation. Other Hoover exhibits include old photos of W. H. Hoover and various Hoover factories around the world, early newspaper and magazine advertisements for Hoover products, and some furnishings used by the family in the farmhouse. Herb and flower gardens surround the museum, which hosts changing exhibits throughout the year.

The Hoover Historical Center is located at 2225 Easton Street, North Canton; (330) 499–0287. It's open Tuesday through Sunday, 1:00–5:00 P.M. No admission charge.

As the mules clip-clop down the towpath, for a moment you can imagine yourself back in the days of Ohio's canal era—people waving, men tossing horseshoes, barefoot boys fishing. The captain points out the sights, such as a drydock where canal boats were built and repaired. In less than thirty minutes, you reach the Lock 4 turning basin. The captain describes how the lock works as the skillful crew poles the boat around for the scenic trip home. You ghost along in *St. Helena III,* a 60-foot replica of the freight barges that slipped through the canal network crisscrossing the state more than a hundred years ago.

Canal Fulton is a living canal town of 3,500 residents, where tourism and historical appreciation have replaced the commerce that once thrived on this section of the Ohio and Erie Canal. In addition to the authentic canalboat rides, Canal Fulton features an inviting nineteenth-century business district, listed on the National Register of Historic Places, with everything from antiques and gifts to candy and ice cream.

Other attractions include a Canal Days Museum and tours of a saltbox-style residence built in 1847. Biking along a section of the Cardinal Trail and canoeing on the Tuscarawas River are popular.

Canal Fulton is between Barberton and Massillon on State Route 93; (330) 854–3808. Canalboat rides are given daily in the summer plus weekends in May, September, and October.

For charming accommodations in the area, try the *Canal House Bed and Breakfast.* This circa 1865 Georgian-style post-and-beam home offers three guestrooms with private baths. A hot tub provides more modern creature comforts.

The Canal House Bed and Breakfast is at 306 South Canal Street, Canal Fulton; (330) 854–6229. Rates: $55 to $65 per night.

If cooking is the way to your heart, you will find just what you're looking for at the *Amish Door Restaurant & Village.* The restaurant features family-style meals as well as a standard menu. This is Amish country, so fresh baked breads and real mashed potatoes have got to be part of your meal, along with a salad and dessert bar. Adjacent to the restaurant is a bakery so you can take some more of those fresh baked goodies with you.

If you're spending some time in the area, the Amish Door Village offers two choices of accommodations. The Hasseman Bed and Breakfast has four guest rooms in an early 1900 Victorian home. The most unusual is the "Attic" room, which is the inn's honeymoon suite. Breakfast is served at the B & B on Sunday; weekdays and Saturday guests breakfast at the Amish Door Restaurant.

The Inn at Amish Door offers fifty Victorian-style rooms in a modern inn. Your stay includes a continental breakfast, and the inn offers such amenities as a heated, indoor pool and a fitness room.

The Amish Door Restaurant & Village is located at 1210 Winesburg Street, Wilmot; (330) 359–5464. Rates: $89 to $170 per night.

Europe's foremost woodcarvers proclaimed Ernest Warther "the world's master carver," and the intricately crafted carvings displayed at **Warther's** museum give credence to that proclamation. Born near Dover, Ohio, in 1885, Ernest started carving at age five, when he found an old pocketknife while tending the family's cow. His formal education ended in the second grade, and at the age of fourteen he went to work in the American Sheet and Plate Company's mill. During his twenty years at the plant, he used his spare time to perfect his craft.

That steel-rolling mill is preserved today in a 3-by-5-foot working model carved by Warther—a model built with thousands of small, handmade walnut parts. Warther mechanized not only the model's steel-rolling equipment, but also many of the workers, including the foreman raising a sandwich to his mouth, a second worker nodding off on the job, and a third "drinking" his lunch by raising a tiny bottle to his lips. An intricate belt-drive system designed by Warther and a sewing-machine motor power the model's many moving parts.

Warther's most widely acclaimed carvings, however, are the series he created tracing the history of steam power, particularly his many steam locomotives and trains. Starting with working models of the simplest steam devices dating from 250 B.C., Warther produced models of the various developmental stages of the steam era. By far the most impressive of these are the dozens of steam railroad locomotives on display at the museum, many with hundreds of moving parts.

Warther used walnut for the dark pieces of his models and, in the early part of his career, pieces of bone for the white pieces. In later years, he could afford ivory and carved entire trains, some with as many as 10,000 parts, from pure white ivory. Warther used arguto, an oil-bearing wood, for the moving parts of his carvings, some of which have run for sixty years without repair.

Of the steam locomotives displayed at Warther's, perhaps the most intriguing is the 8-foot replica of Abraham Lincoln's funeral train. An avid admirer of Lincoln, Warther spent a year at age eighty carving the ebony and ivory locomotive, coal car, funeral car, and passenger cars. Thousands of miniature parts make up the magnificent carving. As an example of the extraordinary detail work done by Warther, outside the rest room in one of the passenger cars even has a tiny ivory key hanging on a hook on the wall.

Warther's exacting craft demanded fine precision knives and blades, and, not satisfied with those commercially available, he created his own custom cutlery. In fact, he supplemented his income by selling this cutlery, a business still operated by his family today. Ernest Warther died at the age of eighty-seven in 1973, leaving his sixty-fourth carving incomplete.

The small original museum behind the present one now houses Mrs. Warther's button collection—more than 70,000 buttons, no two alike. Beautiful Swiss-style gardens surround the museums and the Warther home.

Warther's is at 327 Karl Avenue, Dover; (330) 343–7513. Open daily 9:00 A.M.–5:00 P.M., except for major holidays. Admission: adults $6.00; children, $3.00.

A new century was just beginning when Jeremiah E. Reeves moved his family into a newly remodeled home in 1901. Originally built as a stately eight-room farmhouse around 1870, the house was expanded into a magnificent seventeen-room mansion by Reeves, Dover's wealthiest citizen. Its gleaming white exterior is enhanced by dormers, bays, turrets, classical columns, and a porte cochere. To the rear of this Victorian mansion is a large turreted carriage house.

Today, the Dover Historical Society invites you to tour the *J. E. Reeves Victorian Home and Museum* for a magnificent look at turn-of-the-century elegance. Lush drawing-room draperies, gleaming windows of

Top Annual Events

Hopalong Cassidy Festival, Cambridge,
early May; (740) 439–6688

Dogwood Festival, Coshocton, early May;
(740) 622–0326

Dulcimer Days Festival, Coshocton, May;
(800) 877–1830

Trumpet in the Land, New Philadelphia,
June–August; (330) 339–1132

Bluegrass Festival,
Nova, May; (419) 668–8340

Cows and Curds, Zoar Village State
Memorial, June; (800) 874–4336

National Clay Week Festival,
Uhrichsville, June; (740) 922–1644

The Living Word Outdoor Drama,
Cambridge, June–September;
(740) 439–2761

Strawberry Festival,
Barnesville, June; (740) 425–4300

**Brigade of the American Revolution
Encampment,** Fort Laurens State
Memorial, Bolivar, June;
(800) 874–4336

Civil War Reenactment,
Infirmary Mound Park, Lancaster;
(740) 587–2535

Ohio Hills Folk Festival,
Quaker City, July; (740) 679–2954

Jamboree in the Hills,
Morristown, July; (800) 624–5456

Pro Football Hall of Fame Festival,
Canton, late July–August;
(800) 533–4302, (330) 456–7253

Sandy and Beaver Canal Days,
Magnolia, August; (330) 866–9034

Canal Festival,
Coshocton, August;
(800) 877–1830

Native American Gathering,
Gnadenhutten, August;
(740) 254–4143

**Buckeye Central Fall Foliage
Excursions (rail),**
Hebron, October;
(614) 366–2029

Buckeye Book Fair, Wooster,
November; (330) 264–1125 ext.317

Christmas at the Depot,
Orville, November; (330) 683–2426

Maple Syrup Trail, Newark, late
February to mid-March;
(614) 323–2355

stained and leaded glass, luxurious parquet floors, and artistic mementos of the Reeves family all greet the eye. Nearly all of the furnishings on display belong to the Reeveses and are placed where they were when the family lived here. Other special features include a distinctive hand-carved oak grand stairway and a delightful third-floor ballroom.

Out in the carriage house, built in 1902, the first floor houses a marvelous 1892 two-horse carriage that belonged to the Reeves family, a one-horse sleigh, and a 1922 automobile. Upstairs, visitors find remnants of the old Dover post office, along with displays of early household tools and sports memorabilia, plus historic maps, photographs, and documents. Following the crooked stairs to the Tower Rooms rewards the visitor with collections of old-fashioned cameras and radios.

The J. E. Reeves Victorian Home and Museum is at 325 East Iron Avenue, Dover; (800) 815–2794, (330) 343–7040. Open mid-May through October, Tuesday through Sunday, 10:00 A.M.–4:00 P.M and the first two weeks of December, noon–8:00 P.M. daily. Open other times of the year by appointment. Admission is $4.00 for adults, $2.00 for children.

More than 100 years after this Victorian home welcomed a farm family after a hard day's work, the *1881 Olde World Bed and Breakfast* now welcomes travelers for a peaceful retreat. The home, built with sun-baked brick and hand-hewn hardwood beams, was built, as you might have guessed, in 1881. Original features, such as pocket-doors and the solid walnut staircase, have been restored. The guest rooms have been updated, and the five suites have a private bath and are air-conditioned. Each of the rooms is decorated in a theme: the Victorian, the Parisian, the Oriental, the Mediterranean, and the Alpine. Some have old-fashioned claw-foot tubs, fireplaces, and king-size beds.

Guests are treated to a family-style breakfast every morning and can relax in the hot tub. Reservations are recommended; ask about the innkeeper's specials. Romantic packages are available; so are lunch, dinner, and tea but by reservation only.

The 1881 Olde World Bed and Breakfast is at 2982 State Route 516 NW, Dover; (330) 343–1333. Rates: $55 to $100 per night.

Seeking freedom from the new religious tenets in their native Kingdom of Wurttemburg in Germany, 300 men, women, and children known as Separatists, led by Joseph Baumeler, came to 5,500 acres they purchased along the Tuscarawas River, where they established *Zoar Village* in 1817. Two years later, frustrated by their progress to date, the Zoarites abandoned personal property ownership in order to establish a communal system. Under the new system, all property in the village was owned by the Society of Separatists at Zoar, with men and women each given a vote in the election of a board of trustees. The board governed the day-to-day operations of the community, and under this system, with Baumeler remaining as leader of the group, Zoar flourished.

The community established its own farms for food products, a tin shop, a blacksmith shop, two blast furnaces, a bakery, a garden with greenhouse, and a wagon shop. Many of these enterprises produced more goods than needed by the village, with the surplus sold for profit at a store established by the villagers. The Zoarites even landed the contract to build a section of the Ohio and Erie Canal, which passed through their land.

Cows 'n Curds

Quick, what is the month of June? If you said "Dairy Month" you'd be right. But whether you guessed correctly or not, you are still welcome to celebrate the dairy industry's history at Cows and Curds at Zoar Village Memorial.

The recently renovated dairy at Zoar Village is the backdrop for demonstrations of old-time dairy processing and practices such as butter churning. Cows and Curds is celebrated in June at the Zoar Village Memorial on State Route 212, Zoar. Call (800) 874–4336 for details.

In 1852, the assets of the society were more than a million dollars, and the future appeared bright for this hard-working community. But a year later, Joseph Baumeler was dead, leaving a serious leadership void at Zoar. Baumeler had served as the inspiration of the village, as well as its financial administrator. After his death, Zoar began a gradual decline, which persisted for forty years. Finally, in 1898, having lost its competitive edge both in agriculture and in industry, the community disbanded.

Many of the original Zoar buildings have been restored or reconstructed, allowing visitors to better understand the unique experiment that took place here. Inside the Number One House, an audiovisual presentation provides the history of the village. The rooms in this rambling two-story brick building, which once housed the aged and infirm, contain many original furnishings. In the music room, for example, is Peter Bimeler's magnificent hand-built pipe organ. Bimeler was the village miller, and he powered the organ with the mill's water turbine.

The second-floor windows provide a splendid view of the adjacent gardens and greenhouse. A guide at the greenhouse explains the religious significance of the formal gardens, with the large Norway spruce symbolizing Christ and the twelve slip junipers representing the apostles. The greenhouse, constructed in 1835, utilized a unique heating system—charcoal fires burned under the floor; vents funneled the warm air into the greenhouse—allowing the Zoarites to cultivate a wide variety of fruits and vegetables, including tropical fruits. In the Zoar bakery, huge wooden bins stored flour and meal, and the brick oven baked eighty loaves of bread per day.

Other buildings in the village include a tin shop, which has the tools, patterns, and products used and produced by the tinsmith, and the Bimeler House, with its outstanding collection of wool coverlets woven at the community's woolen mill. Knowledgeable guides provide information and answer questions in each building of the village.

Zoar Village is on Route 212, Zoar; (800) 874–4336, (330) 874–3011. Open from Memorial Day to Labor Day, Wednesday through Saturday, 9:30 A.M.–5:00 P.M.; Sunday, noon–5:00 P.M. Open weekends April,

May, September, and October. Admission: adults, $5.00; children (ages 6 to 12), $1.25.

"Rough it or plush it"—that's Ed and Mary Cowger's motto for their two Zoar bed-and-breakfasts. *The Inn at Cowger House #9* is what they call both nineteenth-century houses. Their 1817 Log Cabin, the second structure erected in Zoar, has three guest rooms, each with handmade quilts and a half bath. Its dining room is used for breakfast and other meals.

If you prefer the plush accommodations, try one of the three suites in the 1833 Manor House, two of which have their own Jacuzzis and fireplaces. Elegant cherry furniture, brass beds, and five working fireplaces add to the atmosphere.

Ed Cowger is a retired history teacher who "lives" the nineteenth century through his character—Edward of Virginia, a Civil War soldier. Mary is a cook and cookbook collector (with thousands of titles) who has assumed the character of Mary Zee of Zoar. They opened the inn in 1984, an alternative to early retirement.

The Inn at Cowger House #9 is on Fourth Street, Zoar; (330) 874–3542. Rates: $50 to $125 per night, double occupancy, including breakfast. Cash, Visa, and MasterCard accepted. Reservations recommended.

Proprietor R. A. Eichel operates the Zoar Tavern and Inn, built in 1831. This structure was once the home of Dr. Clemens Breil, who lived here

Mingo Junction

*G*eorge Washington slept here; actually he camped here in the fall of 1770. He came via canoe to scout the land in the Ohio Valley, and he found rugged country and plenty of Indians. He was here to secure land for the officers and soldiers of the Virginia Regiment before the British tried to claim it.

Upon his arrival in poor weather, Washington and his party heard of a killing down river, the direction they were heading. It was unclear if it was an Indian dispute or a simple homicide. After one night's rest, they left what is today Mingo Junction and paddled downstream.

They arrived at Powhatan Point, from which Washington dispatched several in his party to uncover the truth about the alleged murder. They returned and told Washington that the rumors were untrue; the death had been an accidental drowning. On October 25, 1770, they departed, continuing their journey down the Ohio River.

for many years—in fact, well after the dissolution of the Zoar Society.

Today, the Zoar Tavern and Inn, refurbished with ceiling fans and hardwood floors, serves soups, appetizers, salads, and a wide variety of sandwiches. Entrees such as broasted chicken, broiled scrod, and prime rib of beef au jus are also offered, as are a selection of fresh-cut steaks and broiled seafood. Try a hot apple dumpling topped with ice cream, French silk chocolate pie, or a hot peanut-butter fudge sundae for dessert. Overnight accommodations consist of five guest rooms, each decorated with period antiques, and each with original hand-hewn beams and exposed brick and stone walls. Your stay includes a continental breakfast.

The Zoar Tavern and Inn is at 162 Main Street, Zoar; (330) 874-2170. The tavern is open daily, 11:00 A.M.–10:00 P.M. Lodging rates: $70 to $95 per night. Visa, MasterCard, and American Express are accepted.

> ### Famous People from Little Cadiz
>
> *Little Cadiz boasts an impressive roster of native sons. Clark Gable was from this town, as was Edward Stanton, President Lincoln's Secretary of War during the Civil War, and John Bingham, who also has a Lincoln connection. Bingham, an attorney, worked in William Henry Harrison's presidential campaign and was elected to Congress in 1854. During his tenure in Washington, he served as special-judge advocate in the trial of Lincoln's assassins. He also was minister to Japan from 1873 to 1885.*

Named for Henry Laurens, then president of the Continental Congress, Fort Laurens, Ohio's only Revolutionary War fort, was constructed in 1778 as part of an ill-fated campaign to attack the British at Detroit. The 1,200 troops under the command of General Lachlan McIntosh, who built the fort, dubbed it "Fort Nonsense" since no attack on Detroit was ever executed. Supplying this wilderness outpost proved impossible, forcing the starving troops to survive on boiled moccasins while under siege from British-led Indians for a month. The fort was abandoned one year after it was built.

Today visitors to *Fort Laurens State Memorial* find the outline of the old fort, and a small museum commemorates the conflict both via video and artifacts from the fort's excavation. The remains of soldiers who died defending Fort Laurens are buried in a crypt in the museum wall and at the Tomb of the Unknown Patriot of the American Revolution.

Fort Laurens State Memorial is at 11067 Fort Laurens Road, NW, Bolivar; (800) 283-8914, (330) 874-2059. Open Memorial Day through Labor Day, Wednesday through Saturday, 9:30 A.M.–5:00 P.M.; Sunday, noon–5:00 P.M. Open weekends only in September and October. Admission: adults, $3.00; children (6 to 12), $1.25.

The House That Jack Built

You might know that Bellaire is the site of the original "house that Jack built." But did you know that "Jack" was a mule? Englishman Jacob Heatherington immigrated to this area and worked his way up from a laborer hauling coal to an industrialist. His faithful mule, Jack, helped him move coal in those early years, and Jacob never forgot this. So, when he erected a mansion in 1870, he referred to it as the "house that Jack built" and even took the old mule on a tour of the home's interior, describing the features as they clip-clopped through the magnificent residence. Jack died shortly afterward, and Jacob, grief-stricken, buried him nearby under an apple tree.

Missionary David Zeisberger migrated to the United States in 1737 to work with the American Moravian Church in Bethlehem, Pennsylvania. In 1772, accompanied by a band of Delaware Indians, Zeisberger traveled to the wilderness in Ohio to convert other Indians to Christianity, founding *Schoenbrunn Village.*

The efforts at Schoenbrunn were interrupted by the coming of the Revolutionary War. The village was on the trail between the American outpost at Fort Pitt and the British at Fort Detroit, and neither side trusted the Moravians or their Christian Indians. Harassment eventually forced Zeisberger to abandon Schoenbrunn Village in 1777 and to relocate to a new settlement at nearby Gnadenhutten. Even there, they were not safe. The British arrested Zeisberger and other village leaders and transported them to Detroit for trial on charges of treason. While the leaders were away, American troops, seeking revenge for the death of a settler's wife and children, massacred the Christian Indians at Gnadenhutten by striking them with heavy coopers' mallets.

Schoenbrunn Village today contains eighteen reconstructed rustic log buildings, the original village cemetery, and two and a half acres of planted fields. Log cots with stretched animal skins and a firepit in the center of the floor (with a hole in the roof for smoke to escape) are the only conveniences in some of these cabins. Others feature modest pioneer furnishings such as rough rope-spring beds, wooden baby cradles, spinning and flax wheels, and butter churns. Schoenbrunn's settlers constructed Ohio's first schoolhouse, a one-room building completed in 1773. In addition to the log structures, a museum displays Schoenbrunn artifacts excavated from the site, including nails, knives, horseshoes, and chips of cups, jars, and a kettle used at the village more than two hundred years ago.

Schoenbrunn Village is on the southeast edge of New Philadelphia on Route 259; (800) 752–2711, (330) 339–3636. Open Memorial Day to Labor Day, Monday through Saturday, 9:30 A.M.–5:00 P.M.; Sunday, noon–5:00 P.M. Open weekends in September and October. Admission: adults, $5.00; children (ages 6 to 12), $1.25.

For a dramatic presentation of the story of David Zeisberger and the settlement of Schoenbrunn and Gnadenhutten, attend a performance of Paul Green's ***Trumpet in the Land.*** Staged in a lovely hilltop outdoor amphitheater, this spirited drama uses a mix of song and dance, humor, adventure, and ultimately tragedy to tell of Zeisberger's missionary work in frontier Ohio.

Schoenbrunn Village

Trumpet in the Land is presented at the Schoenbrunn Amphitheatre on University Drive, just off Route 250, New Philadelphia; (330) 339-1132. Performances from late June through late August, Tuesday through Sunday, at 8:30 P.M. Admission: adults, $12.00; children, $6.00. Reserved tickets available. MasterCard and Visa are accepted.

The ***Friends Meeting House,*** set in a field in a hilly section of Jefferson County, housed the annual August meeting of 2,000 Ohio and Pennsylvania Quakers for nearly a century. Constructed in 1814, this impressive three-story brick structure measures 92 feet by 60 feet and has walls 2 feet thick.

The Society of Friends relocated an entire meeting from North Carolina to Jefferson County in 1813 and built the meetinghouse of brick fired right on the site. The interior of the building is one large room, with the original floors, poplar benches, and a large balcony. A massive wooden center divider splits the room—four men in the attic raised and lowered this divider as needed. Men sat on one side of the room during the meetings, women on the other side, and young men and women sat in their respective balconies. The elders and overseers used the facing benches—benches resting on a small platform and facing the congregation. "Strict services" took place here until 1909, with no formal ceremony or music; the group simply meditated in silence until a member felt moved to speak out. The interior of the

Barnesville's "Gay '90s Mansion"

Founded in 1808 by James Barnes, a Quaker from Maryland, Barnesville prospered as a producer of tobacco and strawberries during the nineteenth century. As the town flourished, so did its banks. It was the Bradfields, the owners of the First National Bank, who built the town's most dramatic residence, what's known as the "Gay 90's Mansion."

This elegant, twenty-six room, eleven-thousand-square-foot structure, complete with dramatic turret, took five years to construct at a cost of $60,000 when completed in 1893. During its prime, the mansion hosted Barnesville's most important dinners and parties, guests climbing the massive oak staircase to the third-floor ballroom. Today, the mansion is a museum and the restored home of the local historical society.

meetinghouse is exactly as it was 170 years ago, though it has been more than 70 years since the Quakers last gathered in Jefferson County.

The Friends Meeting House is just off Route 150 in Mount Pleasant. Open by appointment; call Sherry Sawchuk, (800) 752–2631, (614) 769–2893. Admission: adults, $2.00; children, $1.00.

Amish Country

Ohio's largest Amish and Swiss Mennonite communities are in four east central Ohio counties: Holmes, Wayne, Tuscarawas, and Stark. The Amish espouse a simple agrarian lifestyle and reject the use of automobiles and electricity as potentially disruptive to that lifestyle. Living in the twentieth century without electricity creates a demand for unusual products, such as kerosene-powered refrigerators, and one Wayne County business, *Lehman Hardware,* has established itself as the nonelectric appliance and equipment supplier for the area's substantial Amish population.

Although Lehman's stocks the nails, wire, and garden tools found in every hardware store, the bulk of the floor space is dedicated to merchandise such as gas-powered washing machines and gas and kerosene lamps. Wood- and coal-burning cooking and heating stoves fill one large showroom, with many of the cooking stoves ornately trimmed in chrome and costing from $700 to $3,000. Used cooking stoves (trade-ins) are also available.

Other items in Lehman's inventory include hardwood fruit presses, an apple parer, a cherry stoner, and a bottle capper. How many other stores carry a variety of hand-crank butter churns and a hand-powered cream separator that produces eighty-five liters of milk per hour?

The store's crowded hitching posts, used by the Amish to secure their horse-drawn buggies, indicate the popularity of Lehman Hardware with the local Amish population, but in recent years Lehman's has attracted another type of customer—people drawn to wood- and coal-burning appliances because of the increasing cost of utilities. Lehman's sells a 128-page catalog called *Lehman's Non-Electric Good Neighbor Heritage Catalog* for $2.00. It's full of major appliances, small gristmills, copper wash boilers, sausage stuffers, noodle makers, and carbide lamps. And city people have been known to purchase unique nonelectric devices, particularly the fancy chrome cooking stoves, simply for use as decorative pieces.

Lehman Hardware is 2 miles west of Route 94 in downtown Kidron; (330) 857–5441. Open Monday through Saturday, 8:00 A.M.–5:30 P.M.; Thursday until 8:00 P.M.

Just down the street is the **Kidron Town and Country Store,** where you can purchase an array of Amish clothing—men's broadfall barndoor pants, black felt church hats, and wide-rimmed flat or mushroom-top straw hats.

Upstairs you'll find quilting supplies, and the store also offers fresh-cut meats, fresh fruits and vegetables, and other grocery items. It has long been the custom of the Amish to come in from the fields at noon and enjoy *es midaugh.* They continue that tradition at the store, serving a hearty midday meal prepared by local Amish women.

The Kidron Town and Country Store is at 4959 Kidron Road, Kidron; (330) 857–2131, 857–4151. Open Monday, Tuesday, Wednesday, and Saturday, 7:00 A.M.–8:00 P.M.; Thursday and Friday, 7:00 A.M.–9:00 P.M.

After establishing their Christmas tree farm, Robert Dush and his son Roger's next challenge was to convert a barn built in the 1860s into a Christmas shop and country store, the **Pine Tree Barn.** This massive old barn has been designated a Wayne County Historic Landmark, and its original rough-hewn beams and floors create a rustic atmosphere.

What started as a gift shop in 1980 has evolved into a complete home furnishing and accessories center, featuring indoor and outdoor lighting, carpeting, floor covering, and window treatment, plus gifts and accessories, all displayed on three floors in this marvelous historic structure. In fact, Roger Dush and his wife, Rita, today offer a complete interior decorating and design service. The gift shops at Pine Tree include a Colonial Williamsburg shop; a floral shop featuring silk and dried flowers, wreaths, and garlands; and a year-round Christmas shop. Christmas is a special time of year at Pine Tree; you'll find ten or more fully decorated trees in the Christmas alcove, along with hundreds of unique ornaments and baubles.

A similar transformation took place at The Granary, Pine Tree's dining facility. In the early 80s, this former dairy barn's old grain bins were converted into a small kitchen, serving simple refreshments. Today, The Granary presents gourmet lunches of crepes, quiches, soups, salads, fresh breads and muffins, and sandwiches. Top off your meal with a slice of one of the sour cream fruit pies, a Pine Tree Barn tradition for more than a decade.

Large windows along the back wall of the barn provide those eating lunch with a view down the hill to the private forty-acre lake and rows of young Christmas trees. Diners also see antique farm implements on the walls of the barn and the block and tackle that once hauled bales of hay up from the ground level to the second-floor loft.

The Pine Tree Barn is on Route 226, 4 miles south of Wooster, (330) 264–1014. Open daily, 10:00 A.M.–5:00 P.M.

The Charles Randolph Compton family built a Victorian farmhouse in 1881, and the family owned the property for more than ninety years. Two of Compton's descendents, Leila and Mary Belle, lived in this home until 1990. Leila was a recognized authority on herbs, and she and her sister often served syrups and jams made from their garden herbs when they entertained. Their grape arbor, apple and cherry trees, and roses remain to this day.

Jim and Marty Taggart lived in the Taggart family home (built in 1883) next door to the Compton house in 1990 when Leila and Mary were no longer able to live on their own. They purchased the property and began a massive, two-year renovation inside and out. They opened the **Leila Belle Inn** as a bed-and-breakfast in 1993.

Today, visitors enjoy four bedrooms, each with private bath, in this revitalized Victorian home. Its three acres include red bud and dogwood trees, restored gardens, walking paths, porches, and patios. Enjoy a leisurely breakfast of juice, fresh fruit compote, homemade granola with yogurt, and assorted goodies such as blueberry lemon bread, lemon crumb muffins, or apple strudel coffeecake.

The Leila Belle Inn is at 846 East Bowman Street, Wooster; (888) 430–7378, (330) 262–8866. Rates: $55 to $80 per night. Visa and MasterCard accepted.

Set in rolling Wayne County farmland is charming **Quailcrest Farm.** More than six hundred different herbs and perennial plants, both potted and field grown, are cultivated here, ready for transplanting to your backyard garden. Shrubs and trees are also available. April through June is the peak season for plants at Quailcrest, but a good selection is available throughout the summer and into fall.

In addition to two working greenhouses, Quailcrest has three shops for visitors to explore. Inside the Country Gallery (behind the family farmhouse), an extensive selection of hand-thrown pottery competes for attention with jewelry, copper pieces, puzzles, and games. Children's gifts and books fill a second-floor loft.

Down the walk through a flower-lined pergola you will find the new Phoenix Shop, which replaces the barn and shop destroyed by fire in 1986. Herb products, garden books and cookbooks, wreaths and arrangements, woven rugs, and decorative pieces all are available here. The Garden Barn, large and airy, features sculptures and benches for your garden, terra-cotta, and farm-grown dried flowers.

Browsers will enjoy five acres of display gardens overlooking the Killbuck Valley. Included are herb gardens, shade gardens, perennial borders, and water gardens. The first Saturday after Labor Day marks a popular annual event—the Quailcrest Farm Herb Fair. More than sixty craftspeople exhibit the fruits of their labors, including pottery, baskets, stone carvings, and culinary herbs and arrangements.

Quailcrest Farm is off Route 83 at 2810 Armstrong Road, 4 miles north of Wooster (7 miles south of I-71); (330) 345-6722. Open mid-March through December, Tuesday through Saturday, 10:00 A.M.–5:00 P.M.; Sunday (April through June and December only) 1:00–5:00 P.M. (extended hours in May and December).

Out-of-state antique dealers have frequented Jeromesville, Ohio, for years, but most native Ohioans are unaware of the town's reputation as an antiques stop. George Delagrange owns one of Jeromesville's more intriguing shops, *Delagrange Antiques,* which is in an 1870s storefront that originally housed the town's drugstore.

Delagrange's twenty-year-old business specializes in the poplar, cherry, and walnut pieces so in demand with East Coast buyers. Delagrange (whose name means "from the farm" in French) purchases four-poster rope-spring beds, cupboards, tables, and chests from area farms, selling hundreds of major pieces each year. In addition, Delagrange has a modest inventory of exquisite handmade quilts. George and his wife, Susan, always are delighted to chat with visitors about tidbits of local history that pertain to the pieces in the shop.

Delagrange Antiques is at 12 North High Street (Route 89), Jeromesville; (419) 368-8371. Open Saturday and Sunday, noon–5:00 P.M., and often during the week. Call ahead to be sure.

The natural beauty of the Mohican area, with its steep and rolling hills, swift rivers, and deep forests, once prompted world-famous author Louis Bromfield to remark, "I live on the edge of paradise." Visitors to the area quickly realize that statement was no exaggeration. White pines flourish along the ridges of the *Mohican State Park,* while hemlock abounds in the hollows and gorges.

Cabins in Ohio's state parks typically are located in scenic surroundings, but the twenty-five two-bedroom Mohican State Park cabins, isolated from the rest of the park in woodlands along the bank of Clear Fork Creek, may just be in the most picturesque setting of any cabins in Ohio. They come furnished with all linens, blankets, and kitchen equipment and may be rented in the summer for full weeks only. (There are no restrictions on the length of stay the rest of the year.) Canoeing and rafting are favorite summertime activities on Clear Fork Creek, and hiking, fishing, and camping are also popular in the park.

Mohican State Park cabins are on Route 3, just north of Route 97, Loudonville; (800) 282–7275. Open year-round. Rates range from $100 for the first day to $540 per week. Early reservations are a must.

Another lodging option in the lush Mohican State Park is the impressive stone-and-timber Mohican Lodge perched on a bluff overlooking Pleasant Hill Lake. Each room in the lodge has a private balcony or patio, many with views of either the lake or the woods surrounding the lodge. Facilities include an indoor and outdoor pool, two tennis courts, shuffleboard, and a game room. In addition to the meals served in the dining room, poolside barbecues are offered occasionally during summer months.

The Mohican State Park Lodge is on Route 97, 6 miles west of

State Flag/Pennant

*F*lying overhead at public buildings and parks in Ohio, visitors may be surprised to see what appears to be a pennant where they would expect a state flag to fly. That is Ohio's state flag. No other state flag has a pennant shape.

Cleveland designer John Eisenmann created this unusual design in the 1880s. At the wide end of the pennant is a blue triangle with a large circle and seventeen stars. The thirteen stars clustered closest to the circle represent the thirteen colonies. The four stars at the apex of the triangle represent the next four states admitted to the Union, since Ohio was the seventeenth state to join the Union. The circle represents the Northwest Territory, but with a smaller red circle at its center; it also forms an O for "Ohio."

Loudonville; (800) 282–7275. Open year-round. Rates: $104 to $135 per night, double occupancy.

The confluence of Black Fork River and Clear Fork Creek forms the scenic Mohican River, probably Ohio's most popular stream for canoeing, kayaking, and rafting. Canoe liveries rent hundreds of canoes and kayaks in the Loudonville area, from as early as April to as late as November. With prices of $15 and up per canoe and trips lasting from two hours to several days, the liveries provide access to these scenic waterways. One of the liveries, on Route 3 south of Loudonville and north of Route 97, is the Mohican Canoe Livery and Fun Center, which also has go-carts, horseback rides, water slides, and miniature golf; (800) 662–2663, (419) 994–4097. Many other liveries operate in the area, and a complete list is available from the Loudonville Chamber of Commerce, Loudonville, 44842 or by calling (800) BUCKEYE, Ohio's tourism information center.

Another enjoyable way to explore the 4,000-acre Mohican State Forest is on horseback, and **Bit 'N Bridle Stables** offers guided trail rides through sections of this vast wooded preserve. Along the paths, riders enjoy the deer, rabbits, and multicolored wildflowers in this peaceful state forest. Trail rides cost $11.50 for the first hour. For groups of ten or more, Bit 'N Bridle gives hayrides for $4.00 per person.

Bit 'N Bridle Stables is at 996 County Road 3275, off Route 3 south of Route 97, Perrysville; (419) 938–8681. Open daily, April through November.

It's a dream you may have had, too: Purchase one of those charming Victorian houses on a quiet street in a small Ohio town and restore it to create the perfect bed-and-breakfast. City people would flock to your new establishment, attracted by the charm of your stately residence, not to mention your gracious hospitality. You would earn extra income while enjoying the company of "new friends."

I'm sure that's what the couple who originally restored the **Blackfork Inn** believed when they acquired this 1865-vintage property on Water Street in Loudonville. Built by Philip J. Black, this delightful brick three-story home seemed destined to be a fine small inn. And the couple restoring it decided to "do it right" by importing antiques from Europe, installing a complete commercial kitchen, securing accurate reproductions of period wallpapers, and updating the six guest rooms with private baths, while retaining the high ceilings and natural woodwork that make such properties both distinctive and desirable. It's rumored they spent upwards of a half-million dollars on this project, and that may have been their undoing. Less than a year from their grand opening, the Blackfork Inn was closed down and boarded up—its brief resurrection snuffed out.

Blackfork Inn

On Labor Day weekend in 1982, Al and Sue Gorisek arrived at the sheriff's auction at the Blackfork hoping to pick up some good deals on antiques, which they have collected for years. But they walked away as the proud new owners of the entire inn.

Philip Black built his home from the profits he made during the Civil War selling groceries and such to Federal troops. It's said he was instrumental in bringing the railroad to Loudonville, so it seems appropriate that railroad tracks are next door—it's the main line between New York and Chicago, so trains do rumble by!

Both Goriseks are in publishing: Al is an editor for the *Cleveland Plain Dealer,* Sue writes for *Ohio Magazine* and other publications. And the Blackfork has become Sue's other career—she splits her time between their home in Cleveland and the inn. Sue is perhaps the perfect host for such a place, for as a freelance writer, she travels the state extensively and has plenty of tips for guests on where to go and what to see in the area.

Accommodations at the Blackfork Inn include exquisite breakfasts, such as fresh fruit, a breakfast entree, and a raspberry crepe. Although no other meals are routinely served, an area chef is available to prepare elegant meals for guests, with approximately one week's notice.

The Blackfork Inn is at 303 North Water Street, Loudonville; (419) 994–3252. Rates: $43 single, $65 to $75 double, including breakfast. MasterCard and Visa are accepted. Open year-round.

The fertile, rolling farmland of Holmes County is the center of Ohio's largest Amish community, with 20,000 of the 70,000 Amish in the United States living in the area. Amish men and women can be seen in the markets, restaurants, and shops, or driving their black horse-drawn buggies through the pastoral countryside.

Amish restaurants in Holmes and surrounding counties serve simple country cooking at reasonable prices, and shops sell Amish goods, such as quilts. This section of east central Ohio also contains a sizable Swiss Mennonite population, and there are many cheese houses producing Swiss cheese from the milk brought in by Amish dairy farmers.

The Amish split with the Mennonite Church in 1609 to follow the leadership of Jacob Amman, from whom the sect gets its name. Facing religious persecution in their native Germany and Switzerland, they began a migration to the United States in the mid-1700s, settling in Pennsylvania, where many Amish live today. The move to Ohio took place in the 1820s, and the Amish have continued their agricultural traditions for the past 150 years.

Artist Heinz Gaugel painted the history of the Amish-Mennonite-Hutterite people in a spectacular 10-foot-by-265-foot cyclorama called *Behalt*, which means "remembering." Completed in 1992 after four years' labor, Behalt spans the centuries from the time of Christ to the Amish migration to the New World. Behalt is permanently displayed at the Mennonite Information Center, where guides use the cyclorama to educate visitors about Amish history, culture, and lifestyle.

Behalt is at the Mennonite Information Center, 5798 County Road 77, Berlin; (330) 893–3192. Open Monday through Saturday, 9:00 A.M.–5:00 P.M.; extended hours until 8:00 P.M., Friday and Saturday, June through October. Admission: adults, $5.50; children ages 6 to 12, $2.50.

Gloria and Eli Yoder's *Amish Home* is a hundred-acre working farm that can be explored by visitors to Amish country. Children will enjoy the horses, rabbits, chickens, sheep, cows, pigs, and goats that fill the barn. Adults will probably be more interested in the two farmhouses, both built more than a hundred years ago. The first home on your tour contains furnishings typical of an Amish farmhouse in the late 1800s. Built in 1866, this home last served as a residence thirty years ago. Its wood floors, simple heavy furniture, wood-burning stove, and people-powered appliances (such as a pump sewing machine) give a glimpse of the lifestyle of Amish farm families.

The larger home at the Amish Home, constructed in 1885 and occupied for one hundred years, is similarly furnished but contains some unusual items such as gas floor lamps. Religious services have been held here many times, as in most Amish homes and barns. These services take three full hours to complete.

Many who visit here enjoy buggy tours of the property, which even has a hilltop family cemetery. Inside the craft shop, you'll discover quilts, dolls, pottery, woodwork, and many other country favorites. And be

Also Worth Seeing

Salt Fork State Park,
Cambridge

Steubenville Murals,
Steubenville

Fort Steuben, Steubenville

sure to pick up a copy of the *Downhome Shoppers Guide.* This hundred-page magazine-style publication is the guide to Ohio's Amish settlements. It's packed with information on Amish restaurants, tours, crafts, quilts, cheese, and the like, with hundreds of entries and very detailed maps.

Yoder's Amish Home is on Route 515 between Trail and Walnut Creek; (330) 893–2541. Open April through October, Monday through Saturday, 10:00 A.M.–5:00 P.M. Tours: adults, $3.50; children, $1.50. Buggy rides: adults, $2.00; children, $1.00.

If you admire fine handmade quilts, stop by the ***Helping Hands Quilt Shop.*** A nonprofit enterprise with all proceeds donated to charities and missions, the shop stocks hundreds of marvelous quilts in every conceivable pattern and color combination. Many of these are sewn in the large, sunlit quilting room in the back of the shop, where Helping Hands serves a social function in addition to its contributions to charity.

Helping Hands will quilt your quilt top, custom design a quilt for you, or even finish a quilt you have already started. The shop also sells quilted pillow covers, quilting books, embroidery kits and floss, quilting needles, thread, fabrics, stencils, and patterns—in short, everything a quilter could need.

The Helping Hands Quilt Shop is on Route 39 in Berlin; (330) 893–2410. Open Monday through Saturday, 9:00 A.M.–5:00 P.M.

A variety of romantic options await guests of ***Donna's Premier Lodging*** in the heart of Amish country. Along with rooms in the main building, Donna's offers a variety of cottagelike accommodations roughly 1 mile from the main lodge. Honeymoon and anniversary chalets are two-level, brick, free-standing guest cottages located on a wooded hillside. Designed as a luxurious retreat, they feature a main level with a king-sized bed, a brick fireplace, and a heart-shaped Jacuzzi for two. The lower level is a recreation room with another fireplace and a billiard table. Throughout the chalets you will find elegant touches such as leaded glass windows, a chandelier, and homemade cookies for your late-night snack. Chalets are equipped with two televisions, stereo, CD player, microwave, coffee maker, and a refrigerator. The log cabin is similarly equipped but has a queen-sized bed tucked in a loft.

Whether summer or winter, the cabin, cottages, and chalets offer guests natural views and a good opportunity to wander just outside the door to visit with the birds or enjoy the natural woodland displays.

Donna's Premier Lodging is located $\frac{1}{2}$ block off Main Street on East Street, just behind the Helping Hands Quilt Shop, Berlin; (800) 320–3338, (330) 893–3068. Rates: $55 to $225 per night.

Opened for guests in 1996, *Garden Gate Get-A-Way* has a surprisingly long history. Many elements in the home are from a dismantled one-room schoolhouse. The original bell tower now is perched on the roof's south peak, and the original foundation stones now form many of the retaining walls and line the flowerbeds. Inside, lumber, oak flooring, tongue 'n groove ceiling, and wainscoting have found new uses in this modern facility.

Roger and Laverta Steiner (and their children) are your innkeepers, offering four very different guestrooms, each with a garden theme. The Potting Shed Room features a picket fence headboard, a cane chair, and a hickory rocker. A white iron bed is the centerpiece of the Rose Garden Room, flanked by an antique tapestry chair and chest. The Briar Patch Room and the Grape Arbor Room both feature engraved headboards and individual furnishings. All four have private baths, queen-size beds, and coffee makers.

The beautiful gardens include a grape arbor, birdhouses, and porch swings. Roger's design talent is on display with the fieldstone landscaping and winding brick paths through the lush gardens.

Garden Gate Get-A-Way is located just outside Berlin; (330) 893–3999. Rates: $65 to $85 per night.

Established in 1840, the *Rastetter Woolen Mill* is Holmes County's oldest business, and it's still going strong. The mill processes raw wool into wool batting to make its famous wool comforters. Other Rastetter products are rag rugs (in a variety of colors, sizes, and fabrics), goose feather and goose down pillows and comforters, and synthetic comforters. Also sold are sheepskin slippers and mittens and wool socks, plus clothing from Woolrich, Pendleton, Ruff, Wigwam, Fox River, and Uug shoes.

The Rastetter Woolen Mill is on Routes 39 and 62 between Millersburg and Berlin; (330) 674–2103. Open Monday through Saturday, 10:00 A.M.–5:00 P.M.

If you look for an antique dealer at the *Antique Emporium*, you'll be in for more than you bargained for. The shop located 2 blocks west of the Town Square in Millersburg is really two shops five doors apart and home to more than sixty different antique dealers.

The wide range of antique dealers in this historic hardware store building gives the shop a particularly broad range of merchandise. Since dealers are also on the lookout for the next unique item, the stock in the shop is ever changing. The discriminating buyer can seek out china, textiles, Victorian and country furniture, toys, primitives, books, glassware, and a range of collectibles.

Do-it-yourselfers can find great raw material on the second floor of the 113 West Jackson Street shop in the "Furniture in the Rough" section. Those seeking an appraisal of a special object can bring it in the first Sunday of each month between 1:00 and 2:30 P.M. Delivery service is available for shoppers who purchase more than the car trunk or van can handle.

The Antique Emporium is located at 113 West Jackson Street and 155 West Jackson Street, Millersburg; (330) 674–0510. Open Monday through Saturday, 10:00 A.M.–5:00 P.M.; Sunday 10:00 A.M.–4:00 P.M.

When I first heard about a "modern" inn that opened outside Millersburg, right in the heart of Amish country, I must admit I was skeptical. I envisioned a motel-like structure on a bulldozed and paved chunk of earth, and I wasn't thrilled by the prospect.

The Inn at Honey Run does not fit that description in the least. As you motor up a winding county road, through dense vegetation, your curiosity can't help but be aroused. And when you reach the tasteful contemporary structure that is the Inn at Honey Run, it's difficult not to let out a sigh of approval. Carefully blended into the surrounding trees—trees so close that I'm not sure how they managed to get the inn up without disturbing them—is a truly unique getaway. Lots of exposed wood, inside and out, creates a harmony between the inn and the peaceful forest. The inn's twenty-five guest rooms combine a potpourri of styles—everything from Shaker and Early American to very contemporary. Cherry, pine, oak, and walnut furnishings complete these rooms; some feature bi-level floor plans with skylights. All have living areas and tabletop space for work (if absolutely necessary), writing, card playing, or whatever.

Up a hill from the main inn are twelve additional guest rooms in a most unusual setting—dug into the hillside. Called the Honeycomb, this earth-sheltered building looks down onto a peaceful landscape. Each room has a stone patio, wood-burning fireplace, and bath with whirlpool tub. And breakfast is served right to your door. The newest accommodations are two two-bedroom cabins, nestled in the woods.

If you can't stay the night, then come by and enjoy an excellent meal in the dining room, which has a wall of glass for viewing the trees and wildflowers. Amish quilts hang on the walls. The inn prides itself on its from-scratch recipes, including some spectacular pastries and desserts, and regional specialties like Holmes County pan-fried trout. The dining room is open to all for lunch and dinner, by reservation, Monday through Saturday. Overnight guests have the place to themselves on Sundays.

The Inn at Honey Run is 3 miles northeast of Millersburg, off Route 241 on County Road 203; (800) 468–6639 (in Ohio), (330) 674–0011. Lodging rates: $65 to $225 per night for two people, including continental breakfast. Visa, MasterCard, and American Express are accepted. Open year-round.

Charm is the state's only predominantly Amish town, and evidence of that fact includes the popularity of the local icehouse (since the Amish don't use electric refrigerators), the town's harness shop (for the horse-drawn buggies and field horses' leather needs), and the hitching posts behind the popular *Homestead Restaurant.*

This is not the largest Amish restaurant in the county, nor the fanciest, but it does serve authentic Amish cooking at reasonable prices. The menu features a variety of sandwiches, and the dinner entrees include country favorites such as fried chicken, pork chops, steaks, ham, and fish. Family-style dinners of chicken, roast beef, and ham, or any combination of the three, include a choice of vegetables and potatoes. Fresh desserts are one of the trademarks of Amish restaurants, and the Homestead is no exception, offering very tasty peanut butter cream and pecan pies, plus date pudding, sundaes, and Amish cracker pudding. Homemade breads and pastries are also available to carry out.

For a total immersion into the life of Charm, spend the night in the accommodations offered above the restaurant or in the cottage across the street. The three units upstairs are available to a single party and rent for $65 each. The cottage has a private bath, sitting room, a great fireplace, and rents for $80 per night. Both include breakfast and dinner at the restaurant.

The Homestead Restaurant is on Route 557 in Charm; (330) 893–2717. Open Monday through Saturday, 7:30 A.M.–8:00 P.M.

Just up the road is the "home of Ohio Baby Swiss Cheese," the *Guggisberg Cheese Company,* owned and operated by Alfred and Margaret

State Bird/Fish/Insect

The designation of the cardinal as Ohio's state bird was uncontroversial; the Ohio General Asembly unanimously made it official in 1933. Lawmakers deemed the choice appropriate because the cardinal is a permanent resident of the state, its song is pleasing to hear, and its coloring is impressive. But other species have not had it so easy. A debate in the 1980s between fans of the walleye and boosters of the smallmouth bass resulted in a legislative standoff; neither side could muster the votes to be declared Ohio's state fish. One species that did make the cut: the ladybug. Legislators declared it the state insect in 1975.

Guggisberg. Born in Switzerland, Alfred began work in a cheese factory more than forty years ago at the age of sixteen.

Today, their plant produces 1,000 five-pound wheels of baby Swiss each day between 10:00 A.M. and noon, cheese that is then shipped worldwide. Local Amish dairy farmers supply the milk to Guggisberg, which arrives daily in horse-pulled wagons. Visitors to the plant can see the cheese forming in large stainless-steel vats by looking through the windows that connect the plant with the retail store. Guggisberg stocks a wide variety of cheeses in addition to Ohio baby Swiss, and cuckoo clocks, books, gift items, and ice cream are also sold.

Guggisberg Cheese is on Route 557, north of Charm; (800) 262–2505, (330) 893–2500. Open during warm months Monday through Saturday, 8:00 A.M.–6:00 P.M.; Sunday, 11:00 A.M.–4:00 P.M. Open the rest of the year Monday through Saturday, 8:00 A.M.–5:00 P.M.

If you want to unwind after a day of touring Amish country, the *Guggisberg Swiss Inn* is waiting to welcome you with a comfortable room and a country-style breakfast. The inn is a modern structure set in Amish farming country. You can hike or picnic nearby or just take a walk around the inn pond to watch the swans. In the winter months sleigh rides take guests into the rolling countryside.

Rooms are air-conditioned and all have private baths and in-room coffee. Breakfast is included in the room rate and takes advantage of the wonderful, fresh goodies available in farm country.

The Guggisberg Swiss Inn is located at 5025 State Route 557, Charm; (330) 893–3600. Rates: $69 to $145 per night.

One of Ashland's best-known landmark homes is now a delightful bed-and-breakfast, the *Winfield Bed & Breakfast*. Built in 1876 in the Victorian Italianate style, it's perched on two acres of well-manicured lawns and gardens surrounded by green pastures.

Visitors have a choice of two very different rooms, each with private bath. Light pours into the elegant Garden Suite, which features English country decor and a private sitting room. The room's centerpiece is a full-size canopied Shaker bed, and French doors open to a garden terrace. The East Room is more formal, with its magnificent eighteenth-century French armoire and wingback chairs.

Your arrival is greeted with a fresh fruit and cheese plate, and each morning starts with a gourmet breakfast. The nightly turndown service includes fine French chocolate mints.

The Winfield Bed & Breakfast is at 1568 State Route 60, Ashland; (800) 269–7166, (419) 281–5587. Rates: $75 to $90 per night. Visa, Master-Card, and American Express accepted.

Country Charm

The nearly 10,000 acres that constitute *The Wilds* have made a dramatic transformation—from an open strip mine (and blight on the landscape) to North America's largest preserve for endangered species. American Electric Power reclaimed the land and then gave it as a gift to spur the creation of this unique facility. Animals from around the world are free to roam the rolling hills; visitors observe them from buses, which take you past every species imaginable.

The preserve is divided in large sections where African, Asian, and North American wildlife live and thrive. During your visit, you might encounter camel, exotic deer, wild horses, or rhinos. Zebras and giraffes mingle with gazelles and antelopes in the preserve's African environment. During your visit, you'll learn the issues affecting the survival of each species.

The Wilds is at 14000 International Road, Cumberland; (740) 638–5030. Open daily May through October, first tour at 10:00 A.M. last tour at 4:00 P.M. (5:00 P.M. in June, July, and August). Admission: adults, $8.00; children (4 to 12), $5.00.

Eastern Ohio, western Pennsylvania, and northern West Virginia were once the center of the U.S. glassware industry, and Cambridge, Ohio, was an important city for the glass business. The large Cambridge Glass Company dominated glass production in Guernsey County, opening in the spring of 1902 and shutting down half a century later. Although the boom in glassmaking has since passed, the *Degenhart Paperweight and Glass Museum* preserves the heritage of the industry.

By a bequest in her will, Elizabeth Degenhart established the museum. Born in 1889, she had been associated with the glass business most of her life. She went to work at Cambridge Glass at age sixteen and married

John Degenhart in 1908. John's father, Andrew, had been a mold maker in several glass factories, and John worked for the Cambridge Glass Company for forty-six years, until his retirement. John and Elizabeth established the Crystal Art Glass Company, which Elizabeth took over after John's death in 1964.

The museum contains Elizabeth Degenhart's personal collection of paperweights, plus pieces from Cambridge Glass and Crystal Art Glass. Various cut- and blown-glass pieces are displayed, as is an antique glass mold built 150 years ago. An audiovisual presentation explains the history and importance of the glass industry to the area and describes the glassmaking still taking place in Guernsey County.

The Degenhart Paperweight and Glass Museum is on Route 22, just west of I–77, Cambridge; (614) 432–2626. The museum is open Monday through Saturday, 9:00 A.M.–5:00 P.M.; Sunday, 1:00–5:00 P.M., March through December; Monday through Saturday, 9:00 A.M.–5:00 P.M.; Sunday, 1:00–5:00 P.M. January and February. Admission: adults, $1.50; children (under 18), free.

Just down the street from the museum, *Mosser Glass* offers free tours of their factory to the public. Mosser manufactures glass pitchers, goblets, candleholders, lamps, and animal figures such as frogs, owls, cats, and rabbits.

During the tour, guides explain glassmaking, from heating glass powder to 2,000 degrees in the furnace to forming molten glass in a cast-iron mold. After being pressed in a mold, the shaped glass goes under a flame "glazer," which smooths the surface by reheating the exterior. From there, the molded hot glass cools in a special oven called a Lehr, which uniformly reduces the temperature to prevent shattering. Mosser Glass cranks out 150 pieces of glass per hour.

Mosser Glass is one-half mile west of I–77 on Route 22, Cambridge; (614) 439–1827. Tours are given at 8:15, 9:15, 10:15, noon, 1:00, 2:00, and 3:00, Monday through Friday. No tours the first two weeks of July or Christmas week. No admission charge.

Roscoe Village served as an important canal port during the Ohio and Erie Canal's boom years in the 1840s and 1850s, with wheat and wool exports traded for coffee and calico. The 308-mile canal extended from Cleveland to Portsmouth, contained 146 locks, and cost more than $7 million to build. Construction of the canal took seven years, ending in 1832 when the canal completed the link between Lake Erie and the Ohio River.

Located near the confluence of the Muskingum, Walhonding, and Tuscarawas Rivers, the twenty-three brick and frame buildings in the village have been restored to their appearance during the canal's heyday, making Roscoe Village (originally called Caldersburgh) Ohio's only complete canal town restoration. Seven new buildings also have been added to this historic village.

Seven exhibit buildings, a cozy country inn, shops, restaurants, and horse-drawn canalboat rides on the replica *Monticello III* all contribute to the appeal of this unique village. You can purchase tickets to the exhibit buildings and craft demonstrations at the Edward E. and Frances B. Montgomery Visitor Center. This three-story structure offers a wide-screen film presentation of the history of the canal and the village and displays a large, detailed map of the locks and elevation changes along the canal's more than 300-mile span.

Costumed interpreters and craftspeople welcome visitors to the nineteenth-century buildings, including the blacksmith's shop, the print shop, the one-room schoolhouse, and the 1840s period home of Dr. Maro Johnson. You'll see rugs and wall hangings being woven on two antique looms and the village potter throwing pots, bowls, and vases on an old-fashioned kick wheel.

In one of the exhibit buildings, the Toll House, Roscoe's first toll collector, Jacob Welsh, registered incoming canalboats and collected passage fees. Also on display is the compass used in the construction of the canal in the 1820s and 1830s, a canalboat model that travels through a set of double locks, and a working model of a gristmill.

Roscoe Village is on Routes 16 and 83 near Route 36, Coshocton; (800) 877–1830 or (740) 622–9310. Open year-round; festivals and special events are May through December. Admission to exhibit buildings: adults, $8.95; children (5 to 12), $3.95.

The fifty-one-room **Roscoe Village Inn** offers fine dining and overnight accommodations in the heart of the village. The inn is a relatively recent addition to this historic community, but its architecture and decor create a traditional flavor.

A pleasant sitting area is typical of the place—high ceilings, warm woods, a vast fireplace, and a grand piano make this a delightful gathering spot. The inn's tavern, with its rough-hewn wood beams and exposed brick walls, is reminiscent of days gone by.

Perhaps most exciting is the excellent kitchen at the Roscoe Village Inn, serving what is without a doubt the most sophisticated food in the area.

On our last visit, we thoroughly enjoyed coquilles Saint Jacques mornay—Eastern bay scallops braised in white wine, fresh lemon juice, and mushrooms in a mornay sauce, prepared en casserole with fettuccine. Or how about the veal caprice—pan-fried veal cutlets topped with artichoke hearts, Swiss cheese, and a flavorful brown sauce. Fresh seafood du jour, prime rib, chicken, steaks, and lobster tail all await hungry travelers at the Roscoe Village Inn dining room.

The Roscoe Village Inn is located at 200 North Whitewoman Street, Coshocton; (800) 237-7397 (Ohio), (740) 622-2222. Room rates: $89 to $100 per night. Visa, MasterCard, and American Express are accepted. Open year-round.

Those fond of guitars, dulcimers, and the like will want to stop in at **Wildwood Music.** Here you will find one of the largest selections of acoustic guitars in the United States. More than 600 instruments fill five showrooms. Owner and musician Marty Rodabaugh carries a large stock of hand-crafted fretted and hammered dulcimers. Fine mandolins, banjos, autoharps, specialty tapes and CDs, and music books round out the inventory.

Wildwood Music is at 672 Whitewoman Street, by the Roscoe Village Visitor Center; (740) 622-4224. Open Wednesday through Friday, noon–6:00 P.M.; Saturday, noon–5:00 P.M.; Sunday, 1:00–5:00 P.M.

The nationally accredited **Johnson-Humrickhouse Museum,** located in Roscoe Village, contains five major galleries, each with its own theme. North American Indian artifacts including baskets, pottery, beadwork, blankets, and weapons are represented and range from prehistoric to more recent times. Of particular note are the Eskimo totem poles, scrimshaw, and carved argilite, ivory, and bone artifacts.

The Americana Gallery celebrates yesterday in Ohio with a re-created pioneer home and furnishings, plus antique tools, farm implements, rare firearms, dolls, clocks, pottery, and glassware. An extensive treasury of Asian artifacts features Chinese and Japanese porcelains, lacquer ware, embroidery, metals, wood sculptures, and splendid carvings in jade, bone, ivory, soapstone, and horn. A Japanese samurai warrior, fully armored, stands guard beside a case filled with Japanese swords.

One gallery is devoted to fine European and American decorative arts and includes cut and pressed glassware, delicate china, precious metals, wood carvings, and an unusual collection of knife rests.

The Johnson-Humrickhouse Museum is located at 300 North Whitewoman Street, Roscoe Village, Coshocton; (740) 622-8710. Open daily

May through October, noon–5:00 P.M.; November through April, 1:00–4:30 P.M. Admission: adults, $2.00; children (ages 5 to 12), $1.00.

Breathe a relaxed sigh as you gaze from the deck of *A Valley View Inn* across the enchanting valley below. This ten-room inn prides itself on a peaceful, homelike quality. Guests are welcome to walk the trails through the thirty-acre woods behind the inn or try nothing more strenuous than a porch swing.

Rooms each have private baths and queen-size beds. The inn is air-conditioned and smoke-free. There is also a sitting room and a game room for guests to enjoy.

A country breakfast featuring homemade bread and other Amish fare is served Monday through Saturday. Sunday morning breakfast is a buffet.

A Valley View Inn is located at 32327 State Route 7, New Bedford; (330) 897–3232. Rates: $75 to $105 per night.

Farmer and engineer George Crise took three years, from 1915 to 1918, to build the fine old structure that is today the *White Oak Inn.* He used white oak from his land for the soul of his home and red oak to produce intricate flooring. Some of the antiques that complete the ten guest rooms at the White Oak Inn are Crise family originals, and each room in the main building is named for the type of wood that predominates in it. All rooms have private baths; the queen-size first-floor suite features a wood-burning fireplace. The former chicken house has become a spacious guest house with three rooms, two with fireplaces.

Guests congregate in the light and spacious living room, mingling, reading, or just rocking in front of the fire. Innkeepers Ian and Yvonne Martin offer full breakfasts for their guests, and dinners can be arranged by advance reservation. The inn's remote location invites walks or bicycle rides down country roads, far away from city noise and hassle. On clear nights, the sky dazzles with brilliant star displays.

One unusual activity available here is digging for prehistoric artifacts. The inn's grounds have been registered as an official Ohio archaeological site, loaded with arrowheads and stone tools. Kenyon College students regularly dig here, and the Martins have two "dig" weekends a year when they invite guests to join in.

The White Oak Inn is 4 miles east of the junction of Routes 36 and 62, on Route 715 near Millwood; (740) 599–6107. Rates: $75 to $130 per night, double occupancy, with full breakfast. Cash, checks, MasterCard, and Visa are accepted. Reservations and a deposit are required; there is

Yankee Pens "Dixie"

I wonder how Confederate soldiers and sympathizers would have reacted if they had known that a Yankee from Mt. Vernon, Ohio, had written their beloved anthem, "Dixie"? Probably would have spit out their grits.

Daniel Decatur Emmett was a minstrel performer who had moved to New York City when he penned "Dixie" in 1859. It later was played in the South and was quickly adopted as the battle cry for secession. Dan Emmett returned to Mt. Vernon and died there in 1904.

a two-night minimum stay on holiday and peak-season weekends.

Tim and Maureen Tyler undertook a country inn/bed-and-breakfast odyssey; they spent two and a half years and traveled more than 20,000 miles searching for the perfect home to restore as a bed-and-breakfast. Determined to abandon the rat race of New York City, they stumbled on Mount Vernon en route to Kentucky and discovered what is today the *Russell-Cooper House.*

This ornate structure grew in stages over a period of sixty years, originally constructed in 1829 as a modest Federal-style residence. By 1895, the dwelling had been transformed into a one-of-a-kind mansion masterpiece, a Tudor-Italianate Victorian Gothic villa! The Russell-Cooper House is the former home of two prominent Ohio families. Dr. John Russell, physician and surgeon, was the first American to employ a female physician, Dr. Jane Payne, in 1852. His son-in-law, Colonel William Cooper, had a distinguished career as an attorney, U.S. congressman, and Ohio's adjutant general.

When the Tylers acquired the property in 1987, it was no longer the proud residence of the past, but three "modern" apartments. Their restoration of the home's Victorian grandeur was massive, necessitating the removal of thirteen major walls, three baths, five closets, five furnaces, and three water heaters. After nine months of seven-days-a-week restoration, this award-winning mansion inn now boasts six guest rooms with private baths, a cherry-bookcased library, a dining hall with an embossed tin ceiling, a grand ballroom with a restored 1856 hand-painted ceiling, a four-season sunroom, and a professional art gallery and studio.

The inn is furnished almost entirely with nineteenth-century antiques, many recovered from Russell-Cooper descendants. The two third-floor guest rooms, accessed via a new grand staircase of cherry and sassafras, offer a pre-Victorian, primitive style, with hand-hewn beams.

The Russell-Cooper House is at 115 East Gambier Street, Mount Vernon; (740) 397–8638. Rates: $55 to $75 per night, double occupancy, including breakfast. Reservations and a deposit required; cash, Visa, and MasterCard accepted.

Approximately 200 million years ago, a layer of hard flint pushed toward the earth's surface in an area now known as Flint Ridge. Erosion exposed some of the flint, attracting Indians to the area 8,000 to 10,000 years ago. Although the weathered flint was too brittle to be of much value, the Indians discovered a vein of high-quality flint 1 to 10 feet beneath the surface and established crude quarries to extract the material. Using tremendous physical effort and large hammer stones, they pounded bone and wooden wedges into the flint, breaking it into removable chunks.

They used the flint to form arrow and spear points, scrapers, and other tools and to start fires. Because of the demand for flint in prehistoric times, Flint Ridge was considered neutral ground, with members of any tribe allowed to quarry there. White settlers later rediscovered Flint Ridge, using the mineral for buhrstones in gristmills and as roadbed on a nearby section of the National Road.

Today, the **Flint Ridge State Memorial** museum is built around one of the prehistoric Indian quarries, and Indian mannequins stand ready to break up the rock with a stone maul. The museum features an impressive collection of scrapers, drills, hoes, knives, and projectile points. One flint sample contains an excellent impression of a coral animal, created during one of the times when this part of Ohio was under the seas.

A large topographical map illustrates the extent of the ridge in eastern Licking and western Muskingum Counties. Other displays include an explanation of the calendar of geological time and descriptions of the various layers of rock in the region, from the surface to 468 feet underground.

State Gemstone/Fossil

*T*he Columbus Rock and Mineral Society led the charge to honor flint as Ohio's official state gemstone. They pointed to its importance to Native Americans in Ohio for making knives, arrowheads, and spear points, its use for flintlock guns and millstones by early white settlers, and its value as a semiprecious stone when cut and polished. In 1965, the Ohio General Assembly concurred, designating flint as Ohio's state stone.

Twenty years later, lawmakers were at it again, this time to recognize a state fossil. Despite numerous jokes suggesting that some of the older members of the General Assembly were in the running for this honor, the actual winner was the trilobite, an extinct marine crustacean found in the limestone and shale beds of southwestern Ohio, among other places.

A thick forest of beech, maple, and oak surrounds the museum, and hiking trails pass by old Indian quarries and exposed outcroppings of red, yellow, brown, and creamy flint. One trail takes hikers by two small streams, and abundant wildlife, including deer, squirrels, chipmunks, and birds, can be observed in the park.

Flint Ridge State Memorial is on County Road 668, 3 miles north of Brownsville; (800) 283–8707, (740) 787–2476. The museum is open from Memorial Day through Labor Day, Wednesday through Saturday, 9:30 A.M.–5:00 P.M.; Sunday, noon–5:00 P.M. Open weekends in September and October. Admission: adults, $3.00, children (ages 6 to 12), $1.50.

August Heisey was born in Hanover, Germany, in 1842 and came to America with his family a year later. His career in the glass industry began in Pittsburgh in 1861 but was interrupted by his service with the Union Army during the Civil War.

After the war and several sales positions in the glass business, in 1893 Heisey began formulating plans for his own glass company. He chose Newark as the site for this new enterprise because of its abundance of natural gas and low-cost labor. The factory opened in 1896 and grew to employ several hundred workers.

In 1900, the famous "H within a diamond" trademark was designed by Heisey's son, George Duncan Heisey. Two other sons ran the company, which produced the colored glass and glass animals so popular with collectors today. The company closed for Christmas vacation in 1957 and never reopened, no longer competitive in world markets.

Today, the best of Heisey Glass is on display at the **National Heisey Glass Museum.** The museum is housed in what was once the home of Samuel Dennis King, a prominent Newark attorney. It was built in 1831 and was moved to Veterans Park in 1973. The museum is run by the Heisey Collectors of America. In 1993 the collectors constructed a new wing to the museum, adding two large galleries and a media center where a twenty-six-minute video is shown. Inside, you browse through room after room of Heisey glass; hundreds of patterns are displayed, including pieces in all production colors. Examples of experimental pieces, photographs, molds, and tools complete the collection.

The National Heisey Glass Museum is at 169 West Church Street, Newark; (740) 345–2932. Open Tuesday through Saturday, 10:00 A.M.–4:00 P.M.; Sunday, 1:00–4:00 P.M. Admission: adults, $2.00; children, free if accompanied by an adult.

When Joe and Teresa Cooper purchased this historic property in 1985, it had been in the Pitzer family for more than 125 years. Constructed in 1858 by Anthony Pitzer, Jr., the home has been extensively renovated, including all electric, plumbing, and heating, while maintaining its unique character. Pitzer's father, Major Anthony Pitzer, was the original settler on this land, which was granted to him by the federal government in 1804. The major and much of his family are buried in the historic Beard-Green Cemetery at nearby Dawes Arboretum.

The **Pitzer-Cooper House** is an excellent example of the Greek Revival style with some Italianate features. Listed on the National Register of Historic Places, it features solid wood walls, a curved cherry staircase, six-panel doors, and a recessed second-story porch. Antiques and quilts continue the timeless country ambience, as do the porch swings, perennial and herb gardens, and tranquil pond. Two of the home's guest rooms share a bath; the third is a suite with private bath. Start the day with a generous continental breakfast and perhaps a ride down the country roads on available bicycles.

The Pitzer-Cooper House is at 6019 White Chapel Road, SE, Newark; (800) 833–9536, (740) 323–2680. Rates: $45 to $120 per night.

The 1,150-acre **Dawes Arboretum,** established by Bertie Burr and Beman Gates Dawes in 1929, blends rolling meadows, deep woods, and cultivated gardens. Perhaps the most beautiful area is the Japanese garden designed by noted landscape architect Makoto Nakamura. In Nakamura's design, a small lake with islands connected by arched bridges and plantings such as pine, flowering cherries, Japanese yew, and Japanese maple creates a tranquil environment. Another popular area is the cypress swamp, where Southern native bald cypress trees grow and produce "knees."

The holly collection contains more than one hundred distinct types of holly, and the sugar maples at Dawes provide the sap for the annual

There was a time when being called a "buckeye" was an insult, the equivalent of being labeled a "hick." Its origin as a put down comes from the fact that rural Ohio pioneers used wood from buckeye trees to build their cabins and carve their furniture.

Attitudes about the term gradually changed, and its fruit—a brown nut—was described as resembling the eye of the noble buck deer. In 1953, the buckeye was officially designated Ohio's state tree, and Ohio has been the Buckeye State ever since.

The recognition of Ohio's state beverage has been less successful. In 1963, Governor James Rhodes took office and launched a campaign to promote the consumption of Ohio products. Since tomatoes are a significant crop, he encouraged the drinking of tomato juice. What started as a joke—the naming of tomato juice as Ohio's state beverage—became law in 1965. Cheers.

production of maple syrup. One section of the arboretum consists of the deciduous climax forest that once blanketed the entire state of Ohio. In a climax forest, tree seedlings are able to grow in the shade of parent trees, thus reproducing the forest indefinitely in a cycle of growth and regeneration.

One feature of the arboretum can be fully appreciated only from the air—a 2,100-foot-long series of hedges that spells out "Dawes Arboretum." Other collections at Dawes include oaks, crabapples, flowering shrubs, and conifers. In addition to the forests, meadows, and gardens, there are a lake and two ponds. The visitors' center offers nature exhibits, a bird-watching area, an indoor beehive, which the bees enter from the outside through a clear plastic tube, and a fine bonsai display.

Beman and Bertie Dawes moved into the Daweswood House in 1916. Built in 1867, this two-story brick home contains antique furnishings and other of the Daweses' possessions, including portraits of famous family members William Dawes, who rode with Paul Revere, and Charles Gates Dawes, who served as vice president in the Coolidge administration. Guides conduct tours of the home Saturdays and Sundays at 3:15 P.M.

The Dawes Arboretum is on Route 13, 5 miles south of Newark; (800) 44–DAWES, (740) 323–2355. The visitors' center is open Monday through Saturday, 8:00 A.M.–5:00 P.M.; Sunday and holidays, 1:00–5:00 P.M. Grounds are open daylight hours. No admission charge except at Daweswood House.

Perhaps Ohio's prettiest small town, Granville dates its founding in 1805 by settlers from Granville, Massachusetts, and Granby, Connecticut. The nineteenth-century shops and homes in the picture-postcard community are painstakingly maintained. Up on a hill is Denison University, and a more perfect setting for spending college years is difficult to imagine.

In addition to the craft and antiques shops, Granville boasts historic inns providing overnight accommodations. Orrin Granger built the **Buxton Inn** (known as The Tavern in Granger's day) in 1812, and the inn has operated continuously since then. The inn housed Granville's first post office and served as a stagecoach stop on the Columbus-Newark line. An addition in 1851 formed the U-shaped structure with center courtyard that exists today. The Buxton is named for one of its more colorful proprietors, Major Buxton, who owned the inn from the close of the Civil War until his death in 1905. The present owners, Mr. and Mrs. Orville Orr, purchased it in 1972 and spent two years researching and completely restoring this outstanding structure, which is now listed on the National Register of Historic Places.

The Buxton serves fine cuisine in tasteful period dining rooms, each unique in mood and ambience. Antiques are proudly displayed throughout the inn, and the brick-floored center courtyard provides a delightful outdoor dining area. Blooming, hanging plants in baskets and small potted trees combine with the splash of a nearby fountain and candlelit tables to make the courtyard a most pleasing place.

For dinner, choose from seafood such as the fresh catch of the day, coquille of seafood cardinal (shrimp, scallops, crabmeat, mushrooms in mornay), and, one of our favorites, the red snapper with crabmeat au gratin. Other dinner menu options include roast duckling with orange-cranberry sauce; chicken Victoria with mushrooms, cheese, and ham; medallions of pork Fredonia with sautéed pippin apples; and French pepper steak with

Buxton Inn's Bonnie Ghost

*I*f an inn has a ghost or two in residence, it is best if they are happy lodgers! Such is the case at the Buxton Inn. According to legend, and those who have had the pleasure of a meeting, the resident spirits of the Buxton Inn are just continuing to play the role of host and hostess.

If the feminine fragrance of gardenia perfume wafts heavily across the air on the stairway, the Lady in Blue is nearby. This spirit is supposed to be that of Ethel Bounell, better known as "Bonnie." The former actress turned innkeeper was the owner and operator of the inn from 1934 until 1960. She died in room nine. She is reported to have had a theatrical streak and was known for both her gardenia perfume and her love of blue dresses.

In life and death she apparently loves the inn. According to staff and guests, she often is heard walking up and down the stairs or opening and closing doors. Guests have reported being wakened by a woman, who generally expresses concern over their comfort.

While Bonnie may be tending guests, the tales of the inn say that she doesn't have to handle that duty alone. The first innkeeper, Major Buxton, also has appeared to both staff and guests. The nattily attired gentleman sporting a mustache is apt to show up in the bar or come up behind staff, perhaps just to check that all is running smoothly.

While the occasional ghostly footsteps, door banging, or mysteriously rearranged objects sometimes have given visitors a start, the ghosts also give the Buxton a unique character. Since the inn traditionally receives high ratings for service, who can blame the former innkeepers for hanging around just to make sure that your stay is something special.

Buxton Inn

brandy sauce. Be sure to order the special baked potato, which comes stuffed with cheddar cheese, bacon, chopped onions, sour cream, chives, and butter. The tempting desserts include gingerbread with hot lemon sauce and the chef's double dark chocolate cake.

Luncheon selections such as salads, soups, and sandwiches like the croque monsieur (sautéed ham, Swiss cheese, and fresh mushrooms served with warm syrup or light mustard sauce) join entrees that include quiche, crepes, barbecued ribs, eggs Benedict, and seafood Newburg.

Stagecoach drivers once cooked their meals on an open fire in the stone-walled basement of the inn and slept on straw beds around that fire. With its rough beams and imposing stone fireplace, the basement tavern retains the flavor of those early years. The tavern serves a casual menu of sandwiches and appetizers.

The Buxton Inn also offers overnight accommodations in guest rooms furnished with antiques. Lodging ranges in price from $70 to $85 per night for two people.

The Buxton Inn is at 313 East Broadway, Granville; (614) 587–0001. The inn is open for breakfast, Monday through Friday, 6:45–10:00 A.M.; Saturday and Sunday 8:00–11:00 A.M. Lunch is served Monday through Saturday, 11:30 A.M.–2:00 P.M.; Sunday, 11:00 A.M.–2:00 P.M. Dinner hours are Monday through Thursday, 5:30–9:00 P.M.; Friday and Saturday, 5:30–10:00 P.M.; Sunday, 1:00–8:00 P.M. The Buxton Tavern is open Monday through Saturday, 5:00–midnight. MasterCard and Visa are accepted.

Across the street from the Buxton sits the Tudor-style **Granville Inn,** built in 1924 by the president of the Sunday Creek Coal Company, John Sutphin Jones. Offering the elegance of an English manor house, the lobby is furnished with splendid antiques and lush Oriental rugs. The dining room features high ceilings, ornate brass chandeliers, and sandstone fireplaces. In warm weather, meals are also served outside the tall French doors on the flagstone terrace, which is surrounded by a manicured lawn, gardens, and towering trees.

The evening menu at the Granville Inn features a variety of steaks, chops, seafood, chicken, and house specialties such as chicken Oscar and flounder Belle Franklin. Another favorite is the baked trout à la mer, which is stuffed with Alaskan crabmeat, shrimp, and herb-seasoned corn bread dressing. All dinners are served with the much-acclaimed fresh raisin bread and honey butter. For a unique appetizer, try the angels on horseback: oyster wrapped in bacon, baked in lemon butter, and served with hot toast triangles.

Luncheon selections include soups, salads, sandwiches, and entrees such as steaks, crepes, and the fresh catch of the day. With any meal at the Granville Inn, the house specialty desserts are English walnut pie, served warm, and creamy cheesecake.

Individually decorated, the Granville Inn's twenty-seven guest rooms and three suites have an understated charm and dignity. Prices range from $75 to $85 per night, including a continental breakfast.

The Granville Inn is at 314 East Broadway, Granville; (614) 587–3333. Lunch is served Monday through Saturday, 11:30 A.M.–2:30 P.M. Dinner is Monday through Thursday, 5:00–9:00 P.M.; Friday and Saturday, 5:00–10:00 P.M. On Sunday a buffet is served 11:30 A.M.–2:00 P.M. MasterCard, Visa, and American Express are accepted.

For more personal accommodations, spend the night in Kirsten and Jurgen Pape's historic *Follett-Wright House Bed & Breakfast*. Situated at the base of Mt. Parnassus within easy walking distance of all of Granville's charms, this gracious structure was built in 1860 and is now listed on the National Register of Historic Places. Its lovely garden provides a tranquil retreat.

Twelve-foot ceilings typical of the era grace the living and dining rooms, permitting large floor-to-ceiling windows. A breakfast of Danish rolls, coffeecake, and other specialties are served in the dining room, which is furnished with a blend of American and European antiques. The kitchen, originally a porch, now is a modern yet charming functional facility.

The Papes offer a good night's rest in two spacious guestrooms. The upstairs Lincoln Room features Ohio antiques, a queen-size bed, and a view from the bay window of tree-lined East Broadway. Downstairs, the Madison Room includes a stone fireplace added to the property in 1929.

The Follett-Wright House Bed & Breakfast is at 403 East Broadway, Granville; (740) 587–0941. Rates: $60 per night. No credit cards accepted.

Down the street is a red-painted brick home, which is today the **Granville Life Style Museum**. Built in 1870, it remains furnished as it was while the home of Hubert and Oese Robinson, who lived here from 1918 until their deaths in 1960 and 1981 respectively. Nine rooms of this stately residence are filled with personal and household items of the Robinson's. Visitors also enjoy Oese's lush garden.

The Granville Life Style Museum is at 121 South Main Street, Granville; (740) 587–0373. Open Sundays, 1:00–4:30 P.M. Admission: adults, $1.50; children under 12, free.

It was built in 1861 as a wedding gift from George T. Jones for his bride, Belle, but today you can receive the benefits of this gift as a guest in the **George T. Jones House Historic B & B**. The two-story Victorian Home is on the National Register of Historic Places and was restored and remodeled in 1983.

The Jones house has been furnished with period pieces and now contains three guestrooms, each with a double bed and a private bath. Visitors to the area will find the B & B on a quiet street a block south of the downtown.

Breakfast is included in the room rate as well as afternoon tea. This B&B is known for hot apple and hot peach dumplings. They'll even serve them at breakfast time. Teatime also includes wine or a nonalcoholic beverage, fruit, and dessert. If you require a special diet, such as low-fat, vegetarian, or Kosher, your innkeepers can accommodate your needs.

The inn operates only on weekends. Reservations should be made in advance and a minimum stay may be required on some weekends when the local college has special events planned. Children ten years or older are welcome.

The George T. Jones House Historic B&B is located at 21 East Elm Street, Granville; (740) 587–1122. Open: weekends only. Rates: $75 per night.

The growing season in Ohio welcomes a variety of fruits and flowers to **Lynds Fruit Farm** and Lynds Fruit Farm welcomes visitors to pick the best from the fields. Home of Ohio's largest apple orchard, Lynds has 80,000 trees, and during September and October, you can pick your own apples. Fall also brings pumpkins and squash to pick or cornstalks to use for autumn decorating. In July, daylilies are ready for you to scrutinize and then "dig your own."

A "show" apple orchard tells the history of the fruit. Apples from colonial times hang on trees next to the latest test varieties. You may also want to hop on a hayride, and let one of the farm's ten antique John Deere tractors give you a ride around the farm. In addition to these seasonal activities, the farm also hosts other events, such as cooking and plant propagation demonstrations. Call ahead for dates and times.

Lynds Fruit Farm is located at 9090 Morse Road, Pataskala; (740) 927–1333. Open Friday through Sunday, 9:00 A.M.–6:00 P.M. No admission charge.

A devastating fire at *Ye Olde Mill* near Utica in April 1986 completely destroyed the hundred-year-old structure. Only the 18-foot, 2,000-pound waterwheel and the quarry stone survived the blaze.

But the Velvet Ice Cream Company, which operates the mill and has its headquarters next door, set about building a new Ye Olde Mill of rough-sawed oak and poplar. And this new building now sells country crafts and other gift items and, not surprisingly, Velvet Ice Cream, a Dager family tradition since 1914.

The 1870-vintage building destroyed by fire was not the first mill on this site—a sawmill was erected here in 1817, and a larger one went up in 1827. You can find out about this and more at the museum of milling history and ice cream that is part of Ye Olde Mill. In fact, the ice-cream museum, Ohio's first and only, traces the history of ice cream from Roman times to the present.

Once you've picked up a conefull of your favorite ice-cream flavor, step outside to the twenty-acre parklike picnic area. Relax at the picnic tables while watching the ducks frolic in a picturesque pond. The mill also houses a down-home restaurant, complete with deli sandwiches, soup 'n' salad bar, and finger food.

Ye Olde Mill is located 10 miles north of Newark on Route 13, Utica; (800) 589–5000, (614) 892–3921. Open daily, May through October: 11:00 A.M.–9:00 P.M., summer; 11:00 A.M.–8:00 P.M., fall.

Imports dominate the basket industry in the United States today, but one Ohio family continues five generations of handcrafted basket making. Before the turn of the century, John Longaberger began weaving baskets for his neighbors and local potteries, which used them for storing and shipping their fragile products. John's son, J. W. Longaberger, expanded the business after World War I and taught his twelve children the art of basket making in the evening, after he worked a full day at a nearby paper mill. But over the years, inexpensive cardboard, plastic, and metal containers drastically reduced the industrial demand for Longaberger's baskets, and production slowed to a trickle.

In the 1970s, however, J. W.'s son, Dave, with his father's help, revived the business after becoming convinced a new market existed for good quality, handmade baskets. Today, nearly 1,000 weavers produce an average of 100,000 baskets per week at The Longaberger Company. The baskets are constructed of hard maple from Ohio, Michigan, Pennsylvania, and New England. As testament to the emphasis on quality at Longaberger, each weaver initials and dates each basket. More than 14,000 commissioned sales representatives sell the baskets, along with pottery and dinnerware, at in-home shows throughout the United States.

The success of the Longaberger Company has transformed the small town of Dresden. Visitors pour in to view the manufacturing process at the quarter-mile-long factory just outside of town on Route 16, where a mezzanine viewing area gives a glimpse of hundreds of weavers at work. In town, a former bakery now houses the *Longaberger Museum,* where visitors can pick up tickets for the factory tours.

Four Dresden restaurants are Longaberger properties: The Longaberger Restaurant, with lunch and dinner buffets and salad bars; Jayhawks, an upscale pub that celebrates Dresden's former high school sports teams, the Jefferson Jayhawks; the Breakfast Shop, where the first meal of the day is served in a Victorian atmosphere; and Popeye's Soda Shop, which offers a taste of the fifties.

Right across the street from Popeye's is the world's largest basket. It's 48 feet long, 11 feet wide, and 23 feet high. It took ten hardwood maple trees and 2,000 hours of work to create this novelty. Thanks to Longaberger's, busy shops now line the streets of Dresden, selling Longaberger products and other gift items and merchandise.

The Longaberger Museum is at the corner of Fifth and Main Streets, Dresden; (740) 754–6330. Open Monday through Satuday, 9:00 A.M.–6:00 P.M.; Sunday, noon–6:00 P.M. No admission charge. Factory tours available Monday through Friday, 8:30 A.M.–5:00 P.M., no charge.

As the name indicates, the **National Road–Zane Grey Museum** actually houses two museums—one presenting the story of the building of the National Road connecting the western territories with the original eastern states, and the other commemorating author Zane Grey, the Zanesville, Ohio, native known through his travels and writing as the "High Priest of the Outdoors."

Built in stages from 1811 to 1838, the National Road stretched from Cumberland, Maryland, to Vandalia, Illinois. George Washington originally conceived the idea of constructing a road into the new nation's western lands, and the ninth Congress of the United States approved funds for this first federally supported road in 1806.

Workers earned a dollar per day to clear a 66-foot-wide path and to build a 30-foot-wide roadbed of broken stone using hand tools, mules, oxen, and horses. The National Road was vital to the development of the frontier—as each section of the road opened, settlers loaded their Conestoga wagons and headed west.

The museum displays horse-drawn carts, buggies, and wagons (including a Conestoga wagon), plus antique bicycles and automobiles—all methods of transportation utilized on the National Road (which eventually became U.S. 40 and reached all the way to California). A 136-foot diorama depicts the chronology of the road, from its construction and use by early settlers moving west to farmers herding their livestock on the road and the road's revival after the invention of the bicycle and automobile. Other exhibits include photographs of sections of the road under construction and fully equipped interiors of blacksmith and wheelwright shops.

Author Zane Grey, born in 1875, acquired his passion for hunting and fishing around Dillon Falls, near his home in Zanesville. Grey attended dental school at the University of Pennsylvania, where he also played on the college baseball team. But he abandoned his dental career to write, achieving national prominence with his sixty western novels, many of which were later filmed as motion pictures. He used the money from his books and movies to finance his worldwide fishing trips and big-game hunting expeditions.

The museum displays many of Zane Grey's books, magazine articles, and posters from his motion pictures, plus the lures and hunting rifles used on his travels. There is also a complete replica of the study he added to his Altadena, California, home, where he penned many of his works.

The National Road–Zane Grey Museum is at the Norwich exit of I–70, 10 miles east of Zanesville; (800) 752–2602, (740) 872–3143. Open from March through November, Wednesday through Saturday, 9:30 A.M.–5:00 P.M.; Sunday, noon–5:00 P.M. This museum is also open Monday and Tuesday, 9:30 A.M.–5:00 P.M., May through September. Admission: adults, $5.00; children, $1.25.

Speaking of transportation, Zanesville is also the home port for the

Lorena Sternwheeler. Enjoy a cruise along the Muskingum River on this authentic stern-wheeled paddleboat, a cruise that will remind you of an era when Ohio rivers were primary travel arteries.

The Lorena Sternwheeler sails from Zanes Landing Park, Zanesville; (740) 455–8883. She departs on Saturday and Sunday during warm weather at 1:00, 2:30, and 4:00 p.m. Rates: $3.50 per person.

Jack and Sharon Bogart have combined their love of antiques (and their antique business) with their meticulously restored 1830 Federal-style home to create *Bogart's Bed & Breakfast*. The four guestrooms, each with private bath, are furnished with select pieces from the nearby Bogart's Antiques. Visitors cozy up on the massive 70-foot wraparound-screened porch for a morning coffee or an afternoon read. An evening snack and a candlelight breakfast top off your stay.

Bogart's is across the street from the entrance to Muskingum College. New Concord is best known as the hometown of astronaut, senator, and astronaut (again) John Glenn.

Bogart's Bed & Breakfast is at 62 West Main Street, New Concord; (740) 826–7439. Rates: $65 to $75 per night. Visa and MasterCard accepted.

PLACES TO STAY IN EAST CENTRAL OHIO

ASHLAND
The Winfield Bed & Breakfast
1568 State Route 60
(800) 269–7166,
(419) 281–5587

BERLIN
Donna's Premier Lodging
½ block off Main Street on East Street
(800) 320–3338,
(330) 893–3068.

Garden Gate Get-A-Way
just outside of Berling
(330) 893–3999

Pomerance House
Junction of Routes 62 and 39, Main Street
(216) 893–2842

CANAL FULTON
The Canal House Bed and Breakfast
306 South Canal Street
(330) 854–6229

CHARM
The Guggisberg Swiss Inn
5025 State Route 557
(330) 893–3600

COSHOCTON
Rosco Village Inn
200 North Whitewoman Street
(800) 237–7397 in Ohio,
(614) 622–2222

DELLROY
Atwood Lake Resort
2650 Lodge Road
(800) 735–3596

The Candleglow Bed & Breakfast
4247 Roswell Road SW
(330) 735–2407

DOVER
The 1881 Olde World Bed and Breakfast
2982 State Route 516 NW
(330) 343–1333

GRANVILLE
Pollett-Wright House Bed & Breakfast
403 East Broadway
(740) 587–0941

The George T. Jones House
Historic B&B
21 East Elm Street
(740) 587–1122
Open weekends only.

LOUDONVILLE
Blackfork Inn
303 North Water Street
(419) 994–3252

Mohican State Park Lodge
and Cabins
Route 3, just North of
Loudonville
(800) 282–7275

MILLERSBURG
Inn at Honey Run
3 miles northeast of
Millerburg, off Route 214
on Country Road 203
(800) 468–6639 in Ohio,
(330) 674–0011

MILLWOOD
White Oak Inn
4 miles east of junction of
Routes 36 and 62
on Route 715
(740) 599–6107

MOUNT VERNON
Russell-Cooper House
115 East Gambier Street
(740) 397–8638

NEWARK
Pitzer-Cooper House
6019 White Chapel Road SE
(800) 833–9536,
(740) 323–2680

NEW BEDFORD
A Valley View Inn
32327 State Route 7
(330) 897–3232

NEW CONCORD
Bogart's Bed & Breakfast
62 West Main Street,
(740) 826–7439

WOOSTER
The Leila Belle Inn
846 East Bowman Street
(330) 262–8866,
(888) 430–7378

ZOAR
The Inn at Cowger
House #9
Fourth Street
(330) 874–3542

**PLACES TO EAT IN
EAST CENTRAL OHIO**

ELKTON
Lock 24
On Route 154, 1 mile east of
Route 11
(330) 424–3710

GRANVILLE
Buxton Inn
313 East Broadway
(614) 587–0001
Lodging is also available.

Granville Inn
314 East Broadway
(614) 587–3333
Lodging is also available.

WAYNESBURG
Cibo's Restaurant
134 West Lisbon Street
(330) 866–3838

WILMOT
The Amish Door
Restaurant & Village
1210 Winesburg Street
(330) 359–5464
Lodging is also available.

ZOAR
Zoar Inn and Tavern
162 Main Street
(330) 874–2170

Helpful Web Sites

Ohio Division of Travel and Tourism:
www.ohiotourism.com

Canton/Stark County Visitors Bureau:
www.visitcantonohio.com

Holmes County Visitors Bureau:
www.visitamishcountry.com

Tuscarawas County Visitors Bureau:
web.tusco.net/tourism

Wayne County Visitors Bureau:
www.wooster-wayne.com/wccvb

Southeast Ohio

River Region

At the conclusion of the Revolutionary War, Congress passed the "Ordinance of 1787," which opened up new land west and north of the Ohio River for settlement. A group of soldiers and officers from the Revolutionary conflict, along with other New Englanders, formed the Ohio Company of Associates to settle in this frontier territory. On April 7, 1788, a party of forty-eight men on a crude barge followed the Ohio River to the Muskingum River, arriving at today's location of Marietta, Ohio. By July of that year, Governor Arthur St. Clair had established the first civil government west of the Allegheny Mountains in Marietta, with the settlement destined to be Ohio's first city and gateway to the Northwest Territory (Ohio, Michigan, Indiana, Illinois, Wisconsin, and part of Minnesota). The city was named for Queen Marie Antoinette, in gratitude for the support France had provided the colonies during the war with the British.

Rufus Putnam, a general under Washington during the Revolution, led that forty-eight-man party in April 1788 and supervised the construction of a walled fortification with four blockhouses to discourage Indian attacks. Putnam's home was part of that fortification and still exists today, completely enclosed in the **Campus Martius Museum.** Putnam coined the name Campus Martius, which means "field of wars," but the Treaty of Greene Ville in 1795 virtually ended hostilities in the region.

Putnam's 200-year-old home rests on its original foundation and contains furnishings from the Putnam family. Guides describe the hardships of early pioneer life and explain the use of the various kitchen and household implements on display.

The museum also exhibits hundreds of items from Marietta's early days, such as the compasses and surveyors' chains used to plat the city. Other collections include Dr. John Cotton's surgical equipment (he practiced medicine in Marietta from 1815 to 1847), antique musical instruments, and a very unusual studio portrait camera from the early 1900s.

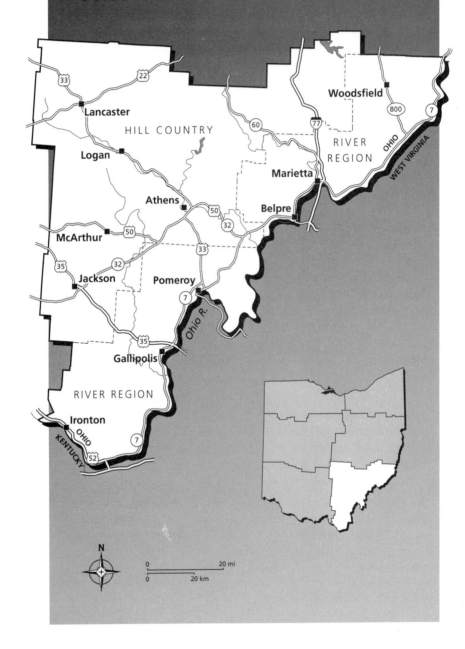

Southeast Ohio

HILL COUNTRY

RIVER REGION

RIVER REGION

Lancaster

Logan

Athens

McArthur

Jackson

Pomeroy

Gallipolis

Ironton

Woodsfield

Marietta

Belpre

Ohio R.

OHIO

WEST VIRGINIA

KENTUCKY

OHIO

N

0   20 mi
0   20 km

SOUTHEAST OHIO

One entire gallery contains nineteenth-century ladies' apparel—the lavish gowns and dresses worn during that era. An outdoor patio features an outstanding assortment of Franklin stoves, a water pumper (circa 1853) used to fight fires, and the enormous pilot wheel from the stern-wheel towboat *J. C. Risher,* which worked the Ohio River from 1873 until it sank in 1919. A military display includes the sword used by General Putnam during the Revolutionary War (he later gave this sword to George Washington), old rifles and muskets used by early settlers in the area, uniforms and dress swords from the War of 1812, and a Confederate flag captured at the Civil War battle of Chancellorsville, plus uniforms, saddlebags, and a fife and drum used by Civil War soldiers.

The Campus Martius Museum is at the corner of Washington (Route 7) and Second Streets, Marietta; (800) 860–0145, (740) 373–3750. The museum is open from March through November, Wednesday through Saturday, 9:30 A.M.–5:00 P.M.; Sunday, noon–5:00 P.M. Also open Monday and Tuesday, 9:30 A.M.–5:00 P.M., May through September. Admission: adults, $5.00; children (ages 6 to 12), $1.25.

With their tall smokestacks puffing black ash and their paddleboards splashing the waters of the Ohio and Muskingum Rivers, the great stern-wheelers plied these waterways carrying freight and passengers during the nineteenth century. Marietta was once a thriving port; its history is interwoven with that of the rivers and the steamboat era.

The **Ohio River Museum** stands on the bank of the Muskingum River, just down the street from Campus Martius. The museum actually consists of four separate buildings connected with covered outdoor walkways. One building's maps, models, and illustrations trace the origins of the Ohio River—the role of glaciers in its development and the natural history of the region. A half-hour multimedia presentation gives the river's more recent past from its early exploration to modern-day commercial and recreational usage.

Ohio's State Song

Ohio's state song, "Beautiful Ohio," was written in 1918 by Ballard McDonald and Mary Earl. But the song is not about the state of Ohio; rather, its focus is the Ohio River. That did not stop the General Assembly fron designating it as Ohio's official state song on October 24, 1969.

Even more curious was the selection of "Hang on Sloopy" as Ohio's state rock song in 1985. Made popular by the McCoys, a Dayton rock band, "Sloopy" is a favorite of the Ohio State University Marching Band.

The most popular building features dozens of detailed models of stern-wheeled paddleboats, with the statistics and a narrative of each vessel provided, plus other riverboat memorabilia such as newspaper clippings, passenger tickets, bills of lading, and stern-wheeler travel brochures. The museum also houses a fine collection of steam whistles and a complete set of woodworking tools used for shipbuilding.

The major outdoor attraction at the Ohio River Museum—the 175-foot, 342-ton *W. P. Snyder, Jr.*—was the last steam-powered stern-wheeled towboat to operate in America. It is now permanently docked on the Muskingum River right behind the museum; visitors walk the gangplank to explore this proud vessel from engine room to pilot house. Built in 1918, the *W. P. Snyder, Jr.* plied America's rivers until 1955.

Other outdoor exhibits include a skiff built in 1885, believed to be the oldest such boat in the inland lakes region, which was used during one of the many floods that rampaged in Marietta prior to the installation of flood-control dams. The museum also has a replica of an early flatboat, the flat-bottomed, square-cornered boats used to float heavy cargoes downstream. Propelled only by the river's current, these boats were dismantled (their wood sold for construction projects) upon arriving at their destination.

The Ohio River Museum is at the corner of Front and Saint Clair Streets, Marietta; (800) 860–0145, (740) 373–3717. Open March through December, Wednesday through Saturday, 9:30 A.M.–5:00 P.M.; Sunday, noon–5:00 P.M. The museum is also open Monday and Tuesday, 9:30 P.M.–5:00 P.M., May through September. Admission: adults, $5.00; children (ages 6 to 12), $1.25.

Given the importance of stern-wheelers to Marietta's past, it seems only proper to survey the city and surrounding area from aboard one—the **Valley Gem,** which docks adjacent to the Ohio River Museum. The ship's captain pilots this 300-passenger excursion vessel down the Muskingum and Ohio Rivers on fifty-minute cruises.

During the trips, he points out the historic places of interest along the shoreline, including the location of Fort Harmar (built in 1785) and the Showboat Becky Thatcher, a popular restaurant that presents

AUTHORS' FAVORITES

Campus Martius Museum

Ohio River Museum

Valley Gem

Betsey Mills Club Dining Room

Levee House Cafe

CLAIRE-E

Rossi Pasta

Lafayette Hotel

Lee Middleton Original Doll Company

Our House

Bob Evans Farm

Buckeye Furnace

Lake Katharine State Nature Preserve

melodrama theater during summer months. Large stone blocks spelling "Marietta" mark the landing once used by arriving steamboats, and this landing is now the site of the annual stern-wheeler festival. Graceful stern-wheelers come from all parts of the inland waterway system to compete in races and generally show off during this annual weekend of activities.

The *Valley Gem* departs from the landing under the Washington Street Bridge at Front Street, Marietta; (740) 373–7862. During the summer, she sails Tuesday through Sunday at 1:00, 2:00, 3:00, 4:00, and 5:00 P.M. In April, May, and September, river trips depart on weekends and holidays at 1:00, 2:00, 3:00, and 4:00 P.M. Rates: adults, $5.00; children, $3.00. Four-hour fall foliage tours leave the landing on Saturdays and Sundays in October at 10:00 A.M. and 2:00 P.M. Rates: adults, $15.00; children, $6.00. (Reservations are recommended for foliage tours.) Dinner cruises are offered every Saturday evening, June through October, from 5:30 to 7:30. Rates: adults, $25; children, $13.

If lunch or dinner is the next priority after your riverboat ride, try the **Betsey Mills Club Dining Room.** A favorite place with local people, this women's club was founded by Betsey Gates Mills in 1911 under the name Girls' Monday Club. The club evolved from a sewing class started by Mrs. Mills in 1898 and later offered instruction in the "household sciences and arts" as well as involvement in social work.

In 1916 Betsey Mills and her husband, W. W. Mills, purchased the home where she was born at the corner of Putnam and Fourth Streets and donated it to the club. Not only was the 1830s structure the birthplace of Mrs. Mills, but her nephew, Charles G. Dawes, was also born there. Dawes served as vice president of the United States under Calvin Coolidge from 1925 to 1929, authored the Dawes Plan for the war reparations after World War I, and was awarded the Nobel Peace Prize.

After Mrs. Mills's death, Mr. Mills expanded the club, joining two adjacent buildings under one roof. Today, the club continues to provide services for the girls and women of Marietta, including the rental of fifteen inexpensive rooms to young working women in the area, organizations for junior high and high school girls, and instruction in everything from art to sports.

The dining rooms in the club are open to the public, each tastefully decorated with cheerful wallpapers and drapes and plenty of potted plants. Looking out the windows, you have a view of the brick patios, well-maintained gardens, and wrought-iron fences and gates that surround this historic two-story building.

With a reputation for quality food at reasonable prices, the Betsey Mills Club serves luncheon entrees such as French toast and sausage, quiche, and liver and onions, plus a choice of sandwiches (Reubens, stacked steak on a kaiser roll, and a dozen others), with fresh fruit salad served in season. The generous dinners at the club include baked stuffed pork chops, steak in brown gravy, cod filet almondine, and scalloped chicken. These include a choice of salad and two vegetables.

The Betsey Mills Club Dining Room is at the corner of Fourth and Putnam Streets, Marietta; (740) 373–3804. The club offers lunch Monday through Sunday, 11:30 A.M.–2:30 P.M. and dinner Monday through Saturday, 5:30 P.M.–8:30 P.M. MasterCard and Visa are accepted.

Another dining option is the *Levee House Cafe,* the only remaining original Marietta riverfront structure. Built in or before 1826 for Dudley Woodbridge, the first merchant in the Northwest Territory, this historic building later served as a hotel, restaurant, and saloon.

Today the menu changes monthly and features entrees as varied as four-cheese pasta, garlic shrimp, chicken sauté au Parmesan, and tenderloin tips in bordelaise sauce. The adventurous might want to sample the enraged pasta—a spicy-hot blend of jalapeño peppers, mushrooms, bacon, and basil, or the mussels mariniere—fresh mussels sautéed in white wine and butter with onions, garlic, and parsley served over pasta with Levee's bran rolls for dipping.

Your dinner starts with appetizers such as fritto calamari, mousse pâté, or picante shrimp and concludes with your choice of freshly baked pies and cakes. For those guests who only want a sample, you can buy desserts "by the inch."

The Levee House Cafe is at 127 Ohio Street, Marietta; (740) 374–2233. Open Monday through Thursday, 11:30 A.M.–9:30 P.M.; Friday and Saturday, 11:30 A.M.–10:00 P.M. Cash, checks, Visa, and MasterCard accepted. Reservations recommended for dinner.

One of the co-owners of the Levee House Cafe, Captain Harley Noland, also offers bed-and-breakfast accommodations aboard his 115-foot stern-wheeler pleasure craft, the *CLAIRE-E.* Moored at Noland's Landing on the west bank of the Muskingum River, the over-sixty-year-old boat is the first of its kind in the nation to be converted to a bed-and-breakfast.

The vessel has three staterooms, a main salon, and two decks for visitors to enjoy. Although the vessel is equipped with central heat and air-conditioning, two wood burners stand ready to cap a romantic evening. Although the *CLAIRE-E* is an operational stern-wheeler, she remains securely moored while guests are aboard. She is the year-round home of Harley Noland.

To book accommodations on the *CLAIRE-E,* contact the Levee House Cafe at (614) 374–2233. Rates: $80 per night, double occupancy, including continental breakfast. Reservations and a deposit required.

Marietta is also home to a world-famous gourmet pasta maker, **Rossi Pasta.** Though most of its pasta is sold by mail or through upscale retailers like Williams-Sonoma, in Marietta you can stop by the Rossi Pasta store and factory.

The success of Rossi Pasta can be attributed to a high-quality product and an intriguing selection of pasta cuts and flavors. These include everything from Artichoke Linguini to Basil Black Pepper Fettuccini, from Wild Mushroom Linguini to Calamari Fettuccini. Not only does Rossi have a half dozen sauces to top off the pasta, they also will recommend the perfect wine and compact disc to complete your meal (they sell CDs and are partial to classic Sinatra).

During the days of the Northwest Territory, the capital of the territory was wherever the territorial governor and judges convened. In July of 1788, Arthur St. Clair, the first territorial governor, arrived in Marietta and instituted the first government under the Ordinance of 1787. By 1790, Governor St. Clair had moved his headquarters to Cincinnati, making it the capital of the Territory.

By 1798, the Territory had 5,000 white male inhabitants, and Congress gave it permission to elect a legislature. In 1799, twenty-two representatives and Governor St. Clair met in Yeatmen's Tavern in Cincinnati. By the September session, when William Henry Harrison was elected the first territorial delegate to Congress, a new two-story frame building on Main Street was the home of the new legislature.

Rossi Pasta is at 114 Greene Street, Marietta; (740) 376–2065. Open Monday through Saturday, 9:00 A.M.–7:00 P.M.; Sunday, noon–5:00 P.M. (Pasta making times are variable, typically before 3:00 P.M.)

During your visit be sure to take a walking or driving tour of Marietta's stately residential neighborhoods. The city contains hundreds of nineteenth-century homes, many on charming brick streets.

For overnight accommodations, the **Lafayette Hotel** is at the landing where steamboats once unloaded their passengers and cargoes on cruises between Pittsburgh and Cincinnati. Nautical memorabilia decorate the lobby, restaurants, and lounge in this building, including brass pilot instruments, a pilot wheel, and paintings and photographs of the stern-wheelers that once prowled the nation's rivers.

The hotel's ninety-one guest rooms feature knotty wood paneling, and three even offer private balconies facing the river. Special Marietta lodging and entertainment packages are also available at the Lafayette, which was built in 1918.

The Lafayette Hotel is at the corner of Front and Greene Streets, Marietta; (800) 331–9337, (740) 373–5522. Rates: $65 to $100 per night. MasterCard, Visa, and American Express are accepted.

Like many innovators, Lee Middleton started work on her dream at her kitchen table. In the late seventies, she began creating porcelain dolls, sculpting her first dolls to resemble her daughter Brynn and her son Michael. Her craftsmanship was obvious to friends, neighbors, and eventually doll collectors, all of whom wanted to order dolls from Lee.

By 1980, Lee had taught others her techniques and moved her operation out of the kitchen and into the basement of a local bank. Five moves

Johnny Appleseed Apparition

*A*s you travel throughout Ohio, you may want to conjure up a mental image of the famous Johnny Appleseed. Many of the state's apple orchards as well as countless lone apple trees stand as a monument to the man who brought seeds to the farmers of Ohio. A more formal monument at the Washington and Noble County line was dedicated to his memory on September 25, 1942, the 168th anniversary of his birth.

Some say that this is not the only reminder of the famous wanderer that a visitor can experience in this area of Ohio. Just after the monument was dedicated, people began reporting that the man himself was coming back to visit. Some folks were pretty amazed to look up into one of Johnny's apple trees to see a smiling man with a long gray beard swinging his legs and calling out a greeting.

Because Johnny adhered to a religious sect that believed in communication with the departed, local tale tellers say it seems natural that he would try to make an appearance in some of his former haunts.

If you travel through Appleseed country, you may catch a glimpse of a shadow of a man in baggy pants held up with one suspender. You may wonder at the appearance of a man who reaches up to adjust the cooking pot he wears for a hat. But whether or not you see Johnny's spirit as an apparition, you certainly will see his spirit in the strong limbs and the glistening fruits of Johnny's apple trees.

later, *Lee Middleton Original Doll Company* began operation in its present 37,000-square-foot factory and doll store.

Today, visitors tour Lee's factory and observe the techniques that make Middleton dolls so distinctive. The most popular part of the tour is when visitors see the hand-painting of each doll's face, the most challenging step in the production process.

Each Lee Middleton doll leaves the factory with a miniature Bible in its hands, and factory visitors also receive one of these tiny Bibles as a memento of their visit. Middleton dolls retail from $120 to $500, but are available at the factory outlet store for $39 to $200.

The Lee Middleton Original Doll Company is at 1301 Washington Boulevard, Belpre; (800) 233–7479, (740) 423–1481. Open Monday through Saturday, 9:00 A.M.–5:00 P.M. (noon–5:00 P.M. weekdays in January and February). Tours Monday through Friday, 9:00 A.M.–3:00 P.M.; March through December, reservations recommended. No admission charge.

The settlement of Gallipolis resulted directly from what had to be one of the first land speculation schemes in the history of the United States. A congressman and his business associates received a congressional grant for 3.5 million acres in southern Ohio. These investors planned to secure the funds to pay for this land by reselling large tracts to Europeans. They formed the Scioto Company and dispatched a sales representative to France, who easily sold tracts to 500 upper-class French citizens ready to leave the turmoil in their country. These 500 men, women, and children set sail for America in 1790, but by the time they arrived in the New World, the Scioto Company had failed, leaving the immigrants without their property.

After negotiations with Congress, the French were given frontier land on the Ohio River. Since these immigrants were largely noblemen, professionals, and artisans, pioneer life quickly took its toll. Half of the party deserted the frontier during the first two years for "more civilized" areas.

But those remaining in what is today Gallipolis endured, and the town's strategic location on the river spurred its growth. In 1819, Henry Cushing constructed a tavern and inn, and that two-story building still exists, now a museum known as *Our House.*

The doors, floors, and even the lock on the front door at Our House are all original. A grandfather clock built in 1780 still keeps time, and the museum contains Chippendale and Hepplewhite furnishings that belonged to early Gallipolis settlers. In the dining room, for example, is a magnificent cherry dining room table set with delicate French plates and serving trays. The second-floor ballroom still has the original carved wooden chandeliers.

The name Our House comes from the sales pitch its owner, Henry Cushing, would give when he met boats arriving at the docks. To keep the newcomers from going to the other inn in town, he would tell them, "Come to our house." The inn's most famous guest was the French general and statesman Marquis de Lafayette. Lafayette, after his first trip to the colonies in 1777 to fight with the Americans against the British, returned to France and convinced his countrymen to enter the war against England. America never forgot Lafayette's aid during the Revolution, and in 1825 he made a triumphant return to the United States, which included a two-and-a-half-hour visit to Gallipolis and Our House on May 22. The coat he wore and one of the violins used to entertain him are displayed at the museum.

Another important Frenchman planned to come to Gallipolis with the original 500 settlers but at the last minute let his fiancée go without him. Had he made the trip to America, history would have been dramatically altered. His name was Napoleon Bonaparte; his fiancée's portrait hangs above a fireplace at Our House.

Our House is at 434 First Avenue, Gallipolis; (800) 752–2618, (614) 446–0586. The museum is open May through October, Saturday, 10:00 A.M.–5:00 P.M.; Sunday, 1:00–5:00 P.M. Also open Tuesday through Friday, 10:00 A.M.–5:00 P.M., June through August. Admission: adults, $3.00; children, $1.00.

Bob Evans has made his mark in two related businesses—as a manufacturer and distributor of his country sausage and as the proprietor of the Bob Evans Restaurants. After World War II, Evans opened a twelve-stool restaurant near Gallipolis. Not satisfied with the sausage available commercially, he started making his own. This blossomed into Bob Evans's sausage business, and he devoted more and more of his time and energy to it. Once Bob Evans Farms Sausage was firmly established in the marketplace, he once again concentrated on the restaurant business, opening a second location in 1962 and coordinating a major expansion in the late 1960s. Today, Bob Evans Farms Sausage is sold in twenty-six states, and more than 400 restaurants serve customers throughout the Midwest.

The 1,100-acre **Bob Evans Farm** consists of fields, woodlands, and scenic Raccoon Creek. Evans purchased the farm in 1953, living there with his family until 1971. Free wagon tours of the property take place four times daily, and local artists display (and sell) handmade gifts such as wood carvings, baskets, and jewelry in the Craft Barn.

Throughout the year, the farm hosts special events, including a bluegrass music festival, an antique car show, a quilt exhibit, and fairs. The most popular is the annual Farm Festival, which features live country music, field exhibits, and craftspeople demonstrating nearly forgotten skills.

The farm offers guided horseback rides on its many bridle trails for $9.00 per hour. Overnight trail rides leave the stable three nights each week during the summer months and on Friday and Saturday nights in September. After a two-and-a-half-hour ride to the campsite, guides serve a campfire supper (including—what else?—Bob Evans sausage). After a night outdoors and a hearty breakfast, riders saddle up and return to the stables. For $50 per person, the farm furnishes horses, meals, and shelters—you just bring your clothing, sleeping bag or bed roll, and perhaps some insect repellent. These popular overnights fill quickly, so reservations are a must.

The farm's canoe livery rents canoes and equipment for trips down Raccoon Creek ranging from two hours to a wilderness overnight trip. The picturesque creek takes canoeists past old gristmills. Canoe rentals range in price from $9.00 per canoe for the shorter trips to $20.00 for longer excursions. The canoeing season is daily in the summer and weekends in September, 8:30 A.M.–4:00 P.M.

Bob Evans Farm is on Route 588, 1 mile east of Rio Grande; (800) 994–FARM, (614) 245–5305. The farm is open daily in the summer and weekends in September, 8:30 A.M.–5:00 P.M. No admission charge.

Hill Country

The 100-mile-long, 30-mile-wide belt of southern Ohio and northern Kentucky known as the Hanging Rock Iron Region once produced the iron demanded by the booming industrial revolution. Eighty charcoal furnaces operated in this region from 1818 to 1916, furnishing iron ingots used to manufacture railroad and farm equipment, heavy machinery, and even the cannons and gunboats used in the Civil War. Abundant quantities of the iron ore, limestone, and timber needed for iron production caused the proliferation of furnaces in the region, and furnace communities sprang up near these facilities.

While many of the region's sandstone stacks today stand in silent memory of this once vital industry, at *Buckeye Furnace*, Ohio's only

More Salt, Please

Long before white settlers explored what is today Jackson County, Native Americans came to Salt Creek for its salt. The first whites to take advantage of the creek did so in 1798. They drew water from 30-foot wells and boiled it away in huge kettles. Due to the low salinity of the water, up to fifteen gallons of water were required to produce each pound of salt. Because of the importance of salt in preserving meats, both Congress and the Ohio Legislature passed laws regulating the Jackson saltworks. The discovery of other saltworks-both more accessible and with higher salinity led to the decline of Salt Creek's commercial value.

restored charcoal furnace, all buildings have been reconstructed. Visitors learn the history of the Hanging Rock region and the basics of iron making by reading the many signs along Buckeye's self-guided tour.

The furnace was built into a hillside, and the raw materials (iron ore, limestone, and charcoal) were brought by wagon to the top of the hill, where the charcoal was stored under a stock shed to keep it dry, and the limestone and ore were graded and sorted. (The charcoal was produced at a separate location by slowly burning timber under mounds of earth.) Laborers mixed and poured enormous quantities of these materials into the top of the furnace: in a twelve-hour shift, they would measure and load 57,000 pounds of ore, 1,900 pounds of limestone, and 800 bushels of charcoal. As the charcoal burned, temperatures in the furnace reached 600 degrees, causing the impurities in the iron ore to mix with the limestone, forming a waste product called slag. Since molten iron is heavier than slag, the iron could be removed from the bottom of the furnace by opening a stone dam at its base. The liquid iron flowed into sand molds known as pigs. The process of loading raw materials (the "burden") and drawing off the slag and molten iron was continuous—the furnaces operated twenty-four hours a day.

Down the hill from the stock shed and loading area, the Buckeye Furnace general store contains merchandise typical of the nineteenth century. The companies often paid the laborers in scrip, rather than currency, which could only be used at the company store or to pay for company lodging. As a result, some workers were continually in debt to their employers.

The discovery of richer and more easily transported Lake Superior iron ore caused the decline of the Hanging Rock Iron Region. Buckeye Furnace shut down for the last time in 1894, closing a chapter in the state's industrial history.

Buckeye Furnace is off Route 124, 10 miles east of Jackson; (800) 860–0144, (740) 384–3537. Open Memorial Day to Labor Day, Wednesday through Saturday, 9:30 A.M.–5:00 P.M.; Sunday, noon–5:00 P.M., plus weekends in September and October. Admission: adults, $3.00; children (ages 6 to 12), $1.25.

Northwest of Jackson, the *Lake Katharine State Nature Preserve* contains 1,400 breathtaking acres of rolling wooded hills, dense vegetation, and a cool, clear lake. Stop by the manager's office for maps of the main hiking trails (which are

Buckeye Furnace

located across the lake from the office) and walk down the path near the office for your first view of tranquil Lake Katharine.

It's a scenic drive to the parking area adjacent to the start of the three main trails on the east side of the lake. The Calico Bush Trail, a favorite in late April and May with wildflower lovers, leads hikers past abundant calico bush (mountain laurel) in full bloom on and between the exposed sandstone formations.

The Pine Ridge Trail crosses Rock Run, a gurgling stream that supplies Lake Katharine's sparkling water, and follows the lakeshore. This 2-mile trail then rises through a ridge of pines to a spectacular overlook.

Ohio's Youth Conservation Corps completed the preserve's newest and most demanding trail in 1979—Salt Creek Trail. Traveling 2 miles of steep hills, wooded ravines, cliffs, and creeks, hikers pass abandoned drift mines, early Indian work sites, and burial pits.

Visitors to this pristine preserve frequently spot varied wildlife, including wild turkey and deer and occasionally a bobcat or king snake. Because this is a nature preserve, no bank fishing, swimming, or picnicking is allowed, and nonmotorized watercraft are permitted on the winding lake by written permit only, with a maximum of five boats allowed per day.

Lake Katharine State Nature Preserve is 3 miles northwest of Jackson, off Route 35 on County Road 59; (614) 286–2487. Open daylight hours; no admission charge.

Just north of Lake Katharine, under a protective roof, rests a large slab of black hand sandstone with some remarkable Indian carvings—the **Leo Petroglyph.** Probably carved by the Fort Ancient Indians more than 700 years ago, the petroglyph has forty different carved figures, with a fish, a bird, and three human feet plainly visible. The most intriguing carving shows an Indian wearing an elaborate headdress. Nature trails penetrate the deep woods and skirt the upper cliffs of the gorges and forests surrounding the petroglyph.

The Leo Petroglyph is on County Road 28, off Route 35, 4 miles northwest of Jackson. Open daylight hours; no admission charge.

Sue and Jim Maxwell have created a most unusual lodging experience in Southeast Ohio: a replica of a twelfth-century Norman castle know as **Ravenwood Castle.** Longtime Anglophiles, the Maxwells have traveled extensively throughout England and Scotland and have always been attracted to castles and the medieval period. Surrounded by the Wayne National Forest and just 7 miles from the Hocking Hills, Ravenwood Castle sits atop a wooded hill. Fifty acres of forest and large rock formations surround the castle.

Ravenwood's crenelated towers contain the guest rooms and suites. Although the building is new, the couple has been collecting architectural antiques for several years. Each guest room or suite has a stained-glass window, usually in the bathroom, a fireplace with Victorian mantle and gas logs, antique light fixtures, and many feature wonderful old doors. The wood moldings around its doors and windows and the castle's five stairways are inspired by centuries-old motifs from Great Britain's stately homes and castles. Each room also has a balcony or private deck overlooking the forest.

Common areas include the Great Hall, with three large stained-glass windows from an old church at one end and a huge arched stone fireplace at the other. Ornate and heavily carved, museum-quality Gothic tables and chairs furnish the Great Hall. On the lower level is a library stocked with books on a wide variety of topics and a game room.

Ravenwood Castle is near the intersection of State Routes 56 and 93, New Plymouth; (800) 477–1541, (740) 596–2606. Rates: $95 to $175 per night, double occupancy, including full breakfast. Visa and MasterCard accepted.

Ohio's state parks offer hundreds of cabins throughout the state, most of them the modern, two-bedroom deluxe model. For those seeking more rustic and less expensive lodging, **Lake Hope State Park** provides the widest selection in types of cabins in the state park system. In addition to deluxe cabins, Lake Hope has twenty-one standard cabins with wood-burning fireplaces. These cabins, available April through October, accommodate up to six people in four rooms and contain complete kitchens. A third type, the sleeping cabins, have one to four bedrooms, fireplaces, and refrigerators, but no cooking facilities. As with the modern deluxe cabins, the sleeping cabins are available year-round.

The 3,000-acre park includes 120-acre Lake Hope, with its large beach and swimming area, in a heavily wooded section of Vinton County. The park's dining lodge serves meals from May through October, and the park has miles of hiking trails, as does the adjacent state forest. Lake Hope State Park also contains the remains of an old charcoal furnace—Hope Furnace.

Lake Hope State Park is on Route 278, 5 miles north of Zaleski; (800) 282–7275 or (740) 596–5253. Cabin rates range from $55 to $80 per day and from $280 to $400 per week.

Southeast Ohio contains thousands of acres of rugged, hilly countryside covered with thick forests, but the most geologically intriguing area may be the 10,000-acre *Hocking Hills State Park and Forest.* Steep hills, deciduous and evergreen forests, caves, rivers, waterfalls, and abundant plant and animal life provide outstanding recreational opportunities.

A warm, shallow ocean covered Ohio some 300 million years ago and deposited the bedrock of shale and black hand sandstone found in the area. Black hand sandstone is so named because of a large black hand drawn on a slab of the stone near Newark. Probably drawn by Indians, the hand may have served as a marker pointing the way to the outcroppings of flint found at Flint Ridge.

Though primitive man may have used the caves, recesses, and cliffs in the Hocking Hills for shelter as long as 7,000 years ago, pottery fragments confirm the Adena Indians lived here from the time of Christ to A.D. 800. White settlers did not discover the lush forests and flowing streams in these hills until the 1790s.

Old Man's Cave, one of the six major formations in the park, so awed Richard Rowe with its natural beauty in the early 1800s that he decided to live at the cave as a hermit for the rest of his days. Rowe was the "old man" for whom this cave is named. A deep gorge runs along the cave, which is actually a major recess in the sandstone cliff, and water flowing through the bottom of the gorge is hurled over two waterfalls and into the Devil's Bathtub, a large pothole formed in the sandstone by

Top Annual Events

Vinton County Wild Turkey Festival,
  McArthur, early May;
  (740) 596–4945

Moonshine Festival, New Straitsville,
  May; (740) 394–2836

Ohio Valley Pow-Wow,
  Nelsonville, May; (740) 753–3591

Bluegrass Festival, between Guysville
  and Steward, June; (740) 662–2051

Regattafest, Ironton, June;
  (800) 416–3223

River Recreation Festival, Gallipolis,
  July 4th weekend; (740) 446–0596

Family Fun Days, Coal Grove,
  July 4th weekend; (740) 532–9427

Summer Festival,
  Gibsonville, July; (740) 385–2216

Lawrence County Fair,
  Proctorville, July; (740) 533–4322

Fireman's Festival,
  Laurelville, July; (740) 332–6033

Morgan County Civil War Encampment
  Days, Malta and McConnelsville,
  July; (740) 962–3431

Lancaster Festival, Lancaster, 12 days
  late July into August; (740) 687–4808

Cruise-in and Sock Hop,
  Nelsonville, July; (740) 753–1931

Jackson County Fair, Wellston, late July
  to early August; (740) 384–6587

Pig Iron Day,
  Jackson, August; (740) 286–3224

All-American Soap Box Derby, Akron,
  early August; (330) 733–8723

Parade of the Hills,
  Nelsonville, August; (740) 753–3553

Sweet Corn Festival, Millersport,
  September; (740) 467–3943

Ohio River Sternwheeler Festival,
  Marietta, September; (800) 288–2577

Civil War Days, Somerset, September;
  (740) 743–2591

swirling rock and gravel in the stream water. Hiking trails follow the ridges on both sides of the gorge, and a third snakes through the hemlocks, beeches, and yews at the bottom of the gorge.

Decades of erosion have created another spectacular sandstone formation called Ash Cave, a 700-foot horseshoe-shaped rock ledge that forms a recess 100 feet deep. Mounds of ash found here by early settlers indicated that this large rock roof was a popular camping site for Indians. Hiking trails run along both ridges and the floor of the gorge, past the 90-foot waterfall.

The Rock House, a massive recess completely enclosed by rock except for the open "windows," is the most cavelike formation in the park—certainly more so than Ash Cave or Old Man's Cave—yet of the three it is the only one not named a cave. Another misnomer is nearby Cedar Falls, a waterfall named by pioneers who mistakenly identified the dense forest as cedar, when, in fact, it is hemlock.

In addition to the six major formations in the park, hiking trails explore thousands of acres in the thickly wooded state forest. The park has forty deluxe cabins in a secluded, peaceful setting and a dining lodge with outdoor swimming pool. The cabins are available year-round but are rented only for full weeks during summer months, with rates ranging from $100 per day to $480 per week. The dining lodge serves meals from May through October. Other park features include campsites, a seventeen-acre fishing lake, and a summer naturalist program, plus picnic tables, barbecue grills, and shelters scattered throughout the area.

Hocking Hills State Park is 14 miles west of Logan, on Route 664; (800) 282–7275 or (740) 385–6841.

Innkeeper Michael Daniel's ambitious goal when he conceived of **Glenlaurel,** his Scottish country inn and cottages, was to build the premier romantic getaway of the Midwest. Situated on 133 wooded acres and backing up to the rocks of Camusfearna Gorge, Glenlaurel welcomed its first guests in 1994.

This full-service resort is a great country escape any time of the year. The eight stone fireplaces of the Manor House and its guest rooms take the chill out of a fall day. A double whirlpool tub in each private bath overlooks the hemlock and trillium. Tucked away in a dense woods, each of the four cottages features an open-air hot tub on a private deck.

Gourmet dining completes this outstanding retreat: The light-as-air Belgian buttermilk waffles topped with maple cream and strawberry-rhubarb sauce are legendary. A "typical" dinner: orange-tomato-basil soup, mixed greens with balsamic vinaigrette, soy-sesame ginger-marinated salmon over basmati rice with roasted vegetables, finished with a slice of mixed berry sour cream pie!

Glenlaurel is 5 miles west of State Route 33, just off State Route 180, at 14940 Mt. Olive Road, Rockbridge; (800) 809–REST. Rates: $110 to $240 per night, double occupancy, including full breakfast. Visa, MasterCard, and American Express accepted.

It took more time and money than its creators ever imagined, but the **Inn at Cedar Falls** was worth the wait. Situated on a hillside meadow, surrounded on three sides by the Hocking Hills State Park, the inn represents two-and-a-half years of work and an investment of a half million dollars.

First, shingle and plaster were removed from an 1850s-vintage farmhouse, purchased from an eighty-six-year-old woman who was born here, to reveal its original log-and-mud construction. A second log building was moved on site, and the union of these structures now houses a gourmet kitchen and indoor dining area. The plank flooring, wood-burning stove, and period pieces give this "common" room a pioneer ambience—it's a place where guests watch culinary artistry in progress. The aromas of American country cooking fill the inn—apple-smoked pork loin, bean soup, bread pudding with whiskey sauce, or chicken with morel sauce.

The inn's garden supplies herbs, beans, edible flowers, peppers, eggplant, cucumbers, and tomatoes, and meals are prepared with the local growing season in mind. Guest chefs from Columbus and elsewhere are invited to spend an evening in the kitchen, explaining their technique to guests as they perform their magic. Exceptional breakfasts and dinners are then served either in the log house or out on the patio.

The Inn at Cedar Falls offers most unusual accommodations for its overnight guests. Housed in a modern, barn-shaped building are nine guest rooms. Though similar in design to contemporary motel rooms, with individual heating and air-conditioning units, they are furnished with antiques and rough wood covers the floors. Each has an up-to-date private bath, but no telephone or television. Rocking chairs and tables make the second-floor balcony a delightful spot for reading or just soaking up the hilly landscape. A new addition is six log cabins scattered throughout the inn's sixty acres, each with privacy, cooking facilities, and its own personality.

A section of the prairie meadow that predominates here has been mowed, so guests can stroll down the hill to an outstanding lookout. An adult-size swing hangs from a tree limb next to an inviting hammock. Here you might encounter deer, fox, or raccoon, while bird-watchers view yellow finches, bluebirds, woodpeckers, ruffed grouse, and wild turkey.

Although the inn occupies a clearing right on Route 374, wooded hiking trails meander nearby. The Buckeye Trail, which connects Old Man's Cave with Ash Cave, is easily joined from here. Or hike to Rose Lake for some trout fishing. Cross-country skiing is a winter favorite.

Innkeeper Ellen Grinsfelder wants her guests to enjoy the natural wonder of this area as much as she does. And although the kitchen primarily serves overnight guests, others are welcome for dinner if they call ahead and make reservations. A single menu is prepared at mealtime, with one sitting when visitors come together to share their day's adventures. Holidays are special times here—the inn provides those without family nearby (or those escaping relatives!) a homey retreat full of holiday spirit.

Also Worth Seeing

Wayne National Forest, Athens

Slate Run Living Historical Farm, Lithopolis

Burr Oak State Park, Glouster

The Inn at Cedar Falls is located at 21190 State Route 374, 10 miles southwest of Logan; (800) 653–2557, (740) 385–7489. Rates: $75 to $185 per night, double occupancy, including full breakfast. Visa and MasterCard are accepted. Open year-round.

Five cabins nestled in the trees around a spring-fed lake, that's **Bookman Woods.** The cabins are well separated from one another, and each has a private dock on the lake—a perfect spot to fish for largemouth bass, yellow perch, and bluegill or to launch one of the rowboats provided for guests. Lake swimming is a favorite summer pastime here, or you can loll and sunbathe out on the diving platform floating in the center of Bookman Lake. Whatever you choose to do here, the limited number of cabins ensures that you will never encounter a crowd.

Cabins here range from one-bedroom single stories to the bi-level Cedar House with two large decks, an indoor hot tub, and two-plus bedrooms. Each cabin at Bookman's has a deck, porch swing, wood-burning stoves with glass fronts for fire watchers (as well as electric heat), and outdoor barbecue grills. All are comfortably furnished in pleasing earth tones, and they have plenty of windows looking out on the dense forest. Complete kitchens round out the facilities here.

Bookman Woods is east of Laurelville, off Route 180; (614) 436–3629. Rates: $80 to $140 per night, depending on the size of the cabin, day of the week, and season. Open year-round. Reservations are required.

Another Hocking Hills lodging option, set on one hundred wooded acres, is **Old Man's Cave Chalets.** These twenty A-frames, sprinkled on a hillside, are three-room structures, complete with lofts. Each chalet sleeps four and has a deck with private hot tub, wood-burning stove (plus central heating and air-conditioning), and a fully equipped kitchen.

In addition to the A-frames, fourteen larger luxury log homes, sleeping four to six people, are seeded in more secluded locations throughout the hills. These deluxe log homes feature large stone fireplaces, private hot tubs, TVs and VCRs, central air, handmade furniture, and fully equipped kitchens. Two large lodges accommodate groups from sixteen to twenty guests.

The quiet, isolated location here makes this an ideal year-round retreat. More than 800 acres of state forest adjoin the property and are available for hiking and exploration.

Old Man's Cave Chalets is at 18905 Route 664, west of Logan; (800) 762–9396, (614) 385–6517. Rates: $119 to $198 per night, double occupancy. Reservations required.

In addition to hiking and camping, canoeing and horseback riding are popular in the Hocking Hills. *Hocking Valley Canoe Livery and Fun Center* provides rental equipment along the picturesque Hocking River, with trips ranging from two hours to three days at rates from $20 to $60 per canoe. The Logan livery is at 31251 Chieftain Drive; (800) 686–0386, (614) 385–8685, 385–2503. Canoe rentals are available April through October, daily June through August, weekend or by appointment April, May, September, and October. Kayaks, rafts, go-carts, miniature golf, and a driving range also are available.

The natural beauty of the Hocking Hills makes them an ideal place for trail riding, and horses are saddled up and ready to go at the stables of the *Hocking Valley Ranch.* The ranch is on Route 93, 8 miles south of Logan; (614) 385–8361, 385–7626. It is open weekends in May, September, and October and daily during the summer, 10:00 A.M.–5:00 P.M.

Nature herself has given this site its name, Wahkenna, which is a Native American word meaning "most beautiful." The 150-acre *Wahkenna Nature Preserve,* at the edge of the Hocking Hills, is blessed with so many natural assets that it serves as a center for both outdoor education and nature study.

But the casual visitor won't have to study too hard to see how the preserve got its name. Much of the area is forested with lovely tulip trees as well as oaks. Mountain laurel, brilliant rhododendron, a host of wildflowers, and more than two dozen kinds of fern grace the landscape. While you may not think of Ohio as home to the exotic orchid, Wahkenna boasts eight native varieties of the flower, including the pink lady's slipper.

Visitors can hike two trails into the preserve. Here you may be able to catch glimpses of the permanent residents: white-tailed deer, woodpeckers, maybe even a hawk or an owl. The land itself is noteworthy, with sandstone cliffs part of the preserve's vista, the famous Black Hand sandstone.

Although you can do your own exploring, naturalists also offer guided hikes and walks focusing on wildlife, plant life, or even the ways of the early pioneers in the area. Check in advance for topics, dates, and times.

The Wahkeena Nature Preserve is located at 2045 Pump Station Road, Sugar Grove; (740) 746–8695. Open April through October, Wednesday through Sunday, 8:00 A.M.–4:30 P.M. Admission: $2.00 per car.

Square 13, a National Register Historic District, is one of the original blocks of Lancaster, a block noted by architectural historians as one of the finest collections of nineteenth-century architecture in a concentrated area in the nation. Within Square 13 on Lancaster's "Main Hill" is the **Sherman House,**

The Georgian

the birthplace and early home of noted Civil War general William Tecumseh Sherman, and his brother, Senator John Sherman, author of the Sherman Anti-Trust Act. This museum is furnished as it would have been when the Sherman family lived there (the home was built between 1811 and 1816) and contains an extensive collection of General Sherman's Civil War memorabilia, mementos, and artifacts. One room is the study of William and John's father, Charles Sherman, who was a justice on the Ohio Supreme Court.

The Sherman House is at 137 East Main Street, Lancaster; (614) 687–5891, 654–9923. Open April through mid-December, Tuesday through Sunday, 1:00–4:00 P.M. Admission: adults, $2.50; students (6 to 18), $1.00.

The Georgian, an elegant two-story brick mansion, sits on a hill looking down on Lancaster's central business district, just as it has for the past 160 years. Constructed in 1833 for prominent businessman Samuel Maccracken, the Georgian mixes Federal architecture with Regency features and Empire furnishings. The Federal influence can be seen in the symmetrical placement of doors, windows, and fireplaces, while the Regency features are exemplified by the curved bay windows along the west wall. Classic Ionic columns, each containing a complete tree trunk for structural support, form the west portico.

Maccracken came to Lancaster from Big Springs, Pennsylvania, in 1810. Later elected to the state legislature, he introduced the bill funding construction of Ohio's canal system. While serving as Ohio Canal Funds Commissioner, Maccracken raised $6 million in Europe for the project.

Ohio's Bulgaria Liberator

The man hailed as one of the greatest figures in the history of Bulgaria was born on a farm near New Lexington in 1844. Januarius MacGahan, the "Liberator of Bulgaria," hoped to be a teacher but was unable to land a job with the local school district. Instead, in the early 1870s, he traveled throughout Europe and eventually became a war correspondent in the Balkans, where he filed eyewitness accounts of Turkish atrocities. His reporting shifted British public opinion regarding their support for Turkey and encouraged Russian intervention. MacGahan crossed the Danube with 100,000 Russian soldiers and received a hero's welcome. MacGahan lived out his life in Constantinople and died there in 1878. His body was returned to the United States; he's buried at New Lexington's Maplewood Cemetery.

This thirteen-room mansion is furnished with handsome pieces dating from the mid-1800s, including some of Maccracken's possessions. The original pine floors and woodwork remain intact, as do the original doors, door frames, and ornate arches. The spiral staircase features a cherry spindle handrail, and a large skylight allows light to spill down the stairs.

Splendid blue marble fireplaces from the quarry in King of Prussia, Pennsylvania, grace the two large parlors, as do matching French chandeliers (circa 1820). One of the upstairs bedrooms contains a fine Regency bed (circa 1800)—the type of bed preferred by generals in the Civil War, since it could be assembled and disassembled easily by the troops. One unique item in the museum is a 1792 senility cradle. Similar in design and function to a baby's cradle, cradles such as this were used by old people who were no longer ambulatory.

Hanging on the wall in one of the stairways are original Fairfield County land grants signed by Presidents Jefferson and Madison. Also on display is an American flag with eighteen stars—the flag of the United States from 1816 to 1820. The basement houses the kitchen, equipped as it was in the 1830s, and a unique dry well, where groundwater from the surface drained by way of pipes and was dispersed into the ground beneath the basement.

The Georgian is at the corner of East Wheeling and North Broad Streets, Lancaster; (614) 654–9923. Open April through December, Tuesday through Sunday, 1:00–4:00 P.M. Admission: adults, $2.50; children (under age 16), $1.00.

After your tour of the Georgian, be sure to walk up East Wheeling Street for a view of the magnificent restored homes in a hilly, shaded section of Lancaster. If lunch or dinner is the next item on your itinerary, try a 1940s hotel that is making a comeback. Just across the street from the Georgian, **Shaw's Restaurant and Inn** features food, libations, and lodging in a delightful setting. Six of the inn's twenty rooms and suites feature whirlpools and themed decor.

With rich wooden doors and trim, potted green-ery, and distinctive floral wall coverings, the main dining room of the hotel has candlelit tables and indirect lighting, creating a cozy atmosphere. The dinner menu changes daily and is known for its sophistication.

Shaw's serves fresh homemade pies and cakes, and the house-made hot fudge sauce is a stand-out. Due to the popularity of lunch and dinner selections, the dining rooms accept reservations for both meals.

Shaw's Restaurant and Inn is at 123 North Broad Street, Lancaster; (800) 654–2477, (614) 654–1842. Rates: $50 to $168 per night, double occupancy, including full breakfast. Visa and MasterCard accepted.

Abundant clay deposits in eastern Ohio, partic-ularly in Perry and Muskingum Counties, encouraged the manufacture of pottery and ceramic wares in this section of the state. Pot-tery production in these counties dates to the early nineteenth century, and twenty-two major pottery companies once generated clay products in the area. Only eight of those firms remain in business, but the *Ohio Ceramic Center* preserves the his-tory of the industry and displays samples of the diverse output of those factories.

Given its name, you might suspect Crooksville is notable for the poor char-acter of its citizenry. That is not the case. Instead, Crooksville made its repu-tation as a center of the pottery business.

The rich clays beneath its soil spawned pottery giants such as Crooksville Pottery Company, the Star Stoneware Company, and the Diamond Stoneware Company in the late nine-teenth century. The arrival of rail service in 1890 established Crooksville as "Clay City," and launched a competition with another Ohio pottery town, East Liverpool.

Set on a hilltop in a cluster of trees, the center consists of five open-air exhibit buildings. Guides provide the background and explain the processes used to produce the assortment of vases, jugs, pots, and pitchers, plus plates, saucers, and other dinnerware—each unique in shape, color, and clay mixture. Some of the older pieces include stoneware jugs and jars from the 1850s and the even older earthenware, which was made from very soft red clay.

The yellow ware, so named because of its yellow hue, came from the East Liverpool, Ohio, area, as did the most unusual brown rocking-ham pottery. Rockingham (also manufactured in Vermont and Great Britain) can be easily identified by the pitcher handles shaped like a dog—a dog that appears to be looking into the pitcher. The guides also explain the obvious similarity in style of pieces from different companies—the firms frequently hired employees away from one

Moonshine Festival

Legal moonshine? Yes, in New Straitsville in late May you can see demonstrations of moonshine brewing as part of the Moonshine Festival. The character of hill country culture of days past comes back to life in the streets as the music of fiddles and banjos fills the air. There always are plenty of games for the kids, as well as displays and sales of local crafts and plenty of local food specialties. The Moonshine Festival takes place in mid-May. For more information call (740) 394–2838.

another, and these employees often brought to their new employer the techniques and processes used by competitors.

Modern pottery displays include samples of dinnerware and decorative pottery currently in production at the remaining local companies. The museum also exhibits pottery-making equipment such as molds and old potter's wheels, plus examples of industrial uses of ceramics—drain tubes, shingles, chimney liners, and even filters for air-pollution devices. A resident potter demonstrates the craft of hand-throwing vases, bowls, and jugs and describes glazing and finishing procedures. Two large shelter houses recently have been added at the center, where antique pottery is sold on special occasions, the proceeds used to help support this facility.

The Ohio Ceramic Center is on Route 93 between Roseville and Crooksville; (614) 697–7021. The center is open mid-May through mid-October, Wednesday through Saturday, 9:30 A.M.–5:00 P.M.; Sunday, noon–5:00 P.M. Admission: $1.00 for everyone over age 12.

Cattle ranch? Ohio? Yep. The **Smoke Rise Ranch Resort** is a working cattle ranch on 2,000 acres in the rolling hills of Southeastern Ohio. Visitors can play cowboy or cowgirl, rounding up strays on horseback, doctoring sick calves, checking fences and water tanks, and driving the herd from pasture to pasture. Or you can just enjoy the scenery, exploring it on foot or in the saddle on the more than 100 miles of trails.

A wildlife management area and the Wayne National Forest, totaling more than 30,000 acres, border the ranch. The terrain ranges from rock bluffs to lush green bottomland. The abundant ponds provide water for your trail horse and a great place to stop and fish away an afternoon.

Accommodations are all rustic, ranging from bunk-style cabins to campsites. And you can cook your own grub (ranch talk for "food"), or dine with the staff at this family-owned resort. Other amenities include a heated swimming pool, a hot tub, and a clubhouse with full kitchen.

Smoke Rise Ranch Resort is at 749 Sweet Gum Road, Murray City; (740) 767–2624, (800) 292–1732. Open for trail riding daily, 8:30 A.M.–6:30 P.M. Lodging is $35 to $120 per night.

It was Harriet and Ora Anderson, she a well-known local artist and he a banker and philanthropist, who decided Southeastern Ohio was in need of a cultural arts center. Their quest for a home for their vision led them to an unlikely structure: a historic dairy barn, built in 1914, once part of a large farm minutes from the heart of Athens.

By the time the Andersons discovered the **Dairy Barn** in 1977, it was scheduled for demolition in nine days. They rallied area residents and artists and saved it from the wrecking ball. In 1978, the facility was placed on the National Register of Historic Places, protecting it from future demolition.

This unique 7,000-square-foot exhibit space today hosts international exhibitions, festivals, performances, and activities for all ages, all consistent with its mission: to promote the arts, crafts, and cultural heritage of Southeast Ohio and to bring into the region the very best of the arts from all over the world. In the international arts community, the Dairy Barn is best known for its contemporary art quilt exhibition. The Dairy Barn is at 8000 Dairy Lane, Athens; (740) 592–4981, 4985. Open year-round, Tuesday through Sunday, 11:00 A.M.–5:00 P.M. (until 8:00 P.M. on Thursday). Admission: adults, $5.00; children, free.

**PLACES TO STAY
IN SOUTHEAST OHIO**

LOGAN
Inn at Cedar Falls
21190 State Route 374
(800) 653–2557,
(740) 385–7489

Old Man's Cave Chalets
18905 Route 664
(800) 762–9396,
(614) 385–6517

MARIETTA
Lafayette Hotel
Corner of Front and
Greene Streets
(740) 373–5522

MURRAY CITY
Smoke Rise Ranch Resort
749 Sweet Gum Road
(740) 767–2624,
(800) 292–1732

NEW PLYMOUTH
Ravenwood Castle
Intersection of State
Routes 56 and 93
(800) 477–1541,
(740) 596–2606

ROCKBRIDGE
Glenlaurel
15402 Mt. Olive Road
(800) 809–REST

ZALESKI
Lake Hope State
Park Cabins
Route 278, 5 miles
north of Zaleski
(800) 282–7275,
(740) 596–5253

**PLACES TO EAT
IN SOUTHEAST OHIO**

LANCASTER
Shaw's Restaurant and Inn
123 North Broad Street
(800) 654–2477,
(614) 654–1842
Lodging is also available.

MARIETTA
Becky Thatcher's
Restaurant and Lounge
237 Front Street
(740) 373–4130

The Betsey Mills Club
Dining Room
At the corner of Fourth
and Putnam Streets
(740) 373–3804

Levee House Café
127 Ohio Street
(740) 374–2233

PORTSMOUTH
Scioto Ribber
1026 Gallia Street
(740) 353–9329

Helpful Web Sites

Ohio Division of Travel and Tourism:
www.ohiotourism.com

Hocking Hills Tourism:
www.hockinghills.com

Athens County Visitors Bureau:
www.athensohio.com

Marietta Visitors Bureau:
www.rivertowns.org

Southwest Ohio

Native Beauty

Two thousand years ago, along the rivers of what is now southern Ohio, a great civilization arose. The Hopewell culture flourished for more than 500 years, leaving behind extensive burial mounds, earthworks, and artifacts. They are preserved at the Mound City site of the *Hopewell Culture National Historic Park.* Excavation and restoration work was conducted by the Ohio State Historical Society in 1920 and 1921, and the site was declared a National Monument in 1923. Additional excavations were conducted in the mid-1960s.

Some of the artifacts discovered and displayed here may have been used to establish trade and diplomatic ties between distant peoples. The territory we now call southern Ohio was the center of a network of peoples extending from Michigan to southern Florida, and from Kansas to the East Coast. The Hopewell included skilled artisans; they fished and hunted, gathered wild foods, and grew a few crops. They lived along river valleys, in permanent or semipermanent villages near the mounds and earthworks they built. By about 500 A.D. the great Hopewell culture ended, perhaps due to social changes, a breakdown in trading patterns, or warfare.

Hopewell Culture National Historic Park is 3 miles north of Chillicothe on State Route 104; (614) 774-1126. Open daily, 8:30 A.M.–5:00 P.M. (open later in the summer). Admission: adults, $2.00; children, free.

Thomas Worthington first came to Ohio from Virginia at the age of twenty-three in 1796, when he and a small band of men arrived to claim the land promised their fathers and friends after the Revolutionary War. Worthington permanently moved his family to Ohio in 1798 and quickly became active in the efforts to achieve statehood for the territory. He succeeded in that endeavor and served as a member of Ohio's Constitutional Convention in 1802. After being elected as one of the state's first United States senators, Worthington built his magnificent hilltop estate, *Adena.* Worthington and his wife, Eleanor, raised their ten children at Adena and entertained distinguished guests such as President James Monroe, Henry Clay, Aaron Burr, and the Indian

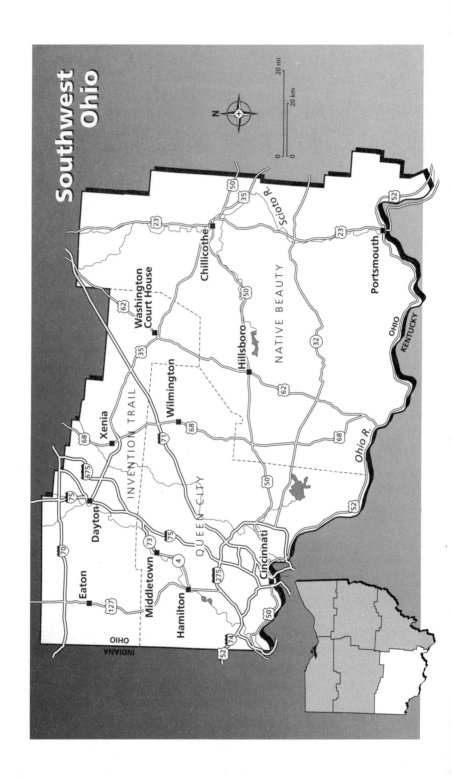

chief Tecumseh. After building Adena, Worthington was reelected to the United States Senate in 1811, and later he served two terms as the governor of Ohio.

More than 300 of the estate's original 5,000 acres are now open to the public, and visitors explore the spacious two-story sandstone home, the barn, the springhouse, and the smokehouse—all located in a rolling meadow above the Scioto River Valley. Self-guided tours of the eighteen-room home allow you to browse at your own pace, appreciating the fine antiques described on the fact sheet, which gives the style and origins of the furnishings in the home. Although many of the pieces on display did not belong to the Worthingtons, they date from the 1780s to 1820s and are typical of the pieces used at Adena.

The large downstairs master bedroom, with its dark ash and oak floors, has a splendid view of the formal gardens. In an adjacent sitting room hangs a most unusual portrait of Thomas Jefferson, created not with paint, but with different colors of wool thread. The enormous state dining room features the actual dining table and chairs used at Adena in 1825. Two large portraits decorate the drawing room; one of Thomas Worthington at age twenty-five and the other of his sister, who married Edward Tiffin, Ohio's first governor.

Two of Adena's most interesting rooms are tucked away down the back stairs: the weaving room, with a large Virginia loom (circa 1790) and wool and flax wheels, and Worthington's private study. On display in the study is a tomahawk given to Worthington by Chief Tecumseh in 1807, and Worthington's musket and his father's sword still hang above the fireplace.

Across the meadow from the home is a scenic overlook of the Scioto River Valley—you can see for miles from this spot. In fact, the splendor of the sunrise over Mount Logan as viewed from Adena is said to have inspired the sunrise design incorporated in the seal of the state of Ohio.

Adena is off Route 104 and Pleasant Valley Road on Adena Road, 3 miles north of Chillicothe, (800) 319–7248, (740) 772–1500. Open from Memorial Day to Labor Day, Wednesday through Saturday, 9:30 A.M.–5:00 P.M.; Sunday, noon–5:00 P.M; plus weekends in September and October. Admission: adults, $5.00, children (ages 6 to 12), $1.25.

State Motto/Animal

*I*n 1866, the Ohio legislature passed a bill adding a motto to Ohio's Great Seal. The motto, Imerium in Imperio, translates from Latin to "an empire within an empire." However, the motto's life span was brief. Critics blasted it as pretentious and feudal, and in 1867 the law authorizing it was repealed. For the next ninety-one years, Ohio had no state motto.

In 1958, Cincinnati sixth-grader Jimmie Mastronardo was disturbed to learn that Ohio was the only state without a motto, and he set about to correct this omission. He decided on a biblical verse from Matthew 19:26: "With God all things are possible." He

and his classmates launched a petition drive aimed at the legislature, a drive that succeeded in 1959 when the new motto officially was adopted.

Students also were the driving force behind the designation of the white-tailed deer as Ohio's state animal in 1988. In this case, it was a fourth-grade class at Worthington Estates Elementary School that lobbied lawmakers. The students argued that the white-tailed deer's abundance (there are more deer today in Ohio than there were at the time of settlement) and gracefulness warranted the recognition. The legislators agreed and deemed it so.

SOUTHWEST OHIO

Shawnee leader Tecumseh dreamed of banding together 50,000 warriors from all the western Indian tribes in a force that he hoped would end the white man's westward expansion. The plan obviously failed, and the whites eventually conquered the land north and west of the Ohio River and beyond. Tecumseh's story is portrayed nightly except Sundays during the summer at Sugarloaf Mountain Amphitheatre in the outdoor drama *Tecumseh!* The Tecumseh Restaurant Terrace serves a buffet dinner each evening prior to the 8:00 curtain. Backstage tours also are offered daily.

Sugarloaf Mountain Amphitheatre is on Delano Road, east of Route 159, 6 miles northeast of Chillicothe; (740) 775–0700. Performances take place from early June to early September. Admission: adults, $13.00 to $15.00, children (ages 10 and under), $6.00. Reservations recommended for weekend performances. MasterCard and Visa are accepted.

> ## Feast of the Flowering Moon
>
> *What child hasn't played at being a Native American or a rugged mountain man? The Feast of the Flowering Moon brings reenactment teams together to return the days of early Ohio to Yoctangee Park in Chillicothe. During the weekend festival you'll marvel at the skills of artisans and feel the beat of drums that fire the performance of Native American dancers.*
>
> *The Feast of the Flowering Moon is held mid- to late May in Yoctangee Park. For more information, write to P.O. Box 879, Chillicothe, Ohio 45601. No admission charge.*

The owner of Chillicothe's first paper mill, John Ingham, built his family a spacious fourteen-room home in 1864. The Italianate residence remained in the Ingham family for more than a century before being acquired by Jack and Katie Sullivan, who now entertain overnight guests in what is today the *Chillicothe Bed and Breakfast.*

Katie grew up in the area but moved to California as a young woman. After catching the bed-and-breakfast bug in England, she returned home in 1982 and opened one a few blocks from the Ingham home. Artist Jack Sullivan, a retired Air Force officer, came to Chillicothe in that same year to show his silk-screen prints, met Katie, and, as they say, the rest is history. They bought the Ingham place and opened Chillicothe Bed and Breakfast in 1984.

The Sullivans' home features high ceilings, four guest rooms—one with private half bath, and a carriage house–garage that Jack uses as his studio. He gladly gives interested guests a peek at his latest masterpiece.

Chillicothe Bed and Breakfast is at 202 South Paint Street, Chillicothe; (740) 772–6848. Rates: $50 to $60 per night, double occupancy, including breakfast. Cash, checks, Visa, and MasterCard accepted. Reservations and a deposit requested.

In an area once inhabited by Shawnee and Delaware Indians, *7 Caves* has intrigued visitors since the turn of the century. The park was established as 7 Caves in 1928 and has been owned by the Miller family since 1981.

Designated as an Ohio Natural Landmark, the 7 Caves wilderness offers a scenic retreat with miles of hiking trails and caves for exploration. The sixty-acre park is home to more than 250 species of plants and more than 60 types of trees, many of which are rare or endangered.

Three well-marked trails lead to the 7 Caves, each with its own unique formation: Cave of the Springs, Witches, Phantom, Bear, McKimie,

Where's the Capital?

*C*ongress divided the Northwest Territory in 1800 and designated Chillicothe as the capital of the eastern half. The territorial legislature met here in November of 1800 in Abrams's Big House, a two-story log cabin and one of the few buildings in the four-year-old village large enough to accommodate the group. The main floor, where the legislature met, also was used for singing schools, dances, and religious services. Upstairs was a bar. Construction began on a state-house, built of stone taken from neighboring hills.

In 1802, when the population of the eastern division of the Territory reached 45,000, Congress authorized the election of delegates to create a state constitution. Thirty-five delegates met in the new Chillicothe statehouse on November 4, 1802, and drafted the document in twenty-five days. Ohio's admission to the Union was in 1803, and the first Ohio General Assembly convened March 1, 1803.

The new constitution called for Chillicothe to remain the capital until 1808, starting an intense competition between towns wanting to be named the permanent capital. Zanesville went as far as building a statehouse and was named temporary capital in 1809 for its efforts. The brick Zanesville statehouse served as the capital until 1812, when the seat of government was shifted back to Chillicothe.

Meanwhile, Worthington, Lancaster, Newark, Mt. Vernon, Delaware, Dublin, and Pickaway Plains all competed for the permanent site. Dublin was believed to be the front runner, but legend has it that Dublin lost the favored spot as a result of a card game the night before the legislature was to act on the siting of the permanent capital. The winner was a plot of land across the Scioto River from the town of Franklinton.

The new capital site was heavily wooded and did not even have a name. Though Ohio City was the favorite name with many, the legislature designated the future capital as Columbus. State offices moved from Chillicothe to Columbus on October 1, 1816, and the legislature met for the first time in Columbus that December.

Marble, and Dancing caves. Rocky Fork Creek flows through the rolling hills of the Paint Valley, known for its crystal clear rapids, waterfalls, precipitous cliffs, and canyons. Also, 7 Caves was one of the filming locations for the CBS miniseries *500 Nations*, a Kevin Costner production that celebrated Native American culture.

Located 4 miles west of Bainbridge, 7 Caves is off U.S. 50 at 7660 Cave Road; (937) 365–1283. Open daily year-round, 9:00 A.M. to dark. Admission: adults, $10.00; children (4 to 14), $5.00.

When you're traveling through southern Ohio, you can't help but notice the dozens of lakes in the region—lakes providing boating, fishing, swimming, and other recreational activities. For this reason I heartily recommend that when you travel off the beaten path in southern Ohio, you always pack a swimsuit—particularly on hot summer days.

One of these alluring lakes is thirteen-acre Pike Lake in *Pike Lake State Park,* which offers a delightful spot for swimming, rowing, fishing, or scuba diving. Lifeguards watch over the sandy beach and swimming area during the summer, and rowboats can be rented. Anglers enjoy the catfish, largemouth bass, crappie, and bluegill, and divers take advantage of the remarkably clear water.

On Christmas morning, 1873, Eliza Jane Thompson and seventy-five other women temperance activists visited every Hillsboro saloon and drugstore that sold alcohol. Thompson, daughter of a former governor and wife of a judge, led the charge into those businesses, where the protestors would kneel, pray aloud, and sing hymns. They informed the shocked owners they'd be back the next day and every day until they stopped selling the devil's brew.

The result: they stopped liquor sales in every Hillsboro store but one. Eliza Jane Thompson's protest movement became the Women's Temperance Crusade, which in turn evolved into the Women's Christian Temperance Union.

Although the state park is a modest 600 acres, a densely wooded 10,600-acre state forest surrounds the park. There are numerous hiking trails in the state forest and 7 miles of trails in the park.

Up a shady hill from the lake sit the park's twenty-five rental cabins—twelve deluxe two-bedroom cabins and thirteen standard cabins. All are set in secluded locations, and the deluxe cabins offer completely equipped kitchens, baths, living areas, and screened porches. The standard cabins contain a single large sleeping and living area with four bunks and a foldout couch, a kitchen, and a bath. Pike Lake also has 112 campsites, and a park naturalist conducts nature programs during summer months.

Pike Lake State Park is at 1847 Pike Lake Road, 7 miles south of Bainbridge; (800) 282–7275 or (740) 493–2212. The standard cabins are available April through October; rates range from $65 per night to $300 per week. Rates for the deluxe cabins, which are open year-round, range from $80 per night to $400 per week. All cabins are rented for full weeks only during summer months. Early reservations recommended.

Bed-and-breakfast accommodations may be secured at nearby **Governor's Lodge** on Lake White. A weekend at Governor's Lodge is like spending time at a friend's spacious lake house. As you journey up the long driveway, you see what appears to be a large two-story residence set on a wooded peninsula overlooking the lake. In fact, the lodge was originally built as a private residence in the 1930s, though it has been expanded and renovated several times over the years.

Since 1966, National Church Residences, a nonprofit senior citizen housing organization, has operated the lodge, which offers a secluded and peaceful getaway. Each of the eight guest rooms has warm wood paneling and a spectacular view of the lake. The homey Lounge Room serves as a comfortable community living room, with unpretentious furnishings and a massive stone fireplace. The Lake Room is another gathering place for guests, and its wall of windows looks out on the tall hickories, buckeyes, and oaks that populate the peninsula. Between the lodge and the lake is a large "backyard" area, with picnic tables and lawn furniture—the perfect place for perusing the Sunday paper or enjoying a good book. A cottage, separated from the lodge, is popular with those celebrating anniversaries, honeymoons, and the like. A light

Fort Hill State Memorial

*F*ort Hill State Memorial offers the traveler a chance to see one of the best preserved Native American earthworks in all of North America. Archaeologists believe that the 1½-mile-long earthen enclosure on the hilltop was constructed by the Hopewell tribe between 100 B.C. and A.D. 500. Experts believe that this area also contained at least two ceremonial buildings and probably a village, located in the Brush Creek Valley.

This 1,200-acre preserve lies just at the edge of the glacial boundary and has

11 miles of hiking trails. The hilly region is home to a wide variety of flowers and plants. Along with the hiking trails, visitors can take a break at the picnic grounds. A museum also offers information and exhibits on the area's geology and on the archaeological findings around the region.

Fort Hill State Memorial is located at 13614 Fort Hill Road, Hillsboro; (937) 588–3221, (800) 283–8905. Open daylight hours. No admission charge.

The Cradle of American Dentistry

Bainbridge was a trendsetter in the early 1800s, when Dr. John Harris opened the first school in the United States for teaching dentistry. Thanks to Harris, the town has been recognized as the "Cradle of American Dentistry." Harris founded the first U.S. dental school in 1825 in a modest one-story brick building on Main Street. The building today houses a dental museum.

breakfast of pastries, cereal, coffee, and juice is the only meal offered at the lodge, but many guests have dinner at the locally acclaimed Lake White Club, which is within easy walking distance of the lodge.

With its unlimited horsepower rating, the 350-acre Lake White is a popular waterskiing and speedboating reservoir during the summer. Governor's Lodge has a private boat dock, and a launching ramp is nearby.

Governor's Lodge is on Route 552, 2 miles south of Waverly; (740) 947–2266. Open year-round. Rates: $58 per night, double occupancy (includes breakfast; no charge for children under 12). MasterCard, Visa, and personal checks are accepted. Reservations recommended, particularly for weekend nights.

The **Lake White Club** dates back to 1936, but the building housing the club was a log cabin on Pee Pee Creek long before construction of the dam and spillway created Lake White. The lobby of the restaurant contains the original rough-hewn wooden beams of the cabin built on this spot in the 1820s. The Ohio and Erie Canal could be seen from the windows of that cabin; the canal followed the creek on its way south to Portsmouth. Pee Pee Creek received its name for the initials of Peter Patrick, which he carved in the trunk of a large beech tree beside the stream as a claim on this land in 1785, when this area was still Shawnee country.

The club specializes in down-home country cooking, and the chicken dinners (either fried or broiled) are a house specialty. Other entrees include half a dozen cuts of steak, roast turkey, chicken livers, hickory-smoked ham in raisin sauce, and ham and turkey smothered with a cheese sauce. If the 180-degree view of the lake whets your appetite for seafood, try the broiled or fried pickerel, the scallops, or the fried shrimp. The club offers prime rib as a special dinner every Saturday night.

The Lake White Club serves generous portions of all its entrees, and the light wood paneling and bentwood chairs give the dining room a pleasant, not-too-formal atmosphere.

The Lake White Club is on Route 552, 2 miles south of Waverly; (740) 947–5000. Open Tuesday through Saturday, 4:00–9:00 P.M.; Sunday, noon–6:30 P.M.

Shawnee State Park, with more than 60,000 acres of parkland and adjoining state forest, consists of ridge upon ridge of thick woods in the splendid southern Ohio countryside. To get perspective on the size of this stunningly beautiful acreage, note that the park contains over 130 miles of roads, not to mention the miles of hiking and bridle paths. Shawnee is particularly popular in October, when the changing leaves produce hillsides bursting with reds, oranges, and golds. A 5,000-acre section of the park has been set aside as the Shawnee Wilderness Area, preserving the unspoiled natural beauty of the land. The park's two small lakes, Turkey Creek Lake and Roosevelt Lake, both have sandy swimming beaches.

A modern stone-and-timber fifty-room lodge provides overnight accommodations in this peaceful park, as do twenty-five deluxe two-bedroom cabins. Facilities at the lodge include an indoor and outdoor pool, tennis courts, a restaurant, a game room, and an 18-hole golf course with putting green, restaurant, and game room. Lodge rates are $95 to $110 per night, double occupancy. The cabins are tucked away in an isolated section of the park and come equipped with all kitchen utensils, linens, and blankets. Cabin rates range from $115 per night to $675 per week. Numerous campsites are also available.

Shawnee State Park is on Route 125, 12 miles west of Portsmouth; (800) 282–7275. Open year-round; reservations recommended.

Impressive but still shrouded in mystery is the **Serpent Mound** in southwest Ohio. The huge snake built of mounded earth stretches for nearly a quarter of a mile. The Serpent Mound is the largest serpent effigy mound in the United States and one of the few effigy mounds in Ohio. Experts believe that the Adena people built this and other mounds and lived in this area in Ohio from 800 B.C. to A.D. 100. Just what purpose the giant, prehistoric mound played in the life and the culture of the Adena remains a question. However, archaeologists believe that the uncoiling snake symbolized some mythical or religious principle. Also on this site are smaller, conical mounds that contain artifacts from the Adena people and also appear to serve as burial sites.

The Serpent Mound is located at 3850 State Route 73, Peebles; (937) 587–2796. Open daily June through August, 10:00 A.M.–7:00 P.M.; weekends only in April, May, September, and October. Admission: per car, $5.00; bicycles, pedestrians, motorcycles, $2.00; RV with eight or more people, $8.00.

Rare plants and impressive geological features are waiting to awe the casual hiker or the serious botanist or geologist at the *Davis Memorial Nature Preserve*. This eighty-eight acre site was donated by Davon Inc., and bears the name of its chairman of the board, Edwin H. Davis.

Visitors enjoy two hiking trails in the preserve. Dolomite cliffs, an impressive geological fault, and a cave are among the geological points of interest. The heavily wooded trails give hikers a chance to see bamboo grass, purple cliff-break ferns, great cane, and a rare plant called Sullivantia, which grew here in preglacial times.

The Davis Memorial Nature Preserve is located at Township Road 126 and 129, Peebles; (614) 297–2630, (800) 686–1535. Open daylight hours. No admission charge.

The redbrick two-story house, with its shake roof and white trim, does not at first appear in any way extraordinary. It does offer a marvelous view down the steep hill to the Ohio River and across the river into northern Kentucky, but there is no outward evidence of this house's role in history. But 150 years ago, rickety wooden steps led from the river up the hillside to this modest home. Those steps became known as the "stairway to liberation," and on moonless nights slaves escaping from plantations in the South crossed the Ohio River and climbed those weathered steps to the *Rankin House,* home of the Reverend John Rankin.

Rankin and his wife, Jean, were conductors on the Underground Railroad, which transported thousands of slaves to freedom in Canada. Rankin's battle against slavery began with his abolitionist preaching as early as 1815, and a series of his letters on the subject were published in a book in 1826. The home he built on "Liberty Hill" protected runaway slaves from the day it was completed in 1828 until 1863. Rankin used an elaborate set of signals with lanterns in his windows to communicate the "all clear" message to Alexander Campbell and other abolitionists in town.

Now open to the public as a museum, the Rankin House contains some of Rankin's possessions, including his personal Bible, published in 1793. The house has dark hardwood floors and high ceilings typical of the period, as well as completely furnished bedrooms and a kitchen stocked with cooking utensils and equipment used in the mid-1800s.

One upstairs room houses a small abolitionist museum, which tells of the more than 2,000 slaves who stayed at Rankin House (often as many as twelve at a time) on their way to freedom. It was Rankin who told Harriet Beecher Stowe the account of a slave named Eliza who carried her children across the frozen, but thawing, Ohio River. Her bravery was rewarded—the bounty hunters pursuing her found the ice broken up by the time they reached the river next morning, forcing them to abandon their chase. Stowe immortalized the story of Eliza in her book *Uncle Tom's Cabin.* Because of his influence in the abolitionist movement and his work as a conductor on the Underground Railroad, southern plantation owners offered a bounty for Rankin's life.

The Rankin House is just off Route 52, west of the central business district in Ripley; (800) 752-2705, (937) 392-1627. Open Memorial Day to Labor Day, Wednesday through Sunday, noon–5:00 P.M., plus weekends in September and October. Admission: adults, $2.00; children, 50 cents.

One of the homes that John Rankin signaled to during those Underground Railroad days was on the corner of Locust and Front Streets in Ripley and is today known as the *Signal House.* Built in the 1830s in Greek Italianate style, this home is now a delightful bed-and-breakfast owned by Vic and Betsy Billingsley.

The Billingsleys first caught sight of the stately white structure while cruising the Ohio River on their houseboat. When they decided they were ready to leave suburban Cincinnati for a more rural environment, they came to Ripley.

Initially they bought the Signal House to be their home and nothing more. But encouraged by friends enchanted with the place, they decided to share it with others and began operation as a bed-and-breakfast in 1989.

Furnished with family antiques, the Signal House features three porches, twin parlors, and river views from every room. The guest rooms share a bath. Breakfast here can range from homemade breads, muffins, jams, and spreads to sausage and cheese strata.

The Signal House is at 234 North Front Street, Ripley; (937) 392-1640. Rates: $75 per night, double occupancy, including breakfast. Reservations recommended; cash, checks, Visa, and MasterCard accepted.

For lunch or dinner in Ripley, stop by **Cohearts Riverhouse.** Sisters Joanne May and Roberta Gaudio, veterans of the Cincinnati restaurant scene, restored this 1840s structure and opened for business in 1989. The second-floor screened porch offers a great view of the river.

Roberta does the cooking, using produce from local farms, handmade pasta, and Amish cheeses. Dinner selections range from pasta and barbecue ribs to chicken, fish, and steaks. Lunch options include soups, salads, and sandwiches.

Top Annual Events

Pumpkin Show, Circleville, mid-
   October weekend; (614) 474–7000

Ohio Folk Festival, Carillon Historical
   Park, Dayton, May; (937) 461–4800

Feast of the Flowering Moon,
   Yoctangee Park, Chillicothe, May;
   P.O. Box 879, 45601

Bluegrass Festival, Hillsboro,
   May; (937) 466–9674

Roy Rogers Festival,
   Portsmouth, June; (740) 353–0900

Canal Days Festival,
   Waverly, June; (740) 947–7131

Tescumseh! Outdoor Historical Drama,
   Chillicothe, June–September;
   (740) 775–0700

Blue Jacket, the Epic Outdoor Drama,
   Xenia, June–September;
   (937) 376–4318

Art and Culture Fest, Miamisburg, June;
   (937) 866–1914

Ohio Arts and Crafts Festival,
   Berea, July; (440) 243–0090

All American Birthday Party,
   Cincinnati, July 4th; (513) 621–9326

Black Cultural Festival,
   Dayton, July; (937) 224–7100

Wheels of Progress Festival,
   Greenfield, July; (937) 981–3302

Zucchini Festival,
   Eldorado; July;(937) 273–4151

Antique and Classic Car Show,
   Hamilton, late July; (513) 863–2334

Clermont County Fair, Owensville, late
   July–early August; (330) 723–9633

Fayette County Fair, Washington Court
   House, late July–early August;
   (740) 335–5856

Cuyahoga County Fair,
   Berea, August; (440) 243–0090

Sweet Corn Festival,
   Fairborn, August; (937) 879–3238

Ohio Renaissance Festival, Waynesville,
   late August–mid-October;
   (513) 897–7000

Highland County Fair,
   Hillsboro, late August–early
   September; (937) 393–9975

Montgomery County Fair,
   Dayton, September; (937) 224–1619

Fall Festival of Leaves, Bainbridge,
   October; (614) 634–2085

Ohio Sauerkraut Festival, Waynesville,
   October; (513) 897–8855

Clifton Mill Legendary Light Display,
   Yellow Springs, December;
   (937) 767–5501

Not So Gold Rush

You missed the Ohio gold rush of 1868? Well, you didn't miss much. The discovery of what was thought to be gold at Batavia right after the Civil War set off a panic and prompted the establishment of the Batavia Gold Mining Company. Speculators sold shares in this venture for $100 each, big money in those days. Oh, there was gold here, but just minute traces too small to ever be profitably mined. The Batavia gold rush was over as quick as it started.

Cohearts Riverhouse is at 18 North Front Street, Ripley; (937) 392–4819. Open Wednesday through Saturday, 11:30 A.M.–8:00 P.M.; Sunday, 11:30 A.M.–7:00 P.M. Personal checks accepted.

Spend a winter evening in front of a wood-burning fireplace or a summer night on the big front porch of the *Misty River B & B.* This homey riverfront bed-and-breakfast is in the heart of Ripley's historic district. President Ulysses S. Grant boarded in this home back in 1838, when he was still a student. While the country atmosphere remains, the home has been modernized to provide guests with up-to-date comforts, including private baths. Breakfast is included in the room rate and features special cinnamon rolls.

The Misty River B & B is located at North Front Street, Ripley; (397) 392–1556. Rates: $75 per night.

The modest roots of Ulysses S. Grant (known as Hiram Ulysses Grant as a boy), commander of the Union forces during the Civil War and eighteenth president of the United States, are obvious when you visit *Grant's Boyhood Home* in rural Georgetown. Built by his father Jesse Grant in 1823, the home is designated a National Historic Landmark. The Grants expanded the home in 1825 and again in 1828.

Early nineteenth-century furnishings and Grant memorabilia are on display. The white gloves President Grant wore to his inaugural ball and a velvet dress belonging to his wife, Julia Dent Grant, are among the more noteworthy items.

Grant's Boyhood Home is at 219 East Grant Avenue, Georgetown; (937) 378–4222, (800) 892–3586. Open Monday through Saturday, 9:00 A.M.–1:00 P.M. and 2:00–5:00 P.M. No admission charge.

Queen City

A three-room cottage was the birthplace of a man who later would become the highest elected official in the land. The *Grant Birthplace* is a simple, one-story home built in 1817. Hiram Ulysses Grant was born in the humble home five years later, April 27, 1822. (Grant did not become "Ulysses S." until his application to West Point incorrectly identified him as such, a mistake with which he concurred.) Grant's father worked at a tannery, which was next to the Grant home.

Before the home was restored and preserved for all of us to visit, it was loaded on a railroad flatcar and transported on a tour around the United States. Now returned to its original site, it is open to the public and is furnished in the style of the early 1800s.

The Grant Birthplace is located at 1591 State Route 232, Point Pleasant; (513) 553–4911. Open April through October, Wednesday through Saturday, 9:30 A.M.–noon and 1:00–5:00 P.M.; Sunday, noon–5:00 P.M. Admission: adults, $1.00; children (6 to 12),.50 cents.

The historic structure that now houses *The Mill Street Manor* has been a centerpiece in Milford, Ohio, for generations. Construction was begun here in 1812, probably by Elijah and Cyrus Pierson, on what would at first be a commercial building. Wealthy John Kugler acquired the property in 1837, first using it as a general merchandise store but later converting it into a palatial residence. The stables behind the Kugler mansion housed not only horses but also liquor—a distillery was one of Kugler's many business interests. The building served a variety of owners and purposes through the years (including a stint as a bordello) before it underwent a complete restoration in 1977.

Today the chef serves fine meals at this charming inn near the banks of the Little Miami River. Fresh flowers, candlelight, the rustic atmosphere of the tavern in the old stable—these elements create a peaceful harmony here. American cuisine is the order of the day, with an emphasis on freshness and meticulous preparation. You might want to lead off with an appetizer, perhaps the pasta du jour. Main course selections include Cajun jambalaya, chicken pecan, steaks, prime rib, and the fresh catch of the day.

The Mill Street Manor is at 203 Mill Street, Milford; (513) 831–7775. Open Tuesday through Saturday, 11:30 A.M.–4:00 P.M. and 5:00–9:00 P.M. Sunday brunch is 9:30 A.M.–2:00 P.M.; Sunday dinner is 5:00–9:00 P.M. MasterCard, Visa, and American Express are accepted. Reservations are recommended on weekends.

After dining at the Mill Street Manor, take time to walk through the historic Milford central business district. Housed in restored commercial buildings, stores on Main Street include Early Antiques and a cheerful gift shop called 100 Main, which happens to be its address.

On the last Thursday, Friday, and Saturday in September, *Valley Vineyards* hosts the annual Ohio Wine Festival, with live entertainment, judging of homemade wines, and other festivities. The rest of the year Ken Schuchter's Valley Vineyards produces more than a dozen fine wines from its forty-five acres of American and French hybrid grapes.

Grape growing and wine making have been popular in southern Ohio for more than 150 years, and the Schuchters planted their first vines at Valley Vineyards in 1969. The winery, in a new chalet-style building, offers a tasting tray with one-ounce servings of twelve different wines—the perfect way to investigate and appreciate the vineyard's quality blends. I particularly enjoyed the Vidal Blanc, the winner of many awards.

The winery has indoor and outdoor seating, with occasional cookout dinners on the large patios. Cheese plates and pizzas are always available.

Valley Vineyards is on Routes 22 and 3, Morrow; (513) 899–2485. Open Monday through Thursday, 11:00 A.M.–8:00 P.M.; Friday and Saturday, 11:00 A.M.–11:00 P.M.; and Sunday, 1:00–6:00 P.M.

On December 23, 1803, Jonas Seaman received a license to operate a "house of public entertainment" at the site today occupied by one of Ohio's premier historic hotels, the *Golden Lamb.* The present building replaced Seaman's cabin in 1815, and the Lamb now provides travelers with fine dining and period accommodations in picturesque Lebanon, Ohio.

During its nearly two centuries, distinguished guests at the Golden Lamb have included ten American presidents, Henry Clay, Mark Twain (who performed at the Lebanon Opera House in the late nineteenth century), and Charles Dickens, who, it is told, complained vociferously during his visit in 1842 when informed that the inn did not serve "spirits." Dickens would maintain his composure if he visited the Golden Lamb today, for the Black Horse Tavern provides complete bar service at the inn. And after some "refreshment," he might well enjoy browsing in the extensive gift shop on the lower level.

With a reputation for serving challenging dishes, the Lamb offers a dinner menu that includes delights such as timbale of filet of sole and salmon mousse with lobster sauce; roast duckling; broiled veal medallion topped with asparagus, crabmeat, and béarnaise sauce; and roast leg of spring lamb with mint jelly. More traditional entrees include steaks, ham, roast pork loin with dressing, and baked filet of haddock. Lunch is also served at the Golden Lamb, with tasty soups, salads, and sandwiches, plus luncheon entrees including broiled petite filet mignon with béarnaise sauce and roasted chicken with dressing.

SOUTHWEST OHIO

Also Worth Seeing

Cincinnati Art Museum

Cincinnati Zoo and Botanical Gardens

Irwin M. Krohn Conservatory, Cincinnati

Dayton Art Institute

After your meal in one of the four cozy downstairs dining areas, venture past the classy blue-gray lobby and up the stairs to the second floor. There you will discover five opulent private dining rooms. One is the Henry Clay Room (he visited the inn frequently on his trips between Kentucky and Washington, D.C.). Decorated in greens and pinks, this room is furnished with a gorgeous dark hardwood table and matching chairs for ten. With their splendid period pieces, these private dining rooms truly conjure up images of a bygone era.

The second floor also has the most expensive guest room at the inn—the Charles Dickens Room. The massive carved headboard towers 12 feet in the air, as do the mirror and frame on the marble-topped washstand. The third and fourth floors contain the other seventeen guest rooms, each unique in its appointments and named for one of the noteworthy guests who have stayed at the Golden Lamb. The De Witt Clinton Room, for example, is named for the New York governor, who traveled to Lebanon in 1825 to attend the opening of the Ohio canal system, and is furnished with a canopied four-poster bed and antique maple chests.

The fourth floor of the Lamb also houses the inn's Shaker museum, which is full of pieces collected from the former Shaker community called Union Village. The Shakers migrated to Warren County from New Lebanon, New York, and established a religious communal village. But one of their religious convictions was celibacy, which doomed the sect to a relatively short existence.

Shaker furnishings are simple and functional, devoid of ornamentation. The Shaker Pantry has the characteristic wall pegs for hanging utensils, herbs, and even chairs not in use. The Shaker Retiring Room contains a simple rope-spring bed with trundle, a maple rocker, a pine cupboard, and a very rare Shaker embroidery hoop. Perhaps the most interesting display room—Sarah's Room—belonged to Sarah Stubbs, a young girl who came to live in the hotel with her aunt and uncle after the death of her father in 1883. The room has the furniture that was Sarah's one hundred years ago.

The Golden Lamb is at 27 South Broadway, Lebanon; (513) 932–5065, (513) 621–8373. Lodging rates: $75 to $95 per night. MasterCard, Visa, and American Express are accepted.

On a bluff overlooking Lebanon just a few blocks south of the Golden Lamb sits one of the best examples of Greek Revival architecture in the

Midwest: *Glendower.* Constructed by John Milton Williams, a young attorney, for approximately $5,000 in 1836, the residence was inhabited by the Williams family during John Williams's career as county prosecutor and state legislator. Brigadier General Durbin Ward, another influential area politician, purchased Glendower from Williams, and the home remained in the Ward family until the turn of the century.

Knowledgeable guides lead visitors through the fourteen rooms and basement, explaining the history and significance of the lavish furnishings, most of which date from the mid-1800s. In the downstairs drawing rooms, the symmetry characteristic of Greek Revival architecture is readily apparent, with matching placement of doors, mirrors, and fireplaces; one side of these rooms is the mirror image of the other. The original brass deadbolt still secures the front door, and the luxurious ash and walnut floors were installed when the home was built. The formal dining room contains a silver sugar bowl with a lock on it (to keep the servants from pilfering this then-expensive commodity), and the old Regina music box plays flat metal discs as it has for decades.

In addition to the furnished bedrooms upstairs, one room has a sizable collection of antique dolls and the 1865 sewing machine that won first prize at the Warren County fair. The basement display cases contain pioneer tools such as axes, woodworking equipment, and a carpenter's vise. Other items include old-fashioned irons, candle molds, boot jacks, spectacles, and snuffboxes, plus the compass used to plat the village of Lebanon and a wonderful assortment of fancy hand-turned horseshoes made by Matt Burdett, the village smith in the 1890s.

Glendower is on Orchard Avenue off Route 48, just south of the business district in Lebanon; (800) 283–8927, (513) 932–5366. Open from June through August, Wednesday through Saturday, noon–4:00 P.M.; Sunday, 1:00–4:00 P.M.; plus weekends in September and October. Admission: adults, $3.00; children (ages 6 to 18), $1.00.

If you are fascinated with unraveling the riddles of pre-history, you should visit **Fort Ancient**. This prehistoric settlement is a significant archaeological site in North America. Two thousand years ago Native Americans, the Hopewells, built a walled enclosure. The walls are earthen and run for 18,000 feet. From the site, archaeologists have determined that parts of the walls were actually designed and constructed to align with the sun and the moon to create a calendar for the community. They believe that Fort Ancient served as a ceremonial and social center for the Hopewells.

Scientists have also uncovered a variety of tools and implements they believe were used to construct the walls. Among them are digging sticks with blades made from animal bones.

Visitors enjoy hiking the trails not only for the historic value of the site, but also for the beauty of the natural surroundings. The site also features the Museum at Fort Ancient, which has numerous interactive exhibits and highlights 15,000 years of Native American history in the Ohio valley.

Fort Ancient is located at 6123 State Route 350, Orgeonia; (513) 932–4421, (800) 283–8904. Open daily 10:00 A.M.–5:00 P.M., March through November. Admission: adults, $5.00; children (6 to 12), $1.25.

Ohio Renaissance Festival

*O*nce upon a time in a kingdom about 5 miles east of Waynesville there was held the Ohio Renaissance Festival. In some ways, to call this a festival is a great understatement. From humble beginnings, a village of sorts has grown up in a farm field. Several streets of a sixteenth-century English village have and continue to evolve into a real town of make-believe.

A king and queen reign over the town and over amazingly realistic jousting matches. Combatants actually mount horses and, in full armor, race toward each other and attempt to knock the opponent from his mount. One generally ends up bouncing on the ground (although we suspect that they probably decided who was going to take the blow before the match began). No blood is spilled, and no bones are broken, although falling from a galloping horse is a little rough on the body, even with choreography.

Throughout the village are more than 150 costumed shopkeepers and entertainers. Modern times do occasionally intrude in interesting ways. There is something a little odd about seeing a gentleman in tights and tunic, holding a crossbow in one hand and a soft drink can in the other. A comical and talented array of performers entertains on several stages scattered throughout the village. Jugglers, tightwire artists, and a variety of clowns, magicians, and musicians take turns entertaining the crowds.

If you want to participant in medieval activities, you can buy a ticket and try the ax throw or spear chuck, or toss over-ripe tomatoes at the guy in the medieval equivalent of a dunk tank. There are plenty of unusual craft and artisan shops. Buy a talisman or a fake sword or a pouch to hang at your waist to hold your ducats. More modern souvenirs such as jewelry, glass art, or candles also are plentiful.

The Renaissance Festival is open weekends from late August through early October. Admission is charged. Be prepared to park in a farm field and walk a bit to the "village gates." For specifics call (513) 897–7000.

Would you like someone to take $150 from you and then push you out of an airplane flying at 3,500 feet? That's precisely what they do at *Waynesville Skydiving.* They offer classes in skydiving every weekend morning at 9:00 (weekdays by appointment), and after four or five hours of expert instruction, you're ready to make your first jump!

Steve Stewart, the founder and owner of Waynesville Skydiving, is a veteran skydiver with 5,000+ jumps and a pilot with thirty years' experience. He is also well known in the sport for developing innovations in parachuting equipment.

Waynesville Skydiving is on State Route 42, just south of State Route 73, Waynesville; (800) 554–JUMP, (513) 897–3851. Classes every Saturday and Sunday, 9:00 A.M. (registration starts at 8:00 A.M.); weekdays by appointment. MasterCard, Visa, and American Express are accepted.

With more antiques shops per square mile than any other city or town in Ohio, Waynesville is a browser's paradise. It has more than forty individual shops, plus three large buildings where dozens of other dealers display their goods on consignment, and it has become a major antiques marketplace, attracting out-of-state buyers and Ohioans alike. Waynesville's antiques boom started inauspiciously in the mid-1960s with the opening of a handful of shops, but the number has grown steadily ever since. Now, many of the town's commercial buildings, a substantial number of former residences, and even one of the town's churches house antiques stores—in fact, in one block on Main Street, there are nine shops in a row!

Among the many quality shops, one favorite is at 274 South Main Street—*Spencer's Antiques.* The two-story house with large front porch and four adjoining buildings hold an impressive inventory. Careful perusal of this 15,000-square-foot shop, with its hundreds of items, takes time, but it will be time enjoyably spent. George and Fay Spencer's inventory includes a large selection of oak—tables, chairs, washstands, chests, wardrobes, and beds—plus many large walnut and poplar pieces. The basement of the main building is filled with old trunks, toys, and stained glass, while the second floor has many antique kitchen gadgets such as meat and sausage grinders, iron pots, and skillets. Spencer's acquires most of its inventory from southwestern Ohio, and this merchandise can be seen from 10:00 A.M. to 5:00 P.M. daily.

Many visitors to Warren County are attracted to the area because of southern Ohio's most popular amusement park complex—*Paramount's Kings Island.* Its seven themed areas, dozens of rides including nine coasters (the Beast has been rated by the *Guinness Book of World Records* as the longest wooden rollercoaster on earth), live shows, international shops, and restaurants delight the millions who visit the park during its April-through-October season. Other favorites include WaterWorks, a fifteen-acre waterpark, and the NICKELODEON themed area. Paramount's Kings Island is on I–71 at Kings Mill's; (513) 573–5800.

A sixty-year-old train station that now houses two superior museums and an OMNIMAX theater? That's the incomparable **Cincinnati Museum Center.** This magnificent, 500,000-square-foot art deco railroad station, built in 1933 as a center of regional travel, is now a center of fine exhibits and spectacular film showings. At its heyday as a rail hub, hundreds of trains arrived and departed from here each day. And while it is still an Amtrak station (one eastbound and one westbound daily, both in the middle of the night), the crowds gather now not to greet passengers, but rather to discover the past.

Exhibits in the Cincinnati History Museum depict the city's founding, its growth as a river and canal town, and its contribution to World War II. Equally impressive is the expansive Museum of Natural History and Science, with its glimpses of everything from the Ice Age Ohio Valley 19,000 years ago to a simulated Kentucky limestone cave, complete with underground waterfalls, streams, fossils, and a live bat colony.

The spectacular Robert D. Linder Family OMNIMAX Theater wraps you in sight and sound, highlighted by a multistory, 72-foot domed screen. Dramatic films that depict flight and rapid travel appear to pull you into the action, while spectacular landscapes completely surround you.

Cincinnati Museum Center is at 1301 Western Avenue, Cincinnati; (513) 287–7000. Open Monday–Saturday, 10:00 A.M.–5:00 P.M.; Sunday, 11:00 A.M.–6:00 P.M. Admission charge. Call for OMNIMAX show times and ticket prices.

European elegance with a musical backdrop graces the intimate **Symphony Hotel.** The full-service bed-and-breakfast welcomes guests into a graceful 1871 building, furnished in turn-of-the-century antiques but modernized to provide private baths, telephones, televisions, and air-conditioning. A European-style breakfast also is included in the room rate.

The Symphony Hotel is across the street from the Cincinnati Music Hall, which was constructed in 1878. The musical theme continues into the hotel. Every guest room is dedicated to a composer, including Mozart, Brahms, Bach, and Beethoven. The dining room serves a special fixed-price, four-course meal prior to performances at the Music Hall. Dinner guests must make reservations in advance. Reservations can also be made for special events such as parties, meetings, or luncheons.

The Symphony Hall is located at 210 West Fourteenth Street, Cincinnati; (513) 721–3353. Rates: $69 to $130 per night.

One of the finest small art museums in the United States, the *Taft Museum* is a National Historic Landmark. Built around 1820, the Taft Museum served first as a residence for Martin Baum. During his ownership of the property from 1829 to 1863, Nicholas Longworth began a tradition of artistic patronage that was expanded by the last private owners of the house, Charles Phelps Taft and Anna Sinton Taft. They acquired and decorated their home with treasures ranging from French Renaissance enamels and Italian decorative arts to Chinese porcelains and European and American oils.

The home and collections were donated as a gift to the people of Cincinnati in 1927, and the house opened as a museum in November 1932. With its slender Tuscan columns, the Taft Museum is a Federal-period country villa. The central section of the structure features delicate elliptical windows, while the southeast façade has a distinctive upper and lower columned porch.

The collection today includes works by such masters as Rembrandt, Hals, Gainsborough, Sargent, Ruisdael, Turner, and Corot. There's an extensive presentation of French Renaissance Limoges enamels and watches of the seventeenth and eighteenth centuries.

The Taft Museum is at 316 Pike Street, Cincinnati; (513) 241–0343. Open Monday through Saturday, 10:00 A.M.–5:00 P.M.; Sunday, 1:00–5:00 P.M. Admission: adults, $4.00; students and seniors, $2.00.

In 1833, the daughter of the new president of Lane Seminary moved into a stately residence on the campus. This house, the *Harriet Beecher Stowe House*, has now been renamed to acknowledge the legacy of the former resident.

Harriet Beecher Stowe wrote the landmark story, *Uncle Tom's Cabin*, which dramatically portrayed the cruel and dehumanizing effects of slavery. The Stowe House is now a Black history education and cultural center.

The Harriet Beecher Stowe House is located at 2950 Gilbert Avenue, Cincinnati; (513) 632–5120. Open Tuesday through Thursday, 10:00 A.M.–4:00 P.M. No admission charge.

Imagine enjoying your breakfast on a private hillside deck overlooking downtown Cincinnati and the majestic Ohio River. You'll see river captains position their barges to "run the bridges," a term meaning to maneuver the five closely spaced bridges. The *Delta Queen, Mississippi Queen,* or *American Queen* stern-wheelers might steam by as you admire the Ohio and Kentucky hills that flank the river.

Cincinnati Suite is the rambling western Cincinnati home of Herb and Sandra Woosley. Adjacent to Mt. Echo Park, the original home was built in 1895, and it has been expanded and remodeled over the years. The guest suite is contemporary in decor and features a sitting room, private bath and dressing room, and a private entrance.

The Woosley's know Cincinnati well; they operated a city limousine service, and Sandra Q. (as she is known) has served as a docent with the Ohio and Cincinnati Historical Societies and has written a column on Cincinnati history.

Cincinnati Suite is at 2510 Gabriel Avenue, Cincinnati; (513) 244–5777. Rates: $65 to $100 per night.

If you're in the mood for mouth-watering barbecued ribs and chicken, plus ice-cold beer, try Ted Gregory's *Montgomery Inn.* This popular restaurant claims to serve the "world's greatest ribs," a designation with which few customers would argue. Although the menu at the Montgomery Inn does include selections such as steaks, pork chops, and filet of sole, the restaurant is known for the tender ribs and chicken dripping with a zesty sauce.

While waiting in the bar for your table, you'll see photographs of the likes of Tommy Lasorda and Billy Carter displayed on the wall, each autographed and extolling the virtues of Ted Gregory's barbecue. On the rough wood paneling in the comfortable dining rooms are photos and paintings of Gregory's other passion—horse racing. You'll even find some bridles and jockeys' shirts displayed throughout the inn.

For those unable to decide between barbecued ribs and barbecued chicken, try some of each with the half-and-half dinner, which is served with crisp tossed salad and their famous Saratoga chip potatoes. The management thoughtfully provides bibs for those partaking of the sauce-laden barbecue.

Mt. Healthy

In 1817, John La Boiteaux and Samuel Hill founded Mt. Pleasant in Hamilton County. Although the town was known as Mt. Pleasant for years, the post office urged the residents to rename it, to avoid confusion with the "other Mt. Pleasant." They did, choosing Mt. Healthy as the new name in gratitude for being spared the cholera epidemic that struck Cincinnati in the late 1840s.

Cincinnati lost 7 percent of its population to cholera in 1849 during the nineteenth century's second global epidemic of this once-terrifying disease. Ohio had become vulnerable for the first time due to increased contact with travelers from other parts of the United States and the world.

If you're not hungry for barbecue (which seems inconceivable once you experience the aroma in this restaurant), other menu selections include Cantonese-style fried Oriental shrimp with sweet 'n' hot sauce, Wisconsin's Pride duckling, and a number of sandwiches (including a barbecued beef sandwich).

The Montgomery Inn is at 9440 Montgomery Road (exit 12 off I–71), Montgomery; (513) 791–3482. Open Monday through Thursday, 11:00 A.M.–10:30 P.M.; Friday, 11:00 A.M.–midnight; Saturday, 4:00 P.M.–midnight; Sunday, 4:00–9:30 P.M. Closed on Sunday during summer months. MasterCard and Visa are accepted.

The founders of the Mariemont Company designed and constructed the village of Mariemont as a totally planned community modeled after the "garden city" villages in England. In the 1920s, they envisioned Mariemont as a rural alternative to bustling Cincinnati nearby.

Although it's no longer in the country (Mariemont is now in the suburban ring surrounding Cincinnati), this quaint village, with its Tudor commercial buildings and peaceful, tree-lined residential neighborhoods, does provide the tranquil existence sought by its founders. The entire village is listed on the National Register of Historic Places.

The *Mariemont Inn* offers visitors a charming place to imbibe, dine, and spend the night. It is set facing the circle in the center of the commercial business district, and the striking Tudor exterior is rivaled by the interior decor in this classic structure. Each of the sixty guest rooms contains the dark, heavy woods and rich colors typical of the Tudor period; the spacious suites come furnished with ornate canopy beds, and there are antiques throughout the inn. Your day starts off with complimentary coffee or juice, delivered to your room at your convenience.

Visitors unwind in the cozy old-English pub, and the popularity of the dining room for breakfast, lunch, and dinner with area residents and businesspeople speaks for the excellent food. An innovative breakfast-brunch-lunch menu featuring omelets, homemade soups, fine salads, and a wide selection of sandwiches is served from 6:30 A.M. until 2:00 P.M.

The varied dinner selections include fresh seafood, pasta, veal, and many great steaks, with appetizers and desserts to accompany these dishes.

The Mariemont Inn is at 6880 Wooster Pike (Route 50), Mariemont; (513) 271–2100 (or call Best Western Reservations, 800–528–1234). Lodging rates: $60 to $95 per night. MasterCard, Visa, and American Express accepted.

After your meal, enjoy a stroll, jog, or bike ride in this picturesque village, or stop by the gift shop, bookstore, ice-cream parlor, or other shops adjacent to the inn. Though downtown Cincinnati is only fifteen minutes from Mariemont, when you're walking through this peaceful community, the big city seems worlds away.

Just east of Mariemont is a trend-setting restaurant known for innovative dishes—*The Heritage.* You name a food trend—nouvelle cuisine, Cajun cooking, free-range chicken, Southwestern cuisine, home-grown

Sorg Opera House Ghost

*S*ince 1891, the Sorg Opera House has been a place where the star struck come and linger. More than one hundred years ago, a wealthy entrepreneur, Paul Sorg, built the theater. Famous actors and grand productions were invited to the Middletown stage to perform with Jeannie Sorg, Paul's wife and a great fan of the performing arts.

Over the life of the theater the likes of George M. Cohen and Bob Hope have taken their place on center stage. It became a movie house in the 1920s and hosted the first "talkie" shown in town. A fire damaged the building in 1935, but it was renovated and reopened four years later.

The legend of the theater centers on Paul Sorg. As owner, the well-dressed business baron is reported to have always claimed the best seat in the house when he attended performances. In the 1890s those seated in

the orchestra or the first balcony arrived at the opera house in full evening dress. Paul Sorg was a fixture at his theater, dressed in fashionable garb and seated in his favorite seat in the first row of the first balcony.

Through the years and even today, staff and patrons sometimes claim they catch a glimpse of the nattily attired Sorg taking his place in the first balcony. When asked to describe the man, many ghost spotters have described him as he appears in his portrait, which hangs in the theater lobby. Sometimes only his footsteps are heard crossing the stage or walking overhead on the catwalks. So, while actors and actresses have come and gone, the first owner maintains his star status as the legend of the Sorg Opera House.

The Sorg Opera House is located at 63 South Main Street, Middletown.

Mariemont Inn

ingredients—and owners Jan and Howard Melvin have been ahead of the crowd.

Casual elegance predominates here—tables topped with pots of fresh herbs, flowers, and cacti. Wall hangings run from John Ruthven paintings and wreaths of dried herbs and flowers to collections of such items as arrowheads and pipes. In one room, a friendly blaze from a fireplace accentuates the massive beamed ceiling.

Heritage appetizers include chile relleno, seafood bisque, shrimp cakes with Texas remoulade, and the renowned Cajun barbecued shrimp. For your main course, in addition to the expected steak, prime rib, and seafood dishes, choose from grilled Jamaican jerked pork tenderloin with tamarind sauce and sun-dried blueberries; stuffed swordfish with spinach, Asiago cheese, and pine nuts; southwestern stuffed tortilla with Texas BBQ brisket and andouille-étoufée sauce; or soft-shell crabs with blackened redfish hollandaise, among other exotic offerings (these change frequently, so call ahead to find out the current menu items).

The Heritage is at 7664 Wooster Pike (Route 50), just east of Mariemont: (800) 814–9963, (513) 561–9300. Open for lunch, Monday through Friday, 11:30 A.M.–2:30 P.M.; for dinner, Monday through Friday, 5:00–9:30 P.M.; Saturday, 5:00–10:00 P.M.; Sunday, 5:00–9:00 P.M.; Sunday brunch, 10:30 A.M.–2:00 P.M. Reservations recommended; cash, Visa, and MasterCard accepted.

Looking for a very different food festival? How about celebrating the wonders of the zucchini? In Eldorado each July, residents and nearby farmers host the Zucchini Festival. Those who appreciate the nutritious and flexible member of the squash family will have a terrific time tasting various zucchini dishes. Games, craft displays, and music are all part of the activities.

The Zucchini Festival is free and held in mid-July in Eldorado. Call (937) 273–4151 for information.

There's no question that small college towns have a different ambience from that of the average Ohio town—a different energy, purpose, and focus. And that difference sometimes means unique dining and lodging that one wouldn't find in a nonacademic town of comparable size.

Such is the case with Oxford's **Alexander House,** nestled on the edge of the Miami University campus. Built in 1869 as the home of the John Shera family, the original L-shaped building was constructed from lumber and clay from Shera's nearby farm. The Shera home was built in the Federalist style, but the property's second owner, Dr. Herschel Hinckley, expanded the structure in a Neoclassic style. The addition housed Dr. Hinckley's reception area, office, surgery, and examining rooms.

In 1894 yet another physician purchased the property Dr. William Alexander. His family resided here for decades until they converted it to student apartments in the 1950s.

The turnaround year for the Alexander House was 1985, when Geraldine del Greco purchased the property—the first time the title had been transferred in nearly a century. Del Greco, an artist, invested a full year and a considerable sum of money to transform the home from a run-down apartment building to its former charm.

Today antiques abound throughout the guest rooms, parlor, and two dining rooms. Some of del Greco's paintings in ornate Victorian frames accent the wall space.

The Alexander House offers overnight accommodations in five guest rooms, each with private bath and each unique in its decor. A continental breakfast is included with your lodging.

The Alexander House is at 22 North College Avenue, Oxford; (513) 523–1200. Lodging rates: $75 to $85 per night, double occupancy, with continental breakfast. Cash, Visa, and MasterCard accepted.

Invention Trail

The community of Miamisburg has the largest conical burial mound in Ohio—the **Miamisburg Mound.** Artifacts excavated from this 68-foot-high mound, which contains 54,000 cubic yards of earth, indicate the Adena Indians built it sometime between 1000 B.C. and A.D. 100. With a circumference of nearly 900 feet at the base, the mound had two burial vaults in it: one 8 feet from the top of the mound that contained a bark-covered skeleton, the other 36 feet down and surrounded by logs but without any skeletal remains.

Visitors to the mound, which today is overgrown with brush and trees, can climb 116 steps to the top of this impressive earthwork for a splendid view of the Miami Valley. A thirty-six-acre park encircles the mound, with picnic tables, barbecue grills, and shelter houses.

The Miamisburg Mound is 1 mile south of Route 725 on East Mound Avenue, Miamisburg. Open daylight hours, no admission charge.

After climbing the mound, you may want to stop for lunch or dinner at Miamisburg's *Peerless Mill Inn.* A huge waterwheel and the flowing Miami and Erie Canal once powered this former lumber mill (built in 1828). The building was converted into a restaurant one hundred years later, called the Peerless Pantry.

Inside this historic structure, the dining rooms have the original heavy beams, flagstone floors, and four great stone fireplaces. Enhancing the nineteenth-century charm of the place, dried flowers hang from the walls, old wagon wheels form the light fixtures, and a flintlock musket is mounted over one of the fireplaces. Fresh flowers trim each table in the five dining areas and in the dark, but friendly, tavern.

Country favorites including roast turkey and celery dressing and steaks dominate the menu, along with classy seafood and sophisticated dishes such as veal Gruyère—veal topped with cheese, tomato, and a light brown sauce. The house specialty is roast duckling, served with wild rice, orange sauce, and corn fritters. If you're having trouble deciding on an entree, pick two or three from six selections and create your own Peerless Mill combination plate. Diners receive a delicious house seven-layer salad with their meals.

Be sure to try the homemade chowder before your dinner and the daily fresh cobbler for dessert. Luncheon selections include burgers, sandwiches, and salads (such as the turkey pecan salad), plus entrees including omelets and shrimp and sea scallop kabob.

The Peerless Mill Inn is at 319 South Second Street, Miamisburg; (937) 866–5968. Open for brunch, Sunday, 10:00 A.M.–2:00 P.M.; and dinner, Tuesday through Thursday, 5:00–9:00 P.M.; Friday and Saturday, 5:00–10:00 P.M.; Sunday, 1:00–7:00 P.M. MasterCard, Visa, and American Express are accepted.

Just south of downtown Dayton, along the Great Miami River, stands the landmark Deeds Carillon, a 151-foot-high, fifty-seven-bell carillon, which stands at the entrance to *Carillon Historical Park.* Dedicated in 1942, the carillon was built by Colonel Edward Deeds and his wife Edith. Free concerts delight audiences from May through October.

In addition to the bells, this sixty-five-acre park has an outstanding group of exhibit buildings, primarily dedicated to Dayton's invention, transportation, and settlement history. The museum's crown jewel has to be the 1905 Wright Flyer III in Wright Hall. Weighing 900 pounds, this plane was the world's first practical aircraft and is one that Orville Wright described as the plane on which he and Wilbur learned to fly. Two years after their historic 1903 flights at Kitty Hawk, Orville stayed aloft in the Flyer III for thirty-eight minutes at an average speed of 40 miles per hour. Orville Wright later supervised the initial restoration of this aircraft.

Deeds Barn, a replica of the carriage house that stood behind Colonel Deeds's home, houses exhibits that underscore the contributions of Deeds and his friend and contemporary Charles F. Kettering. It was on the second floor of the original barn that Kettering and his "barn gang" revolutionized the automobile ignition and lighting systems, and the barn contains a 1912 Cadillac, the first production auto to feature these innovations. Kettering and Deeds went on to found Dayton

Victoria Theater

*S*ome of the attractions of the historic Victoria Theater in Dayton are easy for the visitor to see and appreciate. The turn-of-the-century building is graced by lavish, period touches, such as gilt trim and green marble pillars. But another attraction is a bit more elusive.

According to legend, the ghost of a young actress also occasionally makes an appearance behind the glass and bronze doors of the Victoria. The young lady is winsome, wearing a 1900s black taffeta dress nipped in at the waist and draped softly to the floor. She has a penchant for appearing in the mirror of one of the third-floor dressing rooms.

It is from that dressing room, the legend says, that the ghost, nicknamed Vickie, made her final dramatic exit. In the middle of a production, Vickie is supposed to have forgotten a fan she needed in the next scene and so told the other actors she was returning to the dressing room to get it. She was last seen climbing the stairs. She never returned to the stage. She just vanished.

Did Vickie sneak out of the theater to join a lover? Did she meet with foul play? No one knows for sure, but theatergoers and staff say that she still remains, in spirit. The door to the fabled dressing room seems to have a mind of its own, and feminine footsteps sometimes can be heard tripping lightly on the stairway. If you hear the rustle of taffeta, detect the scent of rose perfume, or feel the light brush of a young lady passing close to you, then you, too, have experienced the continuing performance of Vickie.

Newcom Tavern

Engineering Laboratories Company (later called Delco). Kettering's early inventions at National Cash Register Company and Deeds's later accomplishments in developing the Liberty aircraft engine also are displayed.

The two-story log building called Newcom Tavern, Dayton's oldest building, was the home of George Newcom. It also served as Dayton's first courtroom. The tavern includes many of its original items, such as the pewter ware used by Colonel and Mrs. Newcom and the colonel's favorite rocking chair.

Other displays in Carillon Park include locomotives and railroad cars, a restored canal lock and covered bridge, a working 1930s print shop, and a replica of the Wright brothers' bicycle shop. The Dayton Sales Company automobile showroom has a 1910 Speedwell, a 1923 Maxwell, and a very rare 1908 Stoddard-Dayton.

Carillon Historical Park is at the intersection of Patterson and Carillon Boulevards east of I–75 at the Edwin Moses/Nicholas Road exit, Dayton; (937) 293–2841. The park is open April through October, Tuesday through Saturday, 9:30 A.M.–5:00 P.M.; Sunday, noon–5:00 P.M. Admission: adults, $2.00; children (6 to 17), $1.00.

Art lovers, families, art historians, and those just looking for a glimpse of the unusual can all find just what they're looking for at the *Dayton Art Institute.* Located in downtown Dayton, overlooking the Great Miami River, the impressive Italian Renaissance–style museum underwent an extensive $17 million renovation and re-opened in 1997. The interior was completely renovated. The redesigned and expanded museum nearly doubled the gallery space, which serves as a backdrop for the extensive permanent collections that include American, European, Asian, and African art. In addition, the institute features some new and innovative exhibits, including a "hands-on" family gallery and an "Experiencenter," which let visitors experience art in a new and participatory manner.

The Dayton Art Institute also exhibits some objects never before seen in galleries dedicated to Native American and Oceanic art forms. In addition to the extensive permanent collections, the institute hosts world-class special and traveling exhibits and art-related educational and cultural events. The newly renovated building also houses an Education Resource Center and an Art Reference Library.

The Dayton Art Institute is located at 456 Belmonte Park North, Dayton; (937) 223–5277. Open daily, 10:00 A.M.–5:00 P.M.; Thursday until 9:00 P.M. No admission charge.

The *Dunbar House State Memorial* was the first state memorial in Ohio dedicated to an African-American. This distinction seems fitting, since Paul Laurence Dunbar is often referred to as the poet laureate of African-Americans. The turn-of-the-century home of Italianate design was the poet's final residence.

The son of former slaves, Dunbar used his writing to portray the dilemmas faced by a recently freed but still disenfranchised people. Dunbar died at age thirty-four in 1906, but his mother lived in the Dunbar House until 1934. Thanks to her care in preserving her son's belongings, visitors can view many of his original works and personal items as well as many of the family furnishings.

The Dunbar House State Memorial is located at 219 Paul Laurence Dunbar Street, Dayton; (937) 224–7061. Open June through August, Wednesday through Saturday, 9:30 A.M.–4:30 P.M.; Sunday, noon–4:30 P.M.; September and October, Saturday and Sunday, noon–4:30 P.M. Admission: adults, $3.00; children (6 to 12), $1.25.

For a look at more modern modes of transportation, be sure to see the nearly 300 aircraft and missiles displayed at the impressive *U.S. Air Force Museum.* With ten acres of exhibit space in the two main hangar-type buildings, plus the annex hangars, this has to be the world's most complete aviation museum. From a Wright brothers original to an Apollo space capsule, the museum contains an incredibly comprehensive collection of flying machines. Spads, Camels, Spitfires, Mustangs, the B-29 that dropped the atomic bomb on Nagasaki in 1945, and the enormous Strategic Air Command B-36 bomber—all of these are in one museum.

Located only 3 miles from the place where the Wright brothers tested their early designs, the museum, in addition to the aircraft, balloons, and missiles, has hundreds of exhibits that chronicle the history and milestones of aviation. The Discovery Hangar is an interactive exhibit for children focusing on the how and why of flight. And there is an outstanding IMAX theater, which shows spectacular aviation-related films.

The U.S. Air Force Museum is at Wright-Patterson Air Force Base, off Route 4 northeast of Dayton; (937) 255–3286. Open daily except Christmas, Thanksgiving, and New Year's Day, 9:00 A.M.–5:00 P.M. No admission charge except for the IMAX theater.

Ohio is rich in ancient cultures. One of the best ways to learn more about one of these cultures is to visit *SunWatch,* an outdoor reconstructed village. This twelfth-century village was rebuilt based on the archaeological findings discovered on this site. Wild turkeys gobble around the village, just as they did 800 years ago. You'll see pottery and other artifacts typical of the village's era.

The village is named SunWatch because of the advanced system of charting time developed by the village's original settlers. During summer months, excavations continue at the site, in search of more clues to the past. In season, you'll observe planting, harvesting, house construction, and the manufacture of various artifacts.

SunWatch is at 2301 West River Road, Dayton; (937) 268–8199. Open daily, mid-March through November, 9:00 A.M.–5:00 P.M. Admission: adults, $4.00; children age 17 and under, $3.00.

Daniel Arnold established his 158-acre family farm in 1830 and constructed a farmhouse six years later. The Arnold family worked the farm until 1910, and today this entire farmstead is being restored to its appearance in the 1880s. It's called *Carriage Hill Farm Museum,* and it's part of Carriage Hill MetroPark.

The farmhouse contains furnishings typical of a nineteenth-century conservative farm family—quilting frame, wood-burning cook stove, and a firebox—while bubbles and imperfections in the house's window glass identify it as original. During hot weather, the Arnolds prepared their meals at the outdoor "summer kitchen" to avoid further heating the farmhouse; on many weekends, volunteers now use the cookstove in the summer kitchen to bake fresh bread.

Other demonstrations at Carriage Hill include a blacksmith who operates the old blower and a woodworker who shapes furniture on a foot-powered lathe. Like any 1880s farm, Carriage Hill has a variety of farm animals: cattle, chickens, horses, sheep, and pigs. The horses are used to give hayrides through the reserve's lush meadows and woods. Hiking and bridle trails also wind through the park's acreage. Special events such as square dances, cider pressing, and old-fashioned wheat threshing take place throughout the year at Carriage Hill.

Carriage Hill MetroPark is at 7800 Shull Road, north of I–70 off Route 201, Dayton; (937) 879–0461. The park is open daily except Christmas and New Year's Day, 8:00 A.M.–dusk. The Farm Museum is open weekdays, 10:00 A.M.–5:00 P.M.; weekends, 1:00–5:00 P.M. No admission charge.

You have to give *Clifton Mill* credit—it has burned down twice, but it has always come back. The first water-powered gristmill at this site on the Little Miami River was built in 1803. Called Davis Mill for its founder Owen Davis, this first mill prospered until destroyed by fire in the 1840s. But a year or two later, a second mill was erected here, a mill that did its part for the Union Army by providing cornmeal and flour to Federal troops during the Civil War.

This mill, however, burned down about the time the Confederacy was defeated. In 1869, the Armstrong family built a third mill on this site, which they sold to Isaac Preston twenty years later.

Three generations of Prestons operated the mill until 1948. And although it avoided catching fire again, Clifton Mill did sit idle, deteriorating for fifteen years, until Robert Heller bought it and breathed life into it once again.

Today visitors enjoy self-guided tours of this impressive six-story power plant. The mill generates all its own electricity, and the huge James Leffel Company turbine on the lowest level, installed in 1908, once provided electricity for farms, homes, and businesses in Clifton, Cedarville, and Yellow Springs at a very modest $1.00 per month per customer.

Clifton Mill grinds flour, cornmeal, and pancake mix as it has for decades, a process you observe during your tour. And meal and flour, along with homemade breads, pies, and other pastries, are available for purchase, as are fine jams, jellies, syrups, teas, spices, and other specialties. Clifton Mill also serves breakfast, soups, sandwiches, and salads, plus ice cream. On a nice day, take your meal or snack out on the Millrace Deck, and listen to water rushing under your feet on its way to the turbines. At Christmastime, the mill is radiant with 150,000 lights. There's an enormous collection of Santa Clauses and a 100-foot waterfall of lights.

Clifton Mill is located at 75 Water Street (Route 72), Clifton; (937) 767–5501. Mill tours: adults, $2.00; children, $1.00. Open Monday through Friday, 9:00 A.M.–4:00 P.M.; Saturday and Sunday, 8:00 A.M.–5:00 P.M.

Designated as a National Natural Landmark by the National Park Service, the *Clifton Gorge Nature Preserve* rates as some of Ohio's most beautiful public land. Over the years, the swift Little Miami River has carved a deep gorge through the thick forest, a process started by the raging meltwaters of the last retreating glacier. The power of the river once turned the wheels of two gristmills in the area—Clifton Mill (described above) and a second mill, the remains of which are still visible in the gorge.

With the clean, vertical drops of the limestone cliffs, Clifton Gorge ranked high with rock climbers until that activity was banned in 1982. Concern for the nearly 350 different wildflowers in the park, which provide an unparalleled spring wildflower display, prompted the rock-climbing prohibition.

The preserve has miles of hiking trails along both rims of the gorge and following the river at the floor of the canyon. The adjacent John Bryan State Park contains twelve additional hiking trails, campsites, and picnic areas.

Clifton Gorge Nature Preserve is on Route 343, just west of Clifton. The entrance to John Bryan State Park is on Route 370, near Clifton; (937) 767–1274. Open daylight hours; no admission charge.

Another fabulous natural area is Antioch College's *Glen Helen,* a 1,000-acre preserve and outdoor education center adjacent to the college's Yellow Springs campus. Designated a National Natural Landmark by the National Park Service in 1965, Glen Helen has most of its original forest canopy, a full array of woodland wildflowers, and undisturbed native wildlife. Scenic features include valleys carved by glacial meltwater, ledges, potholes, cascades, and the Yellow Spring, from which the village gets its name. Flowing at seventy gallons per minute, the spring has built a distinctive hill of travertine that extends from cliff line down to the valley floor. Numerous hiking trails permeate the landscape.

Nearly one-third of Glen Helen is thickly wooded, another third is farmland reverting to forest, and the balance is mowed meadow and planted prairie—a diversity that creates varied habitats for many species of animals and birds. A $2^1/_2$-mile stretch of the beautiful, free-flowing Little Miami River courses through the Glen.

One unique feature of this preserve is its Raptor Center. Here injured birds of prey—hawks, owls, falcons, eagles, osprey, and vultures—are nursed back to health for their return to the wild. The center also serves as a public education facility, permitting visitors to view and better understand these marvelous creatures.

Glen Helen is accessible from State Route 343 just east of Yellow Springs or from the Trailside Museum, 505 Corry Street, Yellow Springs; (937) 767–7375. Open year-round, daylight hours. No admission charge.

Known as a hotbed of antiwar and counterculture activity in the sixties and early seventies, Yellow Springs remains slightly eccentric. The marchers and demonstrators have been replaced by potters and shopkeepers, but Antioch College still provides the youthful emphasis of this uncommon community.

A Yellow Springs eatery of note is *Carol's Kitchen.* Here you serve yourself from a spectacular spread of homemade salads and sandwich fixings, but one word of caution: You are charged by the ounce—this isn't an unlimited salad bar as in some fast-food places. And your selections aren't like fast food either—carefully prepared and seasoned salads of every description (including fine crab and shrimp salads), fresh fruits, and innovative soups such as vegetarian cheddar potato (delightful). Carol's is also a complete bakery, so your sandwich starts with slices of just-from-the-oven onion dill, honey wheat, pumpernickel, country rye, or six-grains bread, also sold by the loaf. Top off your meal with a Soho Soda or Perrier.

Once you've made your selections, it's off to the enclosed patio to enjoy them. This fabric-topped area lets in plenty of light while keeping the rain away. And that light is necessary for the plants that fill every available space. There are hanging plants, potted plants, plants on the tables—plants that create a lush, almost tropical, ambience.

Carol's Kitchen is at 100 Corry Street, Yellow Springs; (937) 767–1030. Open Monday through Friday, 7:00 A.M.–9:00 P.M.; Saturday, 9:00 A.M.–9:00 P.M.; Sunday, 9:00 A.M.–5:00 P.M.

If you've decided you need more time to explore the Yellow Springs area, spend the night at the historic *Morgan House.* No Ohio town seems more suited to the bed-and-breakfast concept than this one, and Morgan House fits the bill perfectly. Built in 1921 for the president of Antioch College, Arthur Morgan, this substantial three-story structure has a huge screened porch, a perfect spot to enjoy a morning cup of coffee or the evening breeze.

Innkeeper Marianne Britton has created an appropriately peaceful setting with cozy furnishings, including Ohio antiques. Located on a quiet residential street just a half block from the business district, Morgan House features four guest rooms.

Morgan House is at 120 West Limestone Street, Yellow Springs; (937) 767–7509. Rates: $50 to $55 per night, double occupancy; includes continental breakfast.

Ohio is home to the **National Afro-American Museum and Cultural Center,** a repository for preservation, study, and interpretation of the traditions, values, social customs, and experiences of Afro-Americans. The museum's permanent exhibit, "From Victory to Freedom," chronicles the period from 1945 to 1965—from victory in World War II to freedom through the passage of federal civil rights legislation. Photographs and artifacts re-create a period of social struggle and dramatic change. Particularly impressive is the award-winning film, *Music As Metaphor,* which presents the inspiring Black music of the period.

The first phase of this museum opened in 1988, and it is bordered by a scenic wooded area. Three additional phases of development are planned.

The National Afro-American Museum and Cultural Center is at 1350 Brush Row Road, Wilberforce; (937) 376–4944. The museum is open Tuesday through Saturday, 9:00 A.M. –5:00 P.M.; Sunday, 1:00–5:00 P.M. Admission: adults, $3.50; children and students, $1.50.

What qualifies a theater performance as "an epic drama"? How about a three-acre stage alive with eighteen horses, fifty actors, flaming arrows, and musket and cannon fire? **Blue Jacket** brings Ohio frontier times to life. This is a dramatization about the life of Blue Jacket, a white man adopted by the Shawnee Indians, and his struggle to help his adopted people protect their homeland from frontiersmen, such as the legendary Daniel Boone and Simon Kenton, who were determined to establish settlements in Ohio.

The performance takes place in an outdoor, tiered amphitheater. Dinner and backstage tours also are available, as well as souvenirs and pictures from the gift shop. Reserving tickets in advance is a good idea. When you call you can also find out about other special events that take place throughout the summer season.

Blue Jacket is performed at 520 South Stringtown Road, just east of Xenia; (937) 376–4318. Performances are given Tuesday through Sunday, mid-June through the first week of September, 8:00 P.M. Admission: adults and seniors, Sunday and Tuesday through Thursday, $8.00; Friday and Saturday, $10.00; children, $6.00

**PLACES TO STAY
IN SOUTHWEST OHIO**

CHILLICOTHE
Chillicothe Bed
and Breakfast
202 South Point Street
(740) 772–6848

CINCINNATI
Cincinnati Suite
2510 Gabriel Avenue
(513) 244–5777

The Symphony Hall Hotel
210 West Fourteenth Street
(513) 721–3353

OXFORD
Alexander House
22 North College Avenue
(513) 523–1200

PORTSMOUTH
Shawnee State Park
Route 125, 12 miles
west of Portsmouth
(800) 282–7275

RIPLEY
The Misty River B & B
North Front Street
(397) 392–1556

Signal House
234 North Fourth Street
(937) 292–1640

WAVERLY
Governor's Lodge
Route 552, 2 miles
south of Waverly
(740) 947–2266

WOOSTER
The Mariement Inn
6880 Wooster Pike
(513) 271–2100

YELLOW SPRINGS
Morgan House
120 West Limestone
(437) 767–7509

**PLACES TO EAT
IN SOUTHWEST OHIO**

LEBANON
The Golden Lamb
27 South Broadway
(513) 932–5065,
(513) 621–8373
Lodging is also available.

MIAMISBURG
The Peerless Mill Inn
319 South Second Street
(937) 866–5968

MILFORD
Mill Street Manor
203 Mill Street
(513) 831–7775

MONTGOMERY
Montgomery Inn
9440 Montgomery Road
(513) 791–3482

RIPLEY
Cohearts Riverhouse
18 North Front Street
(937) 392–4819

WAVERLY
Lake White Club
Route 552, 2 miles south
of Waverly
(740) 947–5000

YELLOW SPRINGS
Carol's Kitchen
Corry Street at
Dayton Street
(937) 767–1030

Helpful Web Sites

Ohio Division of Travel and Tourism:
www.ohiotourism.com

Cincinnati Convention and Visitors Bureau:
www.cincyusa.com

Cincinnati Enquirer:
enquirer.com

Dayton Convention and Visitors Bureau:
www.daytoncvb.com

Paramount's Kings Island:
www.pki.com

West Central Ohio

Rural Roots

*J*ust up the road from Yellow Springs' Antioch College (and across the Greene County–Clark County line) is a most remarkable store—***Young's Jersey Dairy Farm Store.*** Located at a working dairy, Young's caters to the nearby college crowd and the area's year-round residents with fresh breads and pastries, fountain service, and dairy-fresh milk and cream.

Young's bakes from scratch the vast selection of doughnuts and pastries—turnovers, brownies, pies, cream horns, pecan rolls, coffee cake, fudge, and cookies, plus glazed, whole wheat, powdered, jelly-filled, and cinnamon doughnuts. The fountain offers shakes, splits, sundaes, and ice-cream sodas created from Young's homemade ice cream. The shakes are particularly good—made in every flavor imaginable using farm-fresh milk. Served regular or extra thick, the calf shake has two scoops of ice cream, the cow shake comes loaded with four scoops, and the diet-busting bull shake contains five scoops.

The selection of fresh breads includes white, whole wheat, raisin, and cinnamon. They also serve country breakfasts and a full lunch menu of sandwiches and side orders. Seating is provided both indoors and at picnic tables not far from the dairy barn. After you eat, check out the farm animal petting zoo, pony rides (Sundays during warmer months), and Young's farm-theme miniature golf course, Udders and Putters.

Young's Jersey Dairy Farm Store is on Route 68 just north of the Greene County–Clark County line, in Hustead; (937) 325–0629. Open daily, 7:00 A.M.–10:00 P.M.

The 6,000-square-foot home that today houses the ***Willowtree Inn*** has seen its share of both good times and bad. The original section of the home, built in 1830, was constructed in the Federal style as a manor house for a family of means and influence. This home and its 160-acre farm were purchased in 1853 by Captain Newell Kerr for $13,000. The Kerrs greatly expanded the place, and an innovative running-water system was installed.

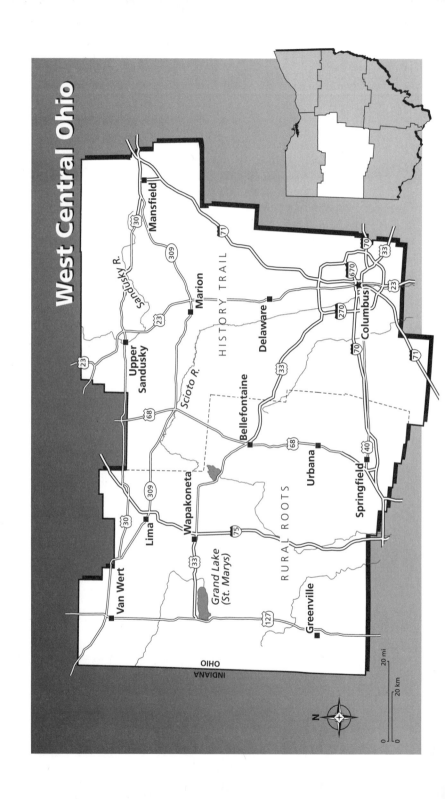
West Central Ohio

WEST CENTRAL OHIO'S TOP HITS

*Young's Jersey Dairy
Farm Store*

Willowtree Inn

Brukner Nature Center

H. W. Allen Villa

Piqua Historical Area

Fort Jefferson

Bear's Mill

Oak Island

*Zane Caverns/Mad
River Mountain*

Piatt Castles/Ohio Caverns

*Neil Armstrong Air and
Space Museum*

Fort Recovery

Allen County Museum

Harding Home

Stengel-True Museum

Indian Trail Caverns

Indian Mill State Memorial

Frederick Fitting House

Malabar Farm

Malabar Inn

*Kingwood Center/Richland
Carrousel Park/Living
Bible Museum*

*Ohio Statehouse/Columbus
Santa Maria/North Market*

At the turn of the century, however, the Kerrs moved out and began renting the farm and house, which eventually fell into disrepair. After numerous tenants and vacancies and several interim owners, the Debold family purchased the house, outbuildings, and five acres in 1973. They transformed the structure to its former glory. They dredged and enlarged the property's spring-fed pond, which had filled with silt and been choked with watercress. And they restored their springhouse-smokehouse, which had been described as one of the county's finest.

Today the Nordquist family owns this historic structure and shares it with guests as a bed-and-breakfast. Furnished with antiques, the Willowtree Inn offers rooms or a suite, some with private baths. Visitors sit by the pond and watch the ducks paddle by, or guests can pull up in front of one of the home's four fireplaces.

The Willowtree Inn is at 1900 West State Route 571, Tipp City; (937) 667–2957. Rates: $70 to $75 per night, which include a full breakfast. Reservations and a deposit required.

With 165 acres and more than 6 miles of trails, the **Brukner Nature Center**'s mission is to preserve and present to the public the splendor of the outdoors. Hardwood and pine forests, ridges, and ravines—all are accessible by the center's nature trails. Visitors observe the flora and fauna while hiking by Cattail and Catface Ponds and while following the banks of the Stillwater River.

The spring woodland flora delights visitors with displays of bluebells, trillium, Dutchman's breeches, and delphinium. In summer, Queen Anne's lace, thin-leaved coneflowers, butterfly milkweed, and prairie roses flourish along the trails. Occasional glimpses of hawks, garter snakes, cottontail rabbits, white-tailed deer, and chipmunks give visitors a sample of Brukner's diverse native fauna.

The Animal Rehabilitation Program nurses back to health injured animals brought to Brukner. Those unable to survive in the wild are kept in the animal room on display for visitors to the center. Brukner also hosts a variety of classes and seminars on topics such as quilting, woodcarving, gems and minerals, photography, beekeeping, and natural history.

The Brukner Nature Center is at 5995 Horseshoe Bend Road off Route 55, west of Troy; (937) 698–6493. Trails are open during daylight hours. The exhibit building is open Monday through Saturday, 9:00 A.M.–5:00 P.M.; Sunday, 12:30–5:00 P.M. Admission charged only on Sundays: adults, $1.00; children, 25 cents; or $2.00 per family.

In 1874, Troy, Ohio, businessman Henry Ware Allen built a large home for his large family—seven children! Allen, half owner of the largest flour mill in the county and president of Troy's only bank, oversaw the construction of the town's most palatial home—three stories high with a tower and cupola.

Henry's son inherited the house in 1915 and set about a major renovation. He added baths and closets, laid oak floors over the original pine, and installed crown molding throughout the first floor. He removed the watchtower but added a spacious front porch and sunroom.

The Hobart Corporation was the next owner of the property, buying it in 1945 and using it as a guest house. In 1984 the corporation decided to sell it, posting a notice on the company bulletin board. Employee Robert Smith and his wife, June, knew "this was the place we'd been looking for."

The Smiths had been collecting Victorian antiques for twenty years, and now they had a place to properly show them—the *H. W. Allen Villa.* The library and study feature the original stencil work, more than one hundred years old. For their restoration efforts, the Smiths were awarded the Troy City Beautification Award in 1987.

The Allen Room, one of four bed-and-breakfast guest quarters, features a queen-size brass bed with hand-crocheted coverlet and a three-piece wicker rocker, table, and sofa bed. In the Royal Room, you'll discover a massive early-1800s high-poster bed. Elegance abounds in the Rose Room, with its matching three-piece Victorian bedroom set and old cranberry swirl chandelier. And finally the Maid's Quarters—a two-room suite with table and chairs for in-room breakfast. All four guest rooms have private baths and fireplaces.

The H. W. Allen Villa is at 434 South Market Street, Troy; (937) 335–1181. Rates: $69 to $74 per night, double occupancy, including breakfast. Reservations and a deposit required; cash, check, Visa, and MasterCard accepted.

WEST CENTRAL OHIO

In 1804, for $5.00 an acre, John Johnston bought the 235 acres he called Upper Pickaway Farms. John and Rachel Johnston, along with their eleven children, lived in the family farmhouse from its completion in 1815 to the 1860s. This historic farm has been restored to its appearance in 1829 and is now part of the *Piqua Historical Area.*

The farmhouse is completely furnished with pieces dating from the early 1800s. The Johnstons used the outdoor fruit kiln to dry apple slices from the farm's two orchards. One feature that attracted Johnston to this property was the flowing spring, and he built a springhouse to utilize the cool spring water to refrigerate meats, milk, and produce. Inside the two-story structure, the clear water circles a stone island in the center of the floor. Items requiring cooling were placed either on the stones or in the flowing water. The spring also provided fresh drinking water for the family. When Johnston advertised the farm for sale in 1857, he estimated the spring's output at ten gallons per minute. The second floor of the springhouse originally contained accommodations for the farm's hired help but today holds an oak loom (circa 1750) on which rug making is demonstrated.

The Johnstons' enormous double-pen log barn, constructed in 1808, is the largest log barn in Ohio. Johnston used it for his flock of one hundred sheep, and the original pens and beams are still plainly visible. Other attractions at the Piqua Historical Area include canalboat rides on a restored section of the Miami and Erie Canal and an Indian museum dedicated to the tribes prevalent in Ohio from the seventeenth to mid-nineteenth centuries.

The Piqua Historical Area is at 9845 North Hardin Road east of Route 66, north of Piqua; (800) 752–2619, (937) 773–2522. Open from Memorial Day to Labor Day, Wednesday through Saturday, 9:30 A.M.–5:00 P.M.; Sunday, noon–5:00 P.M., plus weekends in September and October. Admission: adults, $5.00; children (6 to 12), $1.25.

In October 1791, the forces of General Arthur St. Clair built Fort Jefferson as an outpost, one of the chain of defensive forts constructed to protect army supplies from Indians. Named for Thomas Jefferson, then Secretary of State, the fort served as a supply base for the campaigns of General St. Clair and General "Mad" Anthony Wayne. It was abandoned

Treaty of Greenville

In the summer of 1795, fresh from his victory at the Battle of Fallen Timbers, General "Mad" Anthony Wayne returned to Fort Greenville and waited. By July, twelve tribes with more than 1,300 braves arrived to hammer out a peace treaty with the whites.

On August 3, 1795, the Treaty of Greenville was signed, opening most of Ohio to white settlement. Outgunned, the Native Americans took cash but gave up two-thirds of what is today Ohio. For the native peoples, this was yet another sad chapter in their forced migration west.

in 1796, its location too accessible to the enemy and its water supply too vulnerable.

Today, visitors to the *Fort Jefferson State Memorial* find a monument made of granite field boulders 6 feet square and 20 feet tall. The fort only exists in the imagination of those who travel here; none of the structure survived.

Fort Jefferson State Memorial is on County Road 24, Fort Jefferson; (614) 297–2360. Open daylight hours; no admission charge.

The water of Greenville Creek meanders around a bend in the stream and pushes into a lake surrounded by lily pads. It then cascades over a dam or is forced into the millrace leading to historic *Bear's Mill.*

Built in 1849 by Gabriel Baer, Bear's Mill is an operating water-powered gristmill. The site of the mill, as well as the water rights, were granted to Major George Adams by President James Monroe in 1824. At one time there were 1,200 mills in Ohio; only 7 still operate.

Today Bear's Mill is owned by a local family—Terry and Julie Clark and Mike Johnson (Julie's brother). In 1979 Terry and Julie discovered the mill for sale while taking a leisurely drive in the country. Terry, having a fascination for anything old, was immediately drawn to the property. They decided this rustic, noble building and its property would be perfect for them.

In 1981 the Clarks and their first business partner reopened Bear's Mill. By 1985 Mike replaced that first partner. Julie makes wheel-thrown and hand-built pottery, both functional and decorative, which she sells in the mill's retail area. Her medium is mainly stoneware, although she does occasional firings of raku, earthenware pottery created according to principles that originated in Japan. Among her most popular pieces are large bowls with flared rims, big platters that can be used as tableware and wall decorations, jars, vases, teapots, and pitchers. Also available are selected gift items, ranging from baskets to gourmet coffees.

Mike and Terry oversee the milling of cornmeal, flour, pancake mixes, and wheat bran. All these flours and meals are stoneground on the original 1849 French buhrstones, which have a porous and abrasive quality favored by old-world millers. The grinding process is slow and cool, which prevents the destruction of valuable nutrients.

Bear's Mill

Bear's Mill is off Route 36 at 6450 Arcanum-Bear's Mill Road, 5 miles east of Greenville; (937) 548–5112. Open Friday and Sunday, 11:00 A.M.– 5:00 P.M. and Saturday, 9:00 A.M.–5:00 P.M.

Cedar Bog Nature Preserve has seen it all since its glacial upbringing—mastodons probably fed here and all of Ohio's Native American cultures lived in the area. The bog is the largest and best example of a boreal and prairie fen complex in the state, and as such it supports many rare plants as well as excellent orchid, prairie, and woodland wildflower displays. It is the artesian flow of cool water filtered through limestone gravel that makes this place environmentally unique. Spotted turtles and swamp rattlesnakes also call the bog "home."

Cedar Bog Nature Preserve is at 980 Woodburn Road, Urbana; (937) 484–3744, (800) 860–0147. Open April through September, Wednesday through Sunday, 9:00 A.M.–4:30 P.M.; by appointment the rest of the year. Rates: adults, $3.00; children (6 to 12), $1.25.

Ready to sail away to your own private island? *Oak Island at Indian Lake* could be the place to live out that fantasy. The cottage getaway is a solitary retreat on Oak Island. You'll have to take a boat to reach your private sanctuary.

Whether you are looking for a romantic vacation, family reunion, or family getaway, you can relax at the private beach or on the cottage's covered patios. The cottage has one and one-half baths and three bedrooms, each with a double bed; two rollaway beds are also available. The kitchen comes equipped with a range, oven, refrigerator and freezer, as well as cooking and serving utensils.

Around the area at Indian Lake you'll find restaurants, sailing, waterskiing, golf, and plenty of natural areas for walks, hikes, and exploring. At

Annie Oakley

A teenager with a gun? Today that phrase provokes anxiety, but it was a different story back in 1875. That's when fifteen-year-old Phoebe Ann Moses, born in a log cabin near North Star, challenged champion marksman and showman Frank Butler to a shooting match and won. Annie, as she was called, prevailed over Butler at a place called Oakley near Cincinnati, and hence the legend of Annie Oakley was born.

Annie married Frank Butler a year later, and they began touring together and eventually were featured in Buffalo Bill's Wild West Show. Annie died on November 3, 1926, and she and Frank are still together, in North Star's Brock Cemetery.

the close of summer, generally the first week of September, the residents around the lake set off flares around the rim of the lake to create a "Ring of Fire." This is a reenactment of a Native American tradition that welcomed the coming of autumn.

Oak Island at Indian Lake is accessible only by boat from Russells Point; (937) 843–4653 or voice mail (800) 484–8190, code 5883. Open April through October. Rates: $98 per day to $822 per week; rates vary by season and day of the week.

The 6,000-acre Indian Lake, with its shady islands, peninsulas, and lakefront homes, attracts recreation seekers for fishing, boating, and waterskiing.

Fifteen miles southeast of Indian Lake, a private park, *Zane Caverns,* offers a fascinating cavern, camping, and unique accommodations. A swift underground river eroded the eleven-million-year-old cavern in the limestone, leaving a labyrinth of caves and tunnels and unusual crystal formations. Water seeping through the rock and dripping down on limestone boulders has created the distinctive beehive crystals and, in one case, the rare cave pearls. These pure white crystal balls formed in a small pool of water around tiny pieces of rock and dust. The only other set of similar pearls in existence is in a cave in Switzerland.

Zane Caverns, with its many "rooms," splendid colors, and clear pools of 40° water, was discovered by a young boy in 1892 when his dog fell in a hole and dropped down into the cavern. Early visitors entered through that same hole (which is still visible from inside the cavern); they were lowered in a basket and given a kerosene lamp. In the early 1900s, these self-guided tours cost 10 cents.

Today it takes about forty minutes for the guides to lead a group from one end of the cavern to the other. The tour reaches a depth of 132 feet below the surface, but various tunnels and crevasses shoot off from the main cavern to even greater depths.

Zane Caverns is open daily from May through August and Saturday and Sunday in April, May, September, and October, 10:00 A.M.–5:00 P.M.

Admission: adults, $6.50, children (ages 6 to 12), $3.50.

The cavern's 200 acres of woods, ridges, and ravines also offer camping and lodging for overnight guests. If you're not a tent camper, Zane Caverns has a covered wagon fitted out with seats, carpeting, screens, electric lights, and a double bed for rustic sleeping outdoors. Another delightful place to rest one's head is the Eagles' Nest. Set on stilts in a heavily wooded ravine, this screened sleeping shelter contains a double bed, with a picnic table and barbecue grill adjacent. The Covered Wagon and the Eagle's Nest rent for $25 per night. Two more summer cabins offer accommodations, each with electricity, a table and chairs, a screened porch, and a fire ring in front. Owl's Nest has bunked double beds; Hawk's Nest has one double bed and single bunk beds; each rents for $30 per night for two adults and their children.

Once the site of a Native American settlement, Bellefontaine (pronounced "bellfountain") is most famous for something we take for granted today—paved roads. It was here in 1891 that the Buckeye Cement Company laid an 8-foot strip of concrete on Main Street, America's first concrete street. The company later paved around the courthouse, and this innovation attracted engineers from across the country. A section of the street was displayed at the 1893 Chicago World's Fair, winning a gold medal. We've been pouring concrete ever since.

Zane Caverns is on Route 540, 5 miles east of Bellefontaine; (937) 592–0891. Open April through October. Reservations and a deposit required for accommodations.

Winter recreation in Logan County is centered at ***Mad River Mountain*** ski resort, with eight slopes and trails for skiers open during the November through March season. Ski instruction and rental are offered, and the twenty-three-room lodge provides your favorite beverages and overnight accommodations after a long day on the slopes. During summer months, tennis courts and a swimming pool attract visitors to Mad River's 400 hilly, wooded acres.

Mad River Mountain is on Route 33, 5 miles east of Bellefontaine; (800) 231–SNOW, (937) 599–1015.

Rural Logan County might seem an unusual place for two brothers to build a pair of castles, but that is precisely what Colonel Donn Piatt and General Abram Sanders Piatt did during the mid-1800s. Members of the Piatt family came to America in the 1670s from southeastern France. Donn and Abram's grandfather, Jacob Piatt, served on George Washington's staff during the Revolutionary War. Jacob's son Benjamin, after fighting in the War of 1812, acquired 1,700 acres in the Mac-A-Cheek Valley, named for a local Shawnee settlement. It was Benjamin's sons, Donn and Abram, who built the two stone castles a mile apart in what is today Logan County.

Abram Sanders Piatt built the first of the *Piatt Castles,* patterned after the stone castles of Normandy and France—Castle Piatt Mac-A-Cheek. The three-story home (with five-story watchtower) has walls 2 feet thick made of locally quarried limestone, which was hand-chiseled on the site.

The castle has remained in the Piatt family since its construction, and all furnishings in the castle are family originals. The first stop on guided tours of Castle Piatt Mac-A-Cheek is the spacious drawing room, with its intricate oak, walnut, and cherry floors and splendid ash, pine, and walnut walls. Fine woodwork graces the entire castle, as do the frescoed ceilings painted by French artist Oliver Frey in 1880. These ceilings have survived a century surprisingly well, without so much as a touch-up.

The castle's furnishings include horsehair-stuffed couches and chairs, massive carved beds, and wardrobes—some dating as far back as the Revolutionary War period. The family's historic firearms collection and a private chapel, complete with altar and kneeler, are upstairs.

Down the road, Donn Piatt's Flemish-style Mac-O-Chee Castle (a variation of the name Mac-A-Cheek) contains an outstanding collection of European, American, and Asiatic furnishings and art. The castle was completed in 1881, but the Piatt family lost ownership of this three-story, twin-spired structure in the mid-1890s, when Ella Piatt, Colonel Donn Piatt's widow, sold it. It served briefly as a health spa, but it eventually stood empty and even was used as a barn for more than a decade. Now it's back in the Piatt family and open to visitors. It is an excellent example of a late-nineteenth-century estate.

The Piatt Castles are on Route 245, 2 miles east of West Liberty; (937) 465–2821. Both castles are open daily, noon–4:00 P.M. Admission: adults, $6.00; youths (13 to 21), $5.00; children (5 to 12), $3.00.

Caves and caverns are scattered across (and under) Ohio, but the largest such caverns open to the public are at *Ohio Caverns.* With a constant 54° temperature, a visit to Ohio Caverns can be enjoyed any time of year, no matter what the weather on the "outside."

Inside, you'll discover exquisite crystal-white stalactite and stalagmite formations. Unique coloring and ever-changing shapes make this cave tour a treat. Like many such caverns, the more unusual formations have been named—the "crystal king" and "pathway through the palace of the gods." The real intrigue is not the clever designations, but rather the strange and natural beauty underground. So bring your camera and enjoy.

Ohio Caverns is at 2210 East State Route 245, 4 miles east of West Liberty; (937) 465– 4017. Open daily 9:00 A.M.– 4:00 P.M. Admission: adults, $7.50; children (5 to 12), $4.00.

At 10:56:20 Eastern Daylight Time on July 20, 1969, Neil Armstrong became the first man to step onto the lunar surface. "That's one small step for a man—

Mac-O-Chee Castle

one giant leap for mankind," crackled Armstrong's first radio transmission from Tranquility Base, as he accomplished the goal set by John Kennedy in the early 1960s. It was less than seventy years earlier that Dayton's Wright brothers had conquered powered flight over the sands of Kitty Hawk—from the first successful aircraft to lunar exploration in a little more than six decades.

The *Neil Armstrong Air and Space Museum* in Wapakoneta celebrates the achievements of local boy Armstrong and other Ohioans who contributed to the field of aviation. A NASA F5D Skylancer aircraft flown by Armstrong in the early 1960s greets visitors, and from the Skylancer you simply follow the runway lights to the entrance of the futuristic exhibit building.

Sketches, models, and photographs trace the history of manned flight, from the earliest use of balloons to powered aircraft and space travel. The bright yellow, single-engine Aeronca propeller plane flown by Armstrong at age sixteen and his Gemini Eight space capsule span his accomplishments as an aviator. Other exhibits include spacesuits from the Gemini and Apollo missions, a Jupiter rocket engine, and not particularly tempting packets of astronaut space food. One video projection room continuously shows marvelous footage of American astronauts from various Apollo missions walking, hopping, jumping, and driving on the lunar surface.

The Neil Armstrong Air and Space Museum is at I–75 and Bellefontaine Road, Wapakoneta; (800) 860–0142, (419) 738–8811. Open March

Grand Lake St. Mary's

Stretching from Lake Erie to the Ohio River in western Ohio, the construction of the Miami & Erie Canal was a major catalyst in the state's development. For the canal to succeed, it needed a reliable water source at its high point, near Celina. Some 1,700 men, paid 30 cents a day, labored for years to create Grand Lake St. Mary's, the largest man-made lake in the world when it was completed in 1845. Today, with the canal long gone, the lake is a haven for recreation.

through November, Monday through Saturday, 9:30 A.M.–5:00 P.M.; Sunday noon–5:00 P.M. Admission: adults, $5.00, children (ages 6 to 12), $1.25.

One location on the Wabash River was the site of both one of the worst defeats and one of the most important victories for American troops battling the Indians in the 1790s. Indian warriors led by Little Turtle and Blue Jacket caught General Arthur St. Clair's forces in a surprise attack on November 4, 1791, killing or wounding three-quarters of the soldiers.

But two years after St. Clair's defeat, General "Mad Anthony" Wayne picked that spot on the Wabash to construct a fort consisting of four blockhouses connected by log stockade walls. Each blockhouse measured 20 feet square, and Wayne's troops finished *Fort Recovery* in less than a week. When the Indians attacked on the morning of June 30, 1794, Wayne's forces prevailed, setting the stage for the general's final victory over the Indians at Fallen Timbers on August 20, 1794, and the signing of the Treaty of Greene Ville in 1795.

Visitors to Fort Recovery inspect the two reconstructed blockhouses and view artifacts from the original fort in the two-story stone museum. These artifacts include an army-issue felling ax, bottles, a skillet handle, and bone-handled knives and forks. The museum has other items used in battle here two centuries ago, such as howitzer shells, cannon balls, grapeshot, and parts of muskets and pistols.

One exhibit explains the construction of Fort Recovery, where 13-foot logs with one end axed to a point were placed on end in 3-foot-deep trenches to form the stockade walls. A gap approximately every 6 feet allowed the fort's defenders to point their rifles through the wall and fire on attackers. Other displays include mannequins of an army sergeant and an Indian brave clothed in their respective 1794 battle uniforms, a collection of muskets and military swords from the 1860s, plus Indian artifacts from Mercer County such as tomahawks, leather goods, and arrowheads.

Fort Recovery is near the intersection of Routes 49 and 119, Fort Recovery; (800) 283–8920, (419) 375–4649. Open daily June 1 to Labor Day, noon–5:00 P.M. plus weekends in May and September. Admission: adults, $2.00; children, $1.00.

Lima residents boast of having one of the best county museums in the state—the **Allen County Museum**—and it is. Two floors contain hundreds of items in a modern brick building. Its pioneer kitchen contains old-fashioned butter stamps, molds, and churns, while the pioneer bedroom has a corn-husk mattress on a primitive wooden bed. The mother of the Haller twins (Kathern and Sophie) rocked her infants on the rare double cradle bench during their first year in 1852.

The museum has collected a variety of wagons and buggies, including a covered wagon and a hearse, as well as antique cars such as a magnificent 1909 Locomobile Sports Roadster. Downstairs features a number of muskets and pistols and all manner of Indian items including arrowheads, beads, ornate Hopi dolls and masks, pottery, blankets, and a large ribbed canoe. A nineteenth-century doctor's office and a general store are completely stocked with items typical of the era.

It could have happened anywhere, but it happened here, in 1891. America's first gasoline-powered automobile chugged out of John Lambert's implement store and hit the roads in town, such as they were. No doubt this caused a stir, as the strange, noisy contraption tooled along, dodging trees and potholes. Lambert reportedly ran into a hitching post on one of his early forays, and this very first car was destroyed in a fire later that same year. Lambert continued to tinker with automobiles and held 600 patents related to the invention.

One unusual item is the 1903 Kodak "mugging" camera, used by the Lima police department at the turn of the century (plus sample mugshots demonstrating the policemen's photographic abilities). Other collections include rocks, fossils, and minerals found in the county and a group of antique farm implements.

Next to the museum is the Log House, furnished with primitive pioneer possessions, and the MacDonell House, a Victorian mansion renowned for its handsome woodwork, big game trophies, and period pieces.

The Allen County Museum is at 620 West Market Street, Lima; (419) 222-9426. Open from Tuesday through Sunday, 1:30–5:00 P.M. No admission charge.

History Trail

I n 1890 Warren G. Harding, then twenty-five years old, and his fiancée planned and had built the dark-green home at 380 Mount Vernon Avenue, Marion. From the **Harding Home,** he conducted his famous "front porch" campaign in 1920 and won the presidency. The

Pork Rind, Anyone?

It may not be exactly a celebration of health food, but for the people of Harrod, the food they've chosen for their local celebration is the pork rind. Of course, the Pork Rind Heritage Festival features that legendary snack food, but it also includes a hog roast and a variety of other food fare. And no pork rind fan could leave without cheering on the Pork Rind Parade or staying to enjoy the live entertainment.

The festival is held on Main Street mid-June, Harrod; call (419) 648–2063 for more information.

Harding years in the White House were turbulent ones—his administration was rocked by scandals, including the infamous "Teapot Dome" incident. Harding died in San Francisco in 1923, without completing his term of office.

The eldest son of a doctor, Harding was born in Blooming Grove, Ohio, on November 2, 1865. After working as a printer's apprentice, he bought the *Marion Daily Star* at the age of nineteen. In 1891, he married Florence Kling DeWolfe, daughter of one of Marion's wealthiest and most prominent Republicans, on the stairway of the home they had designed. Harding's election to the Ohio Senate in 1899, as lieutenant governor of Ohio in 1903, and to the United States Senate in 1914 laid the groundwork for his successful presidential campaign in 1920. He used the large front porch of his home, the porch he had expanded in 1900, to speak to the 600,000 voters who traveled to Marion in the summer of 1920 to hear the acclaimed oratory of the Republican candidate.

Inside the entryway sits the small wooden desk where Harding sat on election night reading the latest telegraphed election returns. Nearly all the furnishings and accessories in the Harding home are exactly as the Hardings left them when they went to Washington in 1921. Many of the art objects collected by the Hardings on their three trips to Europe are there, and so is the hat worn by the twenty-ninth president at his inauguration. The small building behind the Harding residence, which served as the press headquarters during the 1920 campaign, now is a museum.

The Harding Home is at 380 Mount Vernon Avenue, Marion; (800) 600–6894, (740) 387–9630. Open Memorial Day to Labor Day, Wednesday through Saturday, 9:30 A.M.–5:00 P.M.; Sunday, noon–5:00 P.M., plus weekends in September and October. Admission: adults, $3.00; children (ages 6 to 12), $1.25.

Not far from the Harding Home are the ten-acre grounds containing the **Warren G. Harding Memorial.** Constructed in 1927 of Georgia white marble, the 52-foot-tall memorial surrounds the graves of President and Mrs. Harding (she died in 1924, a year after her husband). Labrador granite tombstones cover the graves of the Hardings, who were buried here on December 21, 1927. The careful rows of maple trees on the grounds form the shape of a Latin cross.

The Harding Memorial is at the corner of Route 423 and Vernon Heights Boulevard, Marion; open daylight hours; no admission charge.

Marion offers visitors another intriguing museum: the *Stengel-True Museum.* Judge Ozias Bowen built this three-story mansion in 1864 at a cost of $20,000. Bowen arrived in Marion from New York in 1828 and married Miss Lydia Baker, the daughter of Eber Baker, the founder of Marion. Judge Bowen's grandson, Henry A. True, made a provision in his will establishing the museum, and a local optometrist, Dr. Frederick Stengel, contributed many of the collections displayed at Stengel-True.

A wonderful old Regina music box plays waltzes (for a nickel). The front parlor contains a grand piano that once belonged to Florence Kling Harding and one of the ornate marble fireplaces found throughout the museum. Displays include collections of rare and antique guns, all types of early lamps and lighting instruments (from candles to kerosene fixtures), and a wall full of antique clocks (next to a case loaded with old pocket watches).

Tomato juice, tomato soup, tomato sauce—they all are standard fare at the annual Tomato Festival in Reynoldsburg. But you'll find some surprising and different tomato dishes, too, from fried-green tomatoes to tomato brownies.

Reynoldsburg takes special pride in the red fruit, or vegetable, depending on your point of view. You'll see the lovely red round tomato on city signs proclaiming itself, "The Tomato Capital."

It's certain that the tomato is king during the yearly celebration as the city welcomes farmers, cooks, and tomato lovers to town to eat and compete.

The festival is generally held in the early part of September. Call (614) 866–2861 for a tomato festival update.

Pioneer antiques dominate the upper floors—spinning wheels, yarn winders, dough pans, hay forks, and a butter churn. A small staircase on the third floor leads up to the rooftop cupola, with a splendid 360-degree view of Marion.

The Stengel-True Museum is at the corner of South State Street and Washington Avenue (504 South State Street), Marion; (740) 387–6140. Open Saturday and Sunday, 1:00–4:30 P.M. No admission charge.

Richard Hendricks purchased his dream in 1963—the 650-foot *Indian Trail Caverns* he had first visited as a child. Once called the Wyandot Indian Caverns, this bit of underground history first opened in 1927 but closed ten years later. Hendricks, the postmaster in nearby Vanlue, worked nights and weekends whenever the weather would permit, clearing

Top Annual Events

Applefest, Zoar Village State Memorial,
Zoar, early October weekend;
(800) 874–4336

Canal Days, Tipp City, early May;
(937) 667–3696

Chili Cook-Off, Mansfield,
May; (419) 756–1133

Rhythm and Food Festival,
Columbus, May; (614) 645–7995

Columbus Arts Festival,
Columbus, June; (614) 224–2606

Peony Festival, Van Wert,
June; (419) 238–6223

Strawberry Festival,
Troy, June; (937) 339–7714

Camp Chase Memorial Service,
Columbus, June; (614) 276–0060

Pork Rind Heritage Festival,
Harrod, June; (419) 648–2063

Rose Festival,
Columbus, June; (614) 645–6640

National Threshers Annual Reunion,
Wauseon, June; (313) 888–1345
and (419) 335–6006

Boat Parade,
Russells Point, July; (937) 843–5392

Irish Festival, Dublin, late July–early
August; (614) 761–6500

Farmer Merchant Days,
Union City, August; (765) 964–5409

Ohio State Fair,
Columbus, August; (614) 644–3247

Miami County Fair,
Troy, August; (937) 335–7492

All Ohio Balloon Festival,
Marysville, August; (937) 644–8307

Darke County Fair,
Greenville, August; (937) 548–5044

Zucchinifest, Lancaster,
August; (614) 497–2518

Tomato Festival, Reynoldsburg,
September; (614) 866–2861

Popcorn Festival,
Marion, September; (614) 387–3378

Harvest and Herb Festival,
Ada, September; (419) 634–9238
or (419) 674–4590

**Ohio Heritage Days, Malabar Farm
State Park,** Mansfield, September;
(419) 892–2784

Ohio Gourd Show, Mount Gilead,
October; (419) 362–6446

glacial debris from the floor of the caverns, and reopened them in 1975.

Acidic water seeping through the 400-million-year-old rock created the caverns. The formation of the caverns was particularly rapid (in geological time) when this part of Ohio was under a warm, shallow ocean. In fact, Indian Trail was part of a reef millions of years ago. Advancing glaciers dumped sandy debris on the floor of the caverns, and Hendricks removed much of it to increase the height of the caverns. In addition to the 650 feet originally open to the public, Hendricks is continually opening new sections as the excavation continues.

The most recent section of the caverns opened in 1990, in what is called the Sheridan Pit. The University of Cincinnati has been excavating this site since 1992. In it were discovered 11,000-year-old bones of Ice Age animals such as the short-faced bear. This bear was as tall as a quarter horse, could run 40 miles per hour, and was one of the most fierce predators in North America. Other bones found in this pit were from a prehistoric elk-moose, a giant beaver as large as a bear, and an ancient wild boar. In 1995 an 11,000-year-old spear point made from an antler was unearthed, the oldest known artifact in Ohio.

Hendricks has learned a great deal about his caverns from the many geologists and archaeologists who have studied the formation, and he shares his knowledge with those who tour the caves. Smoke-stained walls and ceilings, in addition to artifacts discovered here, indicate that prehistoric humans lived in the caverns, taking advantage of the year-round 52° temperature. Indian Trail has two skylights open to the surface and a natural stone ladder that Indians may have used to go in and out of this unique geological formation. Hendricks delights in pointing out dozens of natural rock sculptures that seem to form shapes such as Abe Lincoln's face and a wolf's head.

Ohio was the site of many conflicts between white settlers and Native Americans. One of the most gruesome was the execution of Colonel William Crawford by Delaware and Wyandot Indians. In 1782, Crawford, a friend of George Washington, led a force of 480 men bent on attacking Indians villages along the Sandusky River.

Not only did his campaign fail, but Crawford was captured and held responsible for the atrocities committed by whites at Gnadenhutten. Crawford literally was burned alive at the stake after being beaten and tortured. Today, Crawford County bears his name as a reminder of this incident.

Indian Trail Caverns is on Route 568, 4 miles northwest of Carey; (419) 387–7773. Open Memorial Day to Labor Day, Tuesday through Sunday, 1:00–6:00 P.M. or by appointment. Admission: adults, $6.00; children, $4.50.

The United States government constructed a saw- and gristmill for Ohio's Wyandot Indians in 1820 in gratitude for their support during the War of 1812. The mill was on the Sandusky River, and government-appointed millers ground flour and cornmeal for the Wyandot reservation until the Indians were relocated to Kansas in 1843, putting the mill out of operation.

A second mill was built 300 feet downstream from the first in 1861 and operated until 1941. This mill had a reputation for particularly good stone-ground buckwheat and cornmeal and has since become the country's first museum of milling—***Indian Mill State Memorial.***

The museum includes a detailed explanation of the four types of mill waterwheels: the overshot, undershot, breast, and horizontal wheels.

Sales Day

Talk about a tradition. London has held a live-stock auction the first Tues-day of every month since 1856. In all those years, only four sales have been canceled: two in 1863, one in 1865, and one in 1868. Farmers bring their herds in for the 10:00 a.m. sale, and then spend the day "in town." Crowds often num-ber two to three thousand people on Public Square for a "sales day."

Exhibits explain the history of gristmills and sawmills and their importance to early Ohio set-tlements. Perhaps the most intriguing feature of the museum is the working model of a water tur-bine mill. This model demonstrates the complex system of "flights" that transported grain and milled meal from floor to floor in the mill—from its entry down a chute to the grinding stones on the lower level to the upper floors for sifting, sep-arating, and sacking. Outside the mill, a three-acre park across the river bridge is a tranquil and picturesque spot for a picnic or just relaxing.

Indian Mill State Memorial is on County Road 47, off Route 67 northeast of Upper Sandusky; (800) 600–7147, (419) 294–3349. Open June through October, Friday and Saturday, 9:30 A.M.–5:00 P.M.; Sunday, 1:00–6:00 P.M. Admission: adults, $1.00; children, 50 cents.

More and more travelers are choosing bed-and-breakfast lodgings in reaction to expensive, impersonal hotels and motels. One of the nicest such accommodations in Ohio opened in 1981 in an 1863 Victorian home—the *Frederick Fitting House.* Built by a prominent Bellville busi-nessman, Frederick Fitting (he brought the railroad to Bellville), the home has three distinctive bedrooms for travelers: the Colonial Room, with its queen-size canopy bed; the Victorian Room, which has an ornate brass bed; and the Shaker Room with twin beds and original Shaker pieces. The three guest rooms have private baths and are on the second floor; the owners, Ramon and Suzanne Wilson, live in an attached car-riage house. The house, painted three shades of green, occupies a corner lot in a quiet residential neighborhood with many tall trees.

Ohio country antiques furnish the first floor, and a fire burns in the fire-place all winter long. The exquisite dining room, with its hand-stenciled walls, is the focal point of the home, and here the Wilsons serve a com-plete gourmet breakfast. The Wilsons purchased the property in 1988 and have added a large country kitchen with informal sitting and eating area and an extensive vegetable, herb, and flower garden. Many guests are drawn to the area by the two nearby ski resorts (Clear Fork in Butler and Snow Trails in Mansfield) during winter months.

The Frederick Fitting House is at 72 Fitting Avenue, Bellville; (419) 886–2863. Rates: $66 to $76 per night. Reservations and a deposit are required.

Humphrey Bogart and Lauren Bacall married and honeymooned on a farm near Lucas, Ohio? Unlikely as that might seem, it did happen on May 21, 1945, at *Malabar Farm,* the 914-acre farm of Pulitzer-winning novelist Louis Bromfield. Bromfield was born in nearby Mansfield in 1896 and graduated from Mansfield Senior High School.

Frederick Fitting House

Though he studied agriculture at Cornell and journalism at Columbia, this prominent author and screenplay writer never received a college degree.

After driving ambulances in World War I, Bromfield remained in Europe and published his first novel, *The Green Bay Tree,* in 1925, launching a literary career that would produce thirty-three books over the next thirty-three years, as well as a number of screenplays. Although dedicated to his writing, Bromfield never lost his interest in agriculture. In 1939, when the outbreak of World War II forced Bromfield and his family to flee France, he began searching Ohio for suitable farm acreage to practice the conservation techniques he had learned from his grandfather and French farmers. He found Malabar or, more accurately, created Malabar (which means "beautiful valley" in an Indian dialect), by purchasing four adjacent farms in the lush, rolling hills of Richland County. Saving only four rooms of the original farmhouse, Bromfield added twenty-eight others, including nine bedrooms, six full baths, and four half baths, to produce the airy rambling estate where he entertained family and friends.

Among the many visitors to Malabar were Hollywood celebrities such as William Powell, Errol Flynn, Dorothy Lamour, and Shirley Temple—all friends of Bromfield's from his work in motion pictures. Bromfield explained his innovative "grass farming" method of agriculture to them, a system of planting grasses in critical areas to arrest soil erosion and reinvigorate the earth. Bromfield distrusted the effects on the soil of using every available acre for grain production; instead he cultivated only enough acreage to support his dairy operation.

The Bromfield home is furnished exactly as it was when the family lived here, with many of the pieces brought back from France in 1939. Bromfield also imported the bright wallpapers from France, and all the oak floors and walnut doors are original. Two Grandma Moses paintings hang in the house, and, because of Bromfield's love of the outdoors, every room on the first floor has an outside door. Bromfield had the twenty-nine-drawer desk in his study custom built, only to discover he was unhappy with the way it "felt." He actually worked at a card table behind the desk.

The family's boxer dogs were important members of the household, and the doors of the house were equipped with special door latches that the dogs could open, giving them free run of Malabar. In addition to guided tours of the house, self-guided tours of the barns, chicken coop, smokehouse, and the farm's active dairy operation are also offered. Cross-country skiing is popular at the farm in the winter, with rental equipment available.

Malabar Farm is west of Route 603 off Pleasant Valley Road, south of Lucas; (419) 892–2784. Open daily year-round, except major holidays. Tours of the house are $3.00 for adults, $1.00 for children ages 6 to 18; wagon tours of the farm are $1.00 for adults, children under 12 free.

Just down the road from Malabar Farm is a former stagecoach stop on the old Cleveland-Marietta line called the *Malabar Inn.* David Schrack and his sons, attracted to this location because of the rapidly flowing spring (later called Niman Spring), built the inn in 1820. The inn had deteriorated badly when Louis Bromfield acquired it in the late 1930s, but he renovated the structure and used it to house the overflow of guests visiting Malabar. Bromfield also took advantage of the springhouse next to the inn, using the cold water flowing through the sandstone troughs to cool the organic produce sold at his roadside market.

The Malabar Inn today serves fine country fare in the brick two-story building, which now has a large deck on three sides. Dinner selections include rainbow trout, smoked Ohio ham, steaks, roast top round of beef, and pan-fried calves' liver with bacon. For lunch, there are salads, sandwiches, homemade soups, and specialty entrees. One dining room is elegantly paneled and trimmed in white; the other features bright wallpaper. Both have a Williamsburg flair, potted plants, and plenty of windows for enjoying the tall trees around the inn. The breads and desserts at Malabar are made from scratch, and the rich cheesecake is particularly good.

The Malabar Inn is at 3645 Pleasant Valley Road, just west of Route 603, south of Lucas; (419) 938-5205. Open 11:00 A.M.–8:00 P.M.on weekends in March, Tuesday through Sunday in April and May, and daily June through October. MasterCard and Visa are accepted.

The late Charles Kelley King, chairman of the board of Mansfield's Ohio Brass Company, spent $400,000 building and furnishing his palatial French Provincial estate in 1926—an estate now dedicated to the study and display of gardening, horticulture, bird study, and related subjects and called *Kingwood Center.*

Fred Sharby was afraid of fire. Two of the theaters he owned burned flat, and he had a terror of dying in a fire. So he tore down his house on the north side of Roxbury Street in Keene and built a new one, all of fireproof materials. Steel girders, stucco, plaster, and fireproof floor tiles, doors of solid metal, and a furnace enclosed in cement walls have indeed lasted to this day without a fire. Fred wasn't so lucky. He chose the night of November 28, 1942, to go to the Cocoanut Grove in Boston and died in the fire.

King joined Ohio Brass in 1893, working his way through the ranks from chief engineer to sales manager, and later from vice president and president to chairman. After his death at age eighty-four in 1952, his will established an endowment for the development and perpetual maintenance of Kingwood. Two of the three floors of the mansion are open to the public. Perhaps the most impressive room is the formal dining room, with its hand-painted French wallpaper, delicate crystal chandelier, and antique chairs and table—a room that any monarch would proudly claim. The mansion also houses an extensive library on horticulture, landscaping, and related topics.

The grounds of the estate include twelve distinct gardens, each designed and arranged by the staff. The center plants 55,000 tulips each year, with the peak blooming season for these during the first two weeks in May. The tulips are replaced with 35,000 annuals to create a summer display. The paths also take you past Kingwood's collections of trees, shrubs, and ferns, and nature trails allow you to enjoy the abundant wildflowers. A variety of ducks and ornamental birds freely roam the grounds, and 130 species of native birds have been sighted on the premises. The greenhouse and orangery feature displays of seasonal flowering plants, cacti, orchids, and tropical plants.

Kingwood Center is at 900 Park Avenue West (Route 430), in Mansfield; (419) 522–0211. Grounds and greenhouse are open daily, 8:00 A.M.–sundown (close at 5:00 P.M. November through March). Kingwood Hall is open Tuesday through Saturday, 9:00 A.M.–5:00 P.M.; Sunday (Easter through October only), 1:30–4:30 P.M. No admission charge.

Mansfield also is home to the first new hand-carved wooden carousel built since the 1930s. Reminiscent of a turn-of-the-century Philadelphia-style carousel, the main attraction at **Richland Carrousel Park** features fifty-two distinctive wooden animals and two chariots. These colorful figures were hand carved and painted in Mansfield.

Lincoln's Last Journey

*A*braham Lincoln journeyed across Ohio in life and death, and some say that the slain president travels Ohio's railways still. Between the time of the popular vote and the formal vote of the Electoral College in 1860, Lincoln visited Ohio. It was, we are told, in the office of Ohio Governor William Dennison that Lincoln actually heard that he had won the presidency. Visitors to the newly renovated Ohio Statehouse can see the very desk at which the Governor and President-elect Lincoln sat that day. The desk has been preserved and the current governor uses it as part of his working office. The rest of the rooms and chambers have also been restored to the style, color, and furnishing that Mr. Lincoln saw during that happy visit.

Lincoln journeyed back across Ohio on the trip that marked the close of his presidency and the end of his life. The funeral train for the slain president stopped in Columbus, and the body of Lincoln lay in state in the statehouse rotunda. The educational center in the lower level of the building documents that sad event and the crowds that packed the statehouse and grounds to pay their respects to the fallen leader.

The Lincoln funeral train also gave people in the farming and rural regions the chance of a glimpse of their assassinated president. A special lead engine, or pilot car, steamed down the rails in advance of the funeral train. People came to the tracks to wait in sad tribute. As the train, draped in black, passed by, some could see the ornate coffin and the men on guard around it.

The image of that somber journey burned itself into the memories of the adults and children who stood in a final tribute along the rail line. But some say that moment was also somehow burned into the fabric of time. Each April 27, legend has it that Lincoln's train again rolls down the track. The muffled sound of the steam locomotive passes through the quiet Ohio countryside. Those who tell the tale of the recurring trip say that the dim light from the funeral train illuminates the ever-vigilant guards who will forever stand over the last journey of their fallen leader.

Music is provided by a Stinson organ, which helps conjure up childhood memories for many of the carousel's riders. Eighteen hand-painted scenery panels adorn the top of the carousel, depicting Mansfield past and present. Also open to visitors is the nearby Carrousel Works, the factory that created the Richland Carrousel.

Richland Carrousel Park is at 75 North Main Street, Mansfield; (419) 522–4223. Open daily, 11:00 A.M.–5:00 P.M. (longer hours in the summer). No admission charge; rides are 60 cents.

A walk through the Bible? That's what you'll find at the ***Living Bible Museum,*** dedicated to "bringing God's word to life." The vision for this unique museum—Ohio's only wax museum—dates back to the early 1970s, when pastor Richard Diamond and his wife, Alwilda, toured a museum in Georgia that depicted the Ascension of Christ. Moved by the exhibit, the Diamonds started planning for a Bible museum. After years of work, the museum opened its doors for the first time on August 15, 1987.

The Living Bible Museum has forty-one vivid life-size re-creations of favorite Old and New Testament stories, including a wax re-creation of the Last Supper. From the Creation of Man to the Judgment of Man, these scenes are complete with narrative and special effects. A second museum—Miracles of the Old Testament—opened in August 1994.

Kelton House

Your tours in the Columbus area may take you to the lovely Kelton House. This grand and charming mansion was built in 1852 and is a fine example of Greek Revival architecture. The home and the lovely surrounding Victorian garden at 586 East Town Street is now a favorite spot, not just for tours, but for special events such as wedding and anniversary celebrations.

The Junior League now operates the mansion, but legend has it that the home still feels the touch of the Kelton family. Fernando Kelton built the home in the mid-1800s, and it remained in the family until 1975. The last of the Keltons to occupy the home was Fernando Kelton's granddaughter, Grace Bird Kelton. She was nationally known in her own right as an interior designer. She preserved the lovely old home's furnishing in the graceful style of her grandfather's era.

The legend surrounding Kelton House is that though Ms. Kelton passed from this world on Christmas Eve, 1975, she just couldn't leave the care of the family manse to outsiders. Tales tell of the former owner returning to rearrange the furniture or move objects or just walk through the house to make sure that the current caretakers don't forget who is really in charge of this piece of Kelton family history.

The Living Bible Museum is at 500 Tingley Avenue, Mansfied; (800) 222–0139, (419) 524–0139. Open April through December, weekdays, 10:00 A.M.–5:00 P.M.; Saturday, 10:00 A.M.–7:00 P.M.; Sunday, 2:00–7:00 P.M. Open weekends only January through March. Admission: adults, $4.50 for each museum, $8.50 for both; students, $3.00 for each museum, $5.75 for both; age 5 and under, free.

Between 1839 and 1861, Ohio inmates constructed the foundation and ground floor of the **Ohio Statehouse**. Built in the Greek Revival style, the statehouse is situated on a ten-acre site donated by four prominent Columbus landowners. Greek Revival was the architecture of choice in nineteenth-century America, with Greece representing one of the world's earliest democracies. The statehouse, with its center rotunda and cupola, mimics the stature of the Greek Parthenon. The large Doric colonnades are typical of Greek Revival structures.

Construction of this significant building did not happen easily; it took seven different architects more than twenty-two years, not to mention a cholera epidemic and an eight-year work stoppage. One of the most important architects on the project was Nathan B. Kelly. He added many flourishes to the building, though his thanks was to be fired

The Lady in Gray

*I*f you take a moment to stroll through the historic Camp Chase Confederate Cemetery in Columbus, some say the Lady in Gray may join you. A grieving young woman with her hair tied back in a bun and dressed in an 1860s-style gray traveling suit is fabled to walk among the gravestones there. Visitors to the site, which rests on what was Camp Chase Union Military Camp during the Civil War, have reported seeing this sad woman, always looking down and weeping.

Adding to the legend, flowers have been placed on the grave of the Unknown Soldier and on the grave of Benjamin Allen, a Confederate soldier in the 50th Tennessee regiment. Since the site is also home to Civil War re-enactments and commemorations, the legend grows. Those participating in the re-enactments and dressed in period garb or uniform have reported either being joined by the Lady in Gray, hearing an otherworldly weeping, or having their commemorations disrupted by violent gusts of wind

So as you stroll among the tombstones, the Lady in Gray could be floating nearby, still grieving for a loved one lost in the great Civil War. The annual Camp Chase Memorial Service for fallen Confederate Soldiers is held at the cemetery at 2900 Sullivant Avenue, Columbus. This commemoration has been held at this site since 1895. For more information call (614) 276–0060.

because the commissioners overseeing the project viewed these same flourishes as both too expensive and too lavish. To Kelly's credit, it was he who realized that the design contained no heating or ventilation system, an oversight he corrected.

During the twentieth century, growth in state government resulted in the building being continuously remodeled, with its magnificent high-ceilinged rooms slowly chopped up and subdivided with new walls and drop ceiling after drop ceiling. Heating and cooling systems produced a ground floor most notable for its exposed (and occasionally leaking) steam pipes and wiring.

The Ohio State Fair

*P*erhaps the carnival rides on the midway aren't your idea of getting away from the crowds and onto the road less traveled. But visitors to the Ohio State Fair, as well as many of Ohio's county fairs, can find the simple pleasures of yesteryear if they look beyond the glare of the midway.

Visiting the animal exhibits takes you back to the time when fairs were truly a celebration of rural life. Here's an example: one of the most charming and whimsical animal competitions is found in the rabbit barn. There is something comical about a judge walking down a row of fluffy bunnies, noses wiggling, whiskers twitching, and tall rabbit ears standing up on alert. You may be amazed at just how many kinds of rabbits are shown at the fairs, from tiny dwarfs to those the size of the average dog, and some with ears that droop like those of a basset hound.

The more traditional farm animals also are a treat for all members of the family to observe. Check the daily schedule for the children's competitions. You'll be charmed by the spunk of a 3-foot-tall girl or boy showing a cow, goat, or pig that has to be twice the child's weight.

Just a trip through the barns can bring a smile to your face. The goats will greet you with grumpy "bleats," and the sheep are forever being groomed and fluffed by their owners. In order to keep the animals clean and fresh looking, some owners will wrap them in blankets, often with a signature color and the name of the family farm. It looks, to the city dweller, as if they are uniformed and suited up for some kind of sheep football game.

The modern fair is awash with food wagons featuring fried just about anything. But if you want something that will keep you in that bygone, farm feeling, just keep walking past the wagons to the Dairy Barn. Not only can you see a huge sculpture of something (it changes every year) made out of pounds and pounds of butter, but you can get a scoop or a cone of some dairy-fresh ice cream or a cheese sandwich that doesn't taste like it came out of a plastic wrapper.

A comprehensive restoration of the statehouse and adjoining Senate Building in the 1990s was long overdue. This massive project, which required the Ohio House and Senate to meet outside the statehouse complex for two years, restored Ohio's most significant government buildings to their earlier grandeur. One addition was the Capitol Atrium connecting the two buildings. It was on this site in1859 that Abraham Lincoln spoke to a small group of Ohioans about the just-completed Lincoln-Douglas debates. The ground floor today hosts a museum and visitors center, with guided tours available.

The Ohio Statehouse is at the corner of Broad and High Streets, Columbus; (614) 752– 6350. Open Monday through Friday, 7:00 A.M.–7:00 P.M.; Saturday and Sunday, 10:00 A.M.– 5:00 P.M. No ad-mission charge.

Moored in the Scioto River downtown in Ohio's capital city is a unique attraction, the *Columbus* **Santa Maria.** Built to commemorate the 500th anniversary of Christopher Columbus's historic voyage, this is the world's most authentic representation of Columbus's flagship. Tours of this historic vessel give one a new appreciation for the hardships endured by early mariners who spent months at sea on craft such as these.

Roses Are for Romance

*R*omance off the beaten path could mean treating your special someone to—not a dozen roses—but a hundred dozen! You can't pick them and take them home, but the two of you can share the sweet smell of romance as you stroll through the rose gardens of Whetstone Park in Columbus.

The park is home to ball fields and to wooded paths and ponds, but the highlight of the area is the impressive display of rose bushes, especially during the month of June, when the park hosts the rose festival. Rose fanciers love to walk among the varieties and see their favorite flowers. The casual gardener also appreciates the rows and rows of roses just for their broad spectrum of colors and light, inviting fragrance.

If you wander the Park of Roses on summer weekends, don't be surprised to see a wedding party using this as a floral background for their most romantic day. The park also hosts many concerts and poetry readings in the spring and summer months.

The poet, Robert Burns, wrote, " My love is like a red, red, rose . . ." The park can't guarantee love, but a romantic ramble through the roses could be a good beginning.

The rose festival is held in early to mid-June at Whetstone Park, 3293 North High Street, Columbus. Call (614) 645–6640 for information.

The *Santa Maria* was constructed from plans provided by the King of Spain in 1990. She measures 98 feet in length, and her 65-foot mainmast was carved from a single Douglas fir tree. Her sails cover 2,700 square feet and her rigging required 4,000 feet of line.

The Columbus *Santa Maria* is moored just north of West Broad Street at Marconi Boulevard, Columbus; (614) 645–8760. Open April through December, Monday through Friday, 10:00 A.M.–3:00 P.M.; Saturday and Sunday, noon–5:00 P.M. Admission: adults, $3.50; children, $1.50.

Looking for fresh food or just a fresh shopping experience? Try **North Market** in Columbus. In operation since 1876, the market is a celebration of food and fun. During the summer months, there is an outdoor market showcasing the best from neighboring farms. Gourmet cooks can find the freshest eggs, poultry, meats, cheeses, vegetables, and fruits. The Allspice Shop offers the gourmet a large assortment of spices and herbs. Fresh herbs are also available at Kanatas Produce.

If you want to add specialty baked goods to your table, or just nibble on a muffin while you shop, stop in at Amanda's Cake Shop, Juergen's Bakery, Delights, Tapatio's Bread Company, or Pie Place. You can even complete your table with fresh flowers from Market Blooms or a bottle of that special wine from the Grapes of Mirth.

International specialties also are within easy reach at the North Market. Flavors of India stocks a full line of Indian foods and spices. The Firdous Express serves Middle Eastern foods including a line of fresh baked goods. Along with the unique shopping experience, the market also hosts special events often featuring live music and contests.

North Market is located at 59 Spruce Street, Columbus; (614) 463–9664. Open all year, Monday, 9:00 A.M.–5:00 P.M.; Tuesday through Friday, 9:00 A.M.–7:00 P.M.; Saturday, 8:00 A.M.–5:00 P.M.; Sunday, noon–5:00 P.M.

The Hanby family and the work done at the **Hanby House** touched the lives of many Americans during the mid-1800s. This house, built in 1846, served as a stop on the Underground Railroad, helping slaves in their flight from the South to freedom. Benjamin Hanby was a minister, teacher, and an abolitionist.

Hanby also was famous as a composer. Among his works are "Darling Nelly Gray" and "Up on the Housetop." The Hanby House contains many family belongings, including the original printing plates for "Darling Nellie Gray" and the composer's flute.

Bishop William Hanby, Benjamin Hanby's father, was a United Brethren minister and co-founder of Otterbein College. Hanby House has been designated a United Methodist shrine.

The Hanby House is located at 160 West Main Street, Westerville; (614) 891–6289. Open May through October, Saturday and Sunday, 1:00–4:00 p.m. Admission: adults, $2.00; children (6 to 12), 75 cents.

Hanby House

PLACES TO STAY IN WEST CENTRAL OHIO

BELLVILLE
The Fredrick Fitting House
72 Fitting Avenue
(419) 886–2863

COLUMBUS
50 Lincoln–A Very Small Hotel
50 East Lincoln Street
(614) 291–5068

RUSSELLS POINT
Oak Island at Indian Lake
accessible only by boat
from Russells Point
(937) 843–4653 or voice
mail (800) 484–8190,
code 5883

TIPP CITY
Willowtree Inn
1900 West State Route 571
(937) 667–2957

TROY
H.W. Allen Villa
434 South Market Street
(937) 335–1181

PLACES TO EAT IN WEST CENTRAL OHIO

BELLVILLE
Der Dutchman
720 State Route 97
(419) 886–7070

COLUMBUS
Handke's
520 South Front Street
(614) 621–2500

Figlio
1369 Grandview Avenue
(614) 481–8850

Rigby's
698 High Street
(614) 461–7888

LUCAS
Malabar Inn
3645 Pleasant Valley Road
(419) 938–5205

Helpful Web Sites

Ohio Division of Travel and Tourism:
www.ohiotourism.com

Columbus Convention and Visitors Bureau:
www.columbuscvb.org

Columbus Dispatch:
www.dispatch.com

Historic Plain

S urrounded by cornfields in the plains of northwest Ohio is a unique historical village—*AuGlaize Village.* Seventeen reconstructed or restored buildings (circa 1860 to 1920) have been gathered from the area and provide visitors with a glimpse of life a century ago in this flat farming region of the state. Self-guided tours of AuGlaize allow you to explore at your own pace.

In Doctor Cameron's office, built in 1874 in Jewell, there are old medical journals and catalogs advertising medical products such as foot and ankle braces and the "Harvard Physician's Chair" rural doctors used for surgery, adjusting it to one of dozens of positions depending on the particular procedure to be performed. Dr. Cameron owned one of these chairs, and it is in the back room of his office.

The Chapel of Crosses Church, which the congregation of Saint John's Lutheran Church in Sherwood built in 1875, is a one-room frame structure containing an antique wooden pump organ. The Story and Clark Company of Chicago manufactured this ornately carved instrument in 1892.

The Sherry School has textbooks from the mid-1800s, including McGuffey's *Eclectic Spelling Book,* teacher Mable Carroll's attendance records from the 1882 school year, and a student's certificate of promotion from 1896. The mailboxes in the front room of the old post office from Mark Centre still have mail in them—a 1906 copy of the *Saturday Evening Post* and a postcard dated 1899 notifying a Defiance man that he owes the Farmer Mutual Fire Protection Association another 25 cents on his insurance policy.

Other restored buildings include a completely equipped 1903 dentist's office (containing some grisly looking instruments), the Ayersville Telephone Company with its old-fashioned switchboard and telephones, a blacksmith's shop, the Minsel Barber Shop, a sawmill, a gas station, a railroad station, an operating smokehouse, and a broom factory.

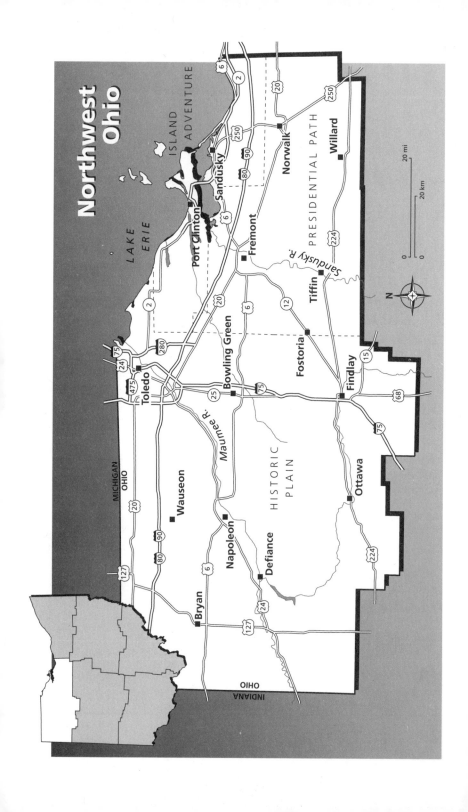

AuGlaize Village's two museums hold a varied collection of pioneer items. One building has an extensive assortment of antique farm implements, such as an elaborate, horse-drawn straw baler, and numerous fruit and tobacco presses. Also in the museum is a 1936 farm tractor, a 1937 four-wheel-drive tractor, and a rare 1919 Defiance Motor Company truck. This local auto and truck manufacturer assembled vehicles for six years until the company failed in 1925. For military buffs, a separate building contains military equipment and hardware, including Civil War uniforms, cannons and mortars, and a variety of pistols and muskets (including a 1763 "Brown Bess" flintlock). Model railroad enthusiasts will enjoy the village's building full of small trains.

Throughout its season, AuGlaize Village hosts special Events Days, such as the annual Harvest Demonstration and the Johnny Appleseed Festival. Craft experts show the old-fashioned way to dip candles and weave rugs and other pioneer skills.

AuGlaize Village is south of Route 24 on Krouse Road, 3 miles west of Defiance; (419) 784–0107, 782–7255, The village is open June through

Fountain City

Bryan was known as "Fountain City" because of its artesian wells. It all started in 1841 when Daniel Wyatt was digging a well next to his log cabin. He stopped digging at the end of one day; when he awoke the next morning, the water was pouring out of the hole. Water would flow from just about any hole dug in the area, and this liquid abundance attracted settlers to Bryan.

But the spouting water was not completely a blessing. In the 1880s a New Yorker claimed the fountains violated a patent he held, and he demanded $10 from each well owner, a claim described locally as the "Great Swindle." And some of the fountains resulted in litigation, as neighbors were flooded out by the spewing discharge. The flow gradually subsided, with the last fountain petering out in 1971.

August, Saturday and Sunday, 11:00 A.M.–4:00 P.M. Admission: adults, $2.00; children, $1.00.

A quiet residential neighborhood in nearby Defiance is the site of a former fortification that played a significant role in this region's history. The bluff at the confluence of the Maumee and Auglaize Rivers was where General "Mad Anthony" Wayne's American troops built **Fort Defiance** in 1794. Wayne launched his campaign against the Indians and British in the area from this fort, which consisted of four blockhouses and a tall stockade fence around the perimeter. It was erected in five weeks, and General Wayne, admiring the completed fortification, is reported to have said, "I defy the British, the Indians and all the devils in hell to take it!" Upon hearing that, a fellow officer suggested, "Then call it Fort Defiance."

It was from here that Wayne's forces marched against the Indians, defeating them at the Battle of Fallen Timbers. Two cannons, one facing each river, are all that remain of the fort today. When you stand on that hill, however, at the junction of those great rivers, the strategic importance of this spot is readily apparent.

The Fort Defiance Memorial is at the end of Washington Avenue in Defiance. It is open daylight hours, and no admission is charged.

East of Defiance in nearby Independence is another historic site. **Independence Dam State Park** is a long, narrow green space between the swift Maumee River and a now-idle section of the old Miami and Erie Canal. This canal, which was built during the 1820s, 1830s, and 1840s, connected Toledo (and Lake Erie) with Cincinnati (and the Ohio River). As part of the canal construction boom in Ohio early in the nineteenth century, the Miami and Erie provided cheap transportation for goods and new settlers, stimulating the economic development of the region. Nevertheless, by as early as the 1850s, the speed and flexibility of the railroad signaled the beginning of the end of the canal era.

Independence Dam was built to divert water from the river to the canal, and this section of the Miami and Erie holds water to this day. The massive wooden gates of Lock 13 at the entrance to the park are the only

Worth Seeing

Toledo Zoo

Toledo Museum of Art

COSI, Center of Science and Industry, Toledo

Maumee Bay State Park, Oregon

such gates still in existence on this canal. In sharp contrast to the boom years, today the banks are overgrown, and the former towpaths have been erased by time.

Visitors to the park can take advantage of the hiking trails, picnic areas, and primitive campsites. Fishing and boating are popular on the wide Maumee River, and the park has boat-launching ramps.

Independence Dam State Park is on Route 424, 3 miles east of Defiance, (419) 784–3263. Open year-round, no admission charge.

For more than two decades, Erie J. Sauder has had an interest in the history of northwest Ohio. First he collected antique woodworking tools to display for his customers at the Sauder Woodworking Company. From woodworking equipment, his collection expanded to include farm tools and household items used in this section of the state in the late 1800s. These were the humble beginnings of the *Sauder Farm and Craft Village* near Archbold. This part of the state was one of the last to be settled because of the 2,000-square-mile Black Swamp. Only after massive drainage and land reclamation in the 1850s was this unhealthy muck transformed into fertile farmland.

Sauder Farm and Craft Village is a well-organized, carefully presented living museum. The village actually consists of three major areas: the restored farmstead, the pioneer craft village, and the museum.

Period pieces furnish the farmhouse, which was built in 1860. Wood cooking and heating stoves, rope-spring beds, and a wooden pump organ are typical of the items found in the two-story home. Costumed guides in each room explain the history and demonstrate the utility of the furnishings and equipmenthow to use a hand-crank apple peeler, for instance. The last stop on the farmhouse tour is the root cellar, where the farm family stored its fruits and vegetables during the winter months. Horses, sheep, turkeys, ducks, geese, and chickens roam the farmyard, and the miniature horses are a particular favorite of the children.

The craft village consists of a cluster of rustic buildings, set in a circle, each housing an expert in a particular craft. Brooms are made the old-fashioned way in the broom shop and are available for purchase, while the blacksmith busily forges candleholders, ladles, gates, and railings. One of the most popular shops belongs to Mark Matthews, the village glassblower. Taking 2,000° F. glass from the bottom of the furnace, Mark adds color chips to the clear glass, then blows and hand shapes this soft, hot glass into beautiful pitchers, vases, and paperweights. As with the other craftspeople in the village, Mark explains each step of the process. Other demonstrations at Sauder's include woodworking, pottery throwing, coopering, spinning, weaving, tinsmithing, and basketry.

The village museum contains an impressive collection of tools, machinery, and household items used by early settlers in this region. A large number of old farm wagons, buggies, and carts are on display, as are farm craft tools, such as woodworking tools, and farm implements, including an 1886 potato digger and an 1860 cultivator. The museum's Conestoga wagon, first designed in 1755 in Conestoga Valley, Pennsylvania, once transported newcomers to the area. Countless meat grinders, butter churns, wood-burning stoves, and foot-powered sewing machines fill this vast exhibit space. A quilting demonstration also takes place there, and finished quilts are sold. If you didn't have time to see it all, spend the night at the thirty-three-room Sauder Heritage Inn or the thirty-seven-site campground, and make it a two-day visit.

Sauder Farm and Craft Village is located on Route 2, northeast of Archbold; (800) 590–9755, (419) 446–2541. Open Monday through Saturday, 10:00 A.M.–5:00 P.M.; Sunday 1:00–5:00 P.M. Admission: adults $9.00; children (ages 6 to 16), $4.50. MasterCard and Visa are accepted.

If you have worked up an appetite touring the Sauder Farm and Craft Village, stop in next door at Erie Sauder's *Barn Restaurant.* This restaurant is housed in an actual poplar barn, which was originally built in 1875, 2 miles northeast of its present location. Sauder saved the barn from being razed and had it moved in 1974.

Country cooking is the order of the day at this restaurant, which serves family-style dinners of chicken, ham, and beef. Or if you prefer, menu items include a selection of steaks, shrimp, and perch. The menu also offers a variety of sandwiches and salads. There are always two fresh soups warming in the large pots, including unusual ones such as Kneppley soup—a ham broth with dough drops. A generous salad bar is loaded with just about every type of salad imaginable, plus a myriad of salad fixings.

The exposed rough beams of this structure, the antique farm implements mounted on the walls, and the period costumes worn by the waitresses all enhance the rustic atmosphere of the Barn Restaurant. All breads and pastries at the restaurant are made fresh daily at the Doughbox bakery, which is next door.

The Barn Restaurant is at the Sauder Farm and Craft Village on Route 2, northeast of Archbold; (800) 590–9755, (419) 445–2231. Open Monday through Saturday, 11:00 A.M.–8:00 P.M.; Sunday buffet, 11:00 A.M.–2:00 P.M. (The Doughbox bakery is open Monday through Saturday, 10:00 A.M.–5:00 P.M.) MasterCard and Visa are accepted.

The Maumee River town of Waterville has a fine restaurant in a historic three-story building—the **Columbian House.** Painted yellow with white trim, the Columbian House was built as a hotel and tavern in 1828 by John Pray, the founder of Waterville. He insisted on black walnut for all the doors and woodwork in his hotel, which served as the center of activity in Waterville for decades. (There was even a jail on the second floor at one time, used to hold prisoners being brought to the courthouse in Maumee.) The third-floor ballroom measures 20 feet by 60 feet and has fourteen carved poplar windows and a 2-inch-thick white ash floor.

Florida, in Ohio?

The town of Florida may or may not be on the site of a Native American village named Snaketown. The tribe of Shawnee Chief Captain Snake did occupy a village in this part of the state from about 1786 until 1794, when confronted by the army of General "Mad" Anthony Wayne. But was it where Florida stands today? An archaeological dig in 1984 sponsored by the Ohio Humanities Council attempted to answer this question, with mixed results. Although the dig did uncover arrowheads, animal bones, and a 40-foot canal boat, no conclusive evidence of Snaketown was discovered. One thing is certain: Jokes about the name, Florida, especially during an Ohio winter, are guaranteed.

The first part of the twentieth century was not kind to the Columbian House, and the inn was even abandoned for a time. In 1927, however, a Toledo antique dealer bought the building and began restoration. The next owner, the late Ethel Arnold of Findlay, purchased the structure in 1943 and, after further restoration, opened it as a restaurant in 1948. Tom and Peggy Parker now operate the Columbian House, which is listed on the National Register of Historic Places.

A large fireplace dominates the entry room, which is furnished with comfortable period pieces. This room has the dark hardwood floors found on the entire first floor, and handsome antiques are scattered throughout. Each of the downstairs candlelit dining rooms has its own color scheme—in one, cool greens; in another, pale reds. The second-floor bedrooms of this former inn, while not available for lodging, are handsomely furnished and left open for visitors to admire.

After your favorite cocktail, it's time to choose from the offerings on the dinner menu, which includes roast chicken and dressing, roast pork, your choice of steaks, and roast prime rib. Seafood lovers can select shrimp curry over rice, stuffed orange roughy, or Lake Erie

Columbian House

walleye (in season), among others. Along with vegetables, potatoes, tossed salad, and fresh bread, all entrees are served with a tasty side dish—the Columbian House tomato pudding. This unusual treat is a sweet tomato concoction, served warm.

A dozen different desserts, including brownies à la mode and strawberries with homemade meringue, tempt those still hungry after the generous entrees. Lunch is also served at the Columbian House; the menu is loaded with salads, soups, sandwiches, and luncheon entrees such as chicken à la king and seafood salad.

The Columbian House is at 3 North River Road in Waterville; (419) 878–3006. Open Wednesday through Saturday, lunch from 11:30 A.M. to 2:00 P.M., dinner 5:30–9:00 P.M.; Sunday, 11:30 A.M.–2:00 P.M. Visa, MasterCard, and American Express are accepted.

Before or after your meal at the Columbian House, you may want to take the scenic train ride that rolls along the tracks of the famed "Nickel Plate Road"—tracks of the Toledo, Lake Erie & Western Railway. The **Bluebird Passenger Train** meanders through the Ohio countryside and across a magnificent 900-foot bridge over the Maumee River at Grand Rapids. Trains on display at the Waterville station include a Baldwin 0-6-0 switcher, a 1908 Porter saddletank switcher, a 1946 Pullman sleeper, and a World War II Pullman troop sleeper.

The Bluebird Passenger Train is operated by the Toledo, Lake Erie & Western Railway and Museum, a nonprofit group dedicated to the preservation and operation of railroad equipment, Box 168, Waterville 43566; (419) 878–2177. The train operates weekends, May through October, with some scheduled weekday runs in summer. Group reservations are accepted and are recommended in October when the leaves are colorful.

One of the top ten museums in the United States is in Toledo, the **Toledo Museum of Art.** Founded in 1901, the museum is a privately endowed nonprofit arts institution with extensive collections of glass, American and European paintings, sculpture, decorative arts, and graphic arts.

In an hour or a day, browse and discover treasures from ancient Egypt, Greece, and Rome; riches within a medieval cloister; and splendors of a room from a French château. Marvel at great works by such masters as El Greco, Rubens, Rembrandt, Gainsborough, Turner, van Gogh, Degas, Monet, Matisse, Picasso, Remington, Hopper, and Nevelson. The museum also has a beautiful and unusual peristyle theater, a 1,710-seat concert hall.

The Toledo Museum of Art is at 2445 Monroe Street, Toledo; (800) 644–6862, (419) 255–8000. Open Tuesday through Thursday and Saturday, 10:00 A.M.–4:00 P.M.; Friday, 10:00 A.M.–10:00 P.M.; Sunday, 1:00–5:00 P.M. No admission charge.

The first Libbey Glass factory was founded in Cambridge, Massachusetts, in 1818, a long way from Toledo. But abundant natural gas lured the factory to Toledo seventy years later, helping to make Toledo "glass capital of the world." Long a pioneer in the development of modern glassmaking, Libbey Glass made its mark internationally in 1893, when the company constructed a house completely built of glass for the World's Columbian Exhibition in Chicago. Many of the other pieces created specifically for the exhibition are now displayed at the Toledo Museum of Art.

But it's not art that draws crowds to the *Libbey Glass Outlet,* rather it's bargains. Here you will find stemware, fountain ware, tumblers and mugs, plates and bowls, canisters and ashtrays, plus L.E. Smith handcrafted glassware, all at factory outlet prices.

The Libbey Glass Outlet is at 1205 Buckeye Street, Toledo; (419) 727–2374. Open Monday through Saturday, 9:30 A.M.–5:30 P.M. (plus Sunday, noon–5:00 P.M., June through December).

Tony Packo's Hungarian hot dogs have been scarfed down by Toledoans for more than sixty years. Billing itself as the place "where man bites dog," *Tony Packo's Cafe* was made famous outside Toledo by Jamie Farr as *M*A*S*H*'s Corporal Klinger, who yearned for the spicy food at his favorite hometown eatery.

Farr and other celebrity visitors to Tony Packo's engage in a local tradition—signing a hot dog bun, which is then mounted and displayed for all to enjoy. In addition to hot dogs, diners find spicy pickles and peppers, steaming hand-rolled stuffed cabbage, spicy chili, Hungarian hamburgers, and homemade vegetable soup with Hungarian dumplings. After dinner on Friday or Saturday night, hang around for foot-stomping Dixieland jazz, performed by the Cakewalkin' Jass Band.

Tony Packo's Cafe is at 1902 Front Street, Toledo; (419) 691–6054. Open Monday through Thursday, 11:00 A.M.–10:00 P.M.; Friday and Saturday, 11:00 A.M.–midnight; Sunday, noon–9:00 P.M.

Lucas County is also the location of one of the state's most scenic parks—*Wildwood Preserve Metropark.* These 460 acres of lush natural beauty, with hardwood forests, ravines, meadows, and the serene Ottawa River, contain wildlife such as deer, fox, mink, muskrat, opossum, and raccoon. Owls, hawks, and pheasant nest here, and wildflowers such as bittercress, buttercups, and wild hyacinth are abundant.

The four primary hiking trails allow visitors to explore the sand dunes along the high ridge and the cottonwood and sycamore trees in the river floodplain. The prairie trail leads hikers through one of the last tallgrass prairie remnants in the state, where some of the grasses reach a height of 10 feet.

The elegant Manor House, a Georgian Colonial brick mansion, is nestled in a clearing and surrounded by deep, cool woods. This stately former residence has twenty-two rooms, with tours offered Wednesday through Sunday from noon to 5:00 P.M. Other facilities in the park include picnic tables, barbecue grills, shelter houses, and playground equipment.

Wildwood Preserve Metropark is at 5100 West Central Avenue (Route 120), east of I–475 and west of downtown Toledo; (419) 535–3050. Open daily, 7:00 A.M.–dark, no admission charge.

On August 20, 1794, General "Mad Anthony" Wayne's army engaged an Indian war party led by Chief Little Turtle at the battleground known as Fallen Timbers, so called because a tornado felled a grove of trees here. *Fallen Timbers State Memorial* is today, two centuries after the battle, a peaceful reminder of that pivotal conflict—a conflict that shaped the future of Ohio's settlement by whites from the East. Wayne's defeat of the Indians here, on a bluff above the north bank of the Maumee River, led to the signing of the Treaty of Greene Ville in 1795, under which the Indians surrendered their claims to most of Ohio.

Turkey Foot Rock, a large boulder at Fallen Timbers, is the subject of Indian lore. According to legend, Chief Turkey Foot of the Ottawa tribe stood at this rock to rally his warriors against General Wayne's troops.

Top Annual Events

Cherry Fest, Providence,
early May; (419) 877–5383

International Migratory Bird Day,
Magee Marsh Wildlife Areas, Oak
Harbor, early May; (419) 898–0960

Springfest, Oregon,
May; (419) 693–0660

Founders Day Ice-Cream Social,
June; (419) 483–6052

Tour of Ohio (bike races),
Fostoria, June; (419) 435–0486

Old Tyme Independence Celebration,
Oak Harbor, July 4th weekend;
(419) 898–0479

Festival in the Park,
Williard, July; (419) 935–1654

Oak Ridge Festival, Attica,
July; (419) 426–2715

Annual Kite Fly, Put-in-Bay,
August; (419) 285–2804

Great Lakes Wooden Sail Boat Regatta,
Sandusky, August; (440) 871–8194

Olde Maumee Summer Fair,
Maumee, August; (419) 893–3256

**National Tractor Pulling
Championships,** Bowling Green,
August; (888) 385–7855

Railroad Days, Deshler,
August; (419) 274–1675

Melon Festival, Milan,
September; (419) 499–2766

Flat Rock Creek Fall Festival, Paulding,
September; (419) 399–4453

Heritage "Living History" Village,
Tiffin, September; (419) 447–1221

Settlers Day, Milan,
October; (419) 499–2968

Christmas by the River, Maumee,
mid-November–December;
(419) 893–9602

Old Home Christmas, Bowling Green,
December; (419) 352–0967

Walleye Derby, Maumee,
April; (419) 893–5805

The chief was later killed on this spot, and for years after the battle, Ottawa braves would come to Turkey Foot Rock and offer tobacco to the Great Spirit for their deceased leader.

Fallen Timbers State Memorial is on Route 24, west of Maumee. Open daylight hours; no admission charge.

A friendly rivalry between Gilead (now Grand Rapids) and Providence—just across the Maumee River—lasted for generations. The Howard family settled at the site of Grand Rapids in 1822, attracted to the location by the great natural beauty and the potential for commerce, thanks to the river.

On the other side of the Maumee, Peter Manor constructed a sawmill in 1822, and Providence took an early lead as the center of development for the area. That original sawmill, along with small gristmill, was razed to make room for the Miami and Erie Canal.

In 1846 a much larger mill went up, and 150 years later, the *Isaac Ludwig Mill* still operates, if only for demonstration purposes. Most of the mill's equipment is more than 75 years old, and some exists from pre–Civil War days. River water diverted to a canal falls through two turbines, creating a combined force of 230 horsepower.

The canal era in this part of Ohio peaked in the 1850s, and when the railroad arrived here, it arrived in Gilead, renamed Grand Rapids, shifting commerce back across the river. An 1848 fire nearly wiped out Providence, and the great cholera epidemic of 1854 took a particularly heavy toll on the town, which today consists of only the mill, a church, and one lone home.

Although the Isaac Ludwig Mill survived the fire of 1848, a blaze a century later, in 1940, destroyed the top floors of this historic structure. The mill bears the name of its second owner, who acquired it in 1865. Isaac Ludwig died in 1906 and is buried in the township cemetery at Mount Pleasant.

Carefully restored and listed on the National Register of Historic Places, Isaac Ludwig Mill today offers a glimpse of Ohio's past. The mill produced flour, meal, and livestock feed commercially until the 1940 fire, and it continues to grind corn into cornmeal and wheat into flour as it has for decades. Visitors not only observe the art of water-powered milling but also may purchase the results. Water power also drives drills and saws, and demonstrations of lumber being cut take place occasionally. Even the mill's electric power comes from water-spinning turbines and a 1910-vintage alternator.

Isaac Ludwig Mill is on Route 24 at Route 578, across the Maumee River from Grand Rapids; (419) 832–8934. Open May through October, Wednesday through Sunday, 10:00 A.M.–5:00 P.M. No admission charge.

After your mill tour, come across the river to charming Grand Rapids, a town that has overcome considerable adversity. Fire has destroyed nearly every building at one time or another during its century-and-a-half history, and spring flooding has done serious damage, especially the floods of 1903 and 1913. As recently as 1957, floodwaters filled downtown in a mere five minutes, sending residents scrambling to rooftops.

Serious restoration of Grand Rapids began in 1975, and what started slowly has picked up momentum, with most structures now in pristine condition. Special events throughout the year, from the spring flood watch, which attracts thousands to view the surging power of the scenic

Maumee, to the October Applebutter Fest, add to the town's interest. Intriguing shops line both sides of Front Street.

LaRoe's Restaurant serves hearty food and relaxing drinks in its restaurant and tavern year-round. Housed in a building dating from the 1890s, this eye- and appetite-pleasing establishment is a local favorite. Tiffany lamps, hanging plants, bentwood chairs, and exposed brick walls create a nostalgic atmosphere. The works of artist Bill Kuhlman, who grew up here and now lives in Whitehouse, Ohio, adorn the walls of the restaurant and tavern. Kuhlman uses oil, pencil, chalk, and watercolor to produce his renderings of past and current residents of the area. And in a town so dominated by a river and its many floods, we suppose it's not surprising to find that the tavern features water-level indicators from some of the floods that have filled the place—water was 4 feet deep in here in 1959!

Owner David LaRoe presents casual dining and straightforward recipes at his eatery. A wide selection of soups, sandwiches, and salads awaits hungry explorers, as do dinners ranging from country ribs and steaks to frog legs and blackened redfish.

Bowling Green Ghost

*T*hose attending a theater production at Bowling Green State University may, according to university legend, meet the theater department's resident ghost—Alice.

This ghost is Ohio's version of Phantom of the Opera, *for Alice must, according to the superstitious, be invited to every theater performance. This must be a formal invitation by the stage manager, who must be alone on stage. If Alice is not consulted or not thanked after the performance, actors report that Alice is given to shows of temper such as knocking over set pieces.*

Just who Alice is—or was—also is a matter of legend. According to one of the most popular stories, Alice was a Bowling Green student and a budding actress. She was on her way to the the-ater to receive an honor as "Actress of the Year" but was killed in a car crash before collecting her prize. Another tale is that she actually was killed in the theater, when a falling object cut short her performance as Desdemona, in Shakespeare's Othello.

Those students and staff who have communed with Alice say that she sometimes appears as a shadowy figure with long, flowing hair. She also has returned in full costume when Othello *is being performed, perhaps to finish the performance that she began so many years ago. So if you attend a Bowling Green State University theater production, just be warned, there is always the possibility of a very special guest appearance by the famous Alice!*

Blanchard River Inspiration

"Down by the Old Mill Stream," Tell Taylor's famous song, was inspired by the Blanchard River. Taylor was born in nearby Vanlue and grew up in Findlay. He moved to New York City in 1897, opening one of Tin Pan Alley's first music publishing houses. During a visit home in 1908, Taylor spent some time along the Blanchard at the Misamore mill. It was this visit that inspired the song, published in 1910. Taylor returned to Findlay for good in 1922 and is buried along the river he made famous.

LaRoe's is located on Front Street (they don't even bother with street numbers in this small town!), Grand Rapids; (419) 832–3082. Open daily, 11:00 A.M.–11:00 P.M.

Standing in the Grand Battery of *Fort Meigs,* with its three twelve-pounder cannons aimed across the Maumee River, you can almost hear the blast of cannon fire and feel the rain of falling earth and timber from shells exploding nearby. The fort was under siege for nine days and nights in May 1813, but the American forces in the fort held off the British attack and repelled them again when the British launched a second invasion three months later.

Ohio's role in the War of 1812 is not given much space in the history books, but the American forces, commanded by General William Henry Harrison, twice turned back British offensives at the fort that Harrison named for Ohio's governor at the time, Return Jonathan Meigs. Harrison's forces constructed the fort in early February 1813, and this fortification became the base for 3,000 troops. On April 28, British forces began to construct a camp and gun batteries opposite Fort Meigs, four batteries across the river and two east of the fort. The British siege began May 1, 1813, and lasted until May 9.

The entire Fort Meigs fortification has been carefully reconstructed, including the seven blockhouses and the 2,000-yard stockade wall. A flat-topped mound of earth built against the inside of the wall forms a banquette (or firing step) where the soldiers stood to fire musket rounds at the invaders attacking the ten-acre fort. Some of the blockhouses today house museums describing the history of the battles here, while others contain twelve-pounder cannons as they did in May 1813. Signs aid visitors taking a self-guided tour of the fort by explaining the significance of various locations inside the stockade. On weekends, costumed soldiers set up camp at Fort Meigs, further enhancing the sensation that one has stepped back in time to the early nineteenth century. Just outside the stockade walls are picnic tables and barbecue grills.

Fort Meigs is on Route 65, west of the intersection with Route 25, in Perrysburg; (800) 283–8916, (419) 874–4121. Open Memorial Day to Labor Day, Wednesday through Saturday, 9:30 A.M.–5:00 P.M.; Sunday, noon–5:00 P.M., plus weekends in September and October. Admission: adults $5.00; children (ages 6 to 12), $1.25.

Fort Meigs

Island Adventure

Gardens, especially traditional Japanese gardens, are havens for contemplation and peace. The *Schedel Foundation Arboretum and Gardens* welcomes guests into such a quiet place. An extensive seventeen-acre arboretum surrounds a gracious home that was formerly the residence of Joseph and Marie Kreuz.

The home, built in 1888, and the extensive gardens were the beneficiary of the Kreuz's loving attention and now serve as their living memorial. They created a foundation to support the home and grounds after their deaths in the 1980s. The home features many unusual items purchased by the couple on their extensive world travels. These include Japanese silk embroideries, Persian rugs, and a Hereke silk prayer rug.

The grounds are home to a wide variety of native and exotic plant life. The Japanese garden tends to draw the visitor's attention to its stone lanterns, bridges, and a stupa—a stone memorial tower shaped like a pagoda. The landscaped grounds also host sixteen different species of pine trees, including the bristlecone pine, which is believed to be the oldest species on earth.

A waterfall, a pool, and two lakes add the relaxing sounds of water to the landscape. They also provide a home for fish, ducks, blue heron, and white egret.

The Schedel Foundation Arboretum and Gardens is located at 19255 West Portage Street, Elmore; (419) 862–3182. Open Monday through Friday, 10:00 A.M.–4:00 P.M.; Sunday, noon–4:00 P.M. Admission: grounds, $4.00; house, $2.00; both house and grounds, $5.00.

A half dozen islands are sprinkled in Lake Erie just north of Catawba and Marblehead peninsulas. Easily accessible by air or ferry, Put-in-Bay is the center of activity on South Bass Island. A large protected harbor attracts boaters, who often dock their vessels overnight.

This safe harbor also attracted Commodore Oliver Hazard Perry in 1813. His fleet lay at anchor here before defeating the British fleet commanded by Captain Robert H. Barclay in the Battle of Lake Erie on September 10, 1813. To commemorate Perry's triumph and to pay tribute to the subsequent decades of peaceful relations between the United States and Canada along their lengthy, unfortified border, a monument was constructed at Put-in-Bay. This 352-foot column, built of pink Milford, Massachusetts, granite, has a 45-foot-diameter base. It was built between 1912 and 1915 and is the world's largest Doric column. *The Perry Victory and International Peace Memorial*'s observation deck is open to the public daily from late April to late October.

First-class nautical memorabilia abound at Robert Stone's and William Timmerman's *Cargo Net.* You can find (and purchase) everything from authentic ships' wheels and massive brass bells to pottery and nautical art in this fabulous shop. Many antique pieces are available—an 1850s-vintage harpoon gun was priced at $6,500 during our last visit here. Also displayed were a spectacular 1870s telescope ($6,200) and a 135-pound ship's bell ($950), plus a World War II diver's suit. For those who hear the call of the sea, a visit to the Cargo Net is a must!

After a walking tour of the town of Put-in-Bay, it's time to explore other points on this small, wooded island. Bicycles and golf carts are two of the most enjoyable ways to survey South Bass, and rentals are available. Trams, buses, and taxis also transport visitors around the island.

About halfway across the island from Put-in-Bay (ten minutes by bicycle) on Catawba Road is *Heineman's Winery and Crystal Cave.* Heineman's offers tours of both a unique geode cave and its winery, as well as selling wine by the glass, bottle, or case. The cave, 40 feet beneath the surface, is actually an unusually large geode. Geodes (stones with a cavity lined with crystal) are relatively common in nature, but they are normally no larger than a baseball or softball. The Crystal Cave geode is large enough to hold thirty people. It was created under pressure over 4.5 million years. The cave remains a cool 52° year-round, and guides explain the history and geology of this unique formation.

After the cave tour, another guide takes you on a tour of the winery. Heineman's grows approximately 40 percent of the grapes they need, purchasing the rest from other island vineyards. From eight different kinds of grapes, Heineman's produces thirteen wines, plus fresh grape juice, with an output of 30,000 gallons of wine and juice annually. The

Lake Erie islands are ideally suited for vineyards because of the soil's high limestone content and a relatively late frost, thanks to the warming influence of Lake Erie.

On the winery tour, visitors see large presses that squeeze 180 gallons of juice from each ton of grapes. The grapes ferment in oak barrels, some holding as much as 1,680 gallons, or in stainless-steel tanks. Other stops on the winery tour include the bottling, labeling, and packing areas.

After your tour, enjoy a glass of Heineman's wine in the wine garden, which has picnic tables, a fountain, and nicely kept gardens. Cheese plates are also served.

Heineman's Winery and Crystal Cave tours are given from mid-May through mid-September, 11:00 A.M.–5:00 P.M. daily; (419) 285–2811. Admission for the combined tour is $4.00 for adults and $1.50 for children ages 6 to 11, and it includes a complimentary glass of wine or grape juice.

Across the street from Heineman's is another cave, a much larger one, known as **Perry's Cave.** Commodore Oliver Hazard Perry is credited with the discovery of this limestone cavern, which measures 208 feet by 165 feet and is 52 feet below the surface. Perry used water from the cave to fill the water kegs for his ships prior to the Battle of Lake Erie in 1813.

Along the north wall of the cave is a large lake of crystal-clear water, which rises and falls with the level of Lake Erie. The luxurious Victory Hotel, once the largest hotel in the world, pumped water from this lake for its drinking water. The hotel burned down in 1919, and its ruins are on the south side of the island on the grounds of South Bass Island State Park.

Perry's Cave is open weekends in spring and fall, daily during summer months, 10:30 A.M.–6:00 P.M.; (419) 285–2405. Admission: adults, $4.50; children (ages 6 to 11), $2.25.

The Lake Erie islands bustle with modern-day visitors during the summer season, but the **Stonehenge Estate Tour** on South Bass Island allows you a quiet retreat to life on the island one hundred years ago.

The estate is an example of the type of family farm and winery common on the island in the late 1800s. Both the historic stone farmhouse and the winepress cottage are on the National Register of Historic Places. Antiques, photographs, and island memorabilia in the house and the cottage help you catch the spirit of turn-of-the-century island life.

The estate covers seven acres. Visitors tour the landscaped grounds, as well as search for souvenirs in the gift shop. A self-guided audio tour also is available.

Stonehenge Estate

Stonehenge Estate Tour is located on South Bass Island, 808 Langram Road, Put-in-Bay; (419) 285–6134. Open daily during the summer, 11:00 A.M.–5:00 P.M. Admission: adults, $3.00; children, $1.50.

Given Put-in-Bay's reputation for nightlife and partying, the appropriately named ***Stagger Inn*** provides quality overnight lodging for visitors not ready to ferry back to the mainland. This home, within walking distance of "downtown," dates from the island's early settlement in the mid-1800s and features ornate flourishes.

The inn's guest rooms each can accommodate up to four people and share a bath. A continental breakfast is included.

The Stagger Inn is at 182 Concord Avenue, Put-in-Bay; (419) 285–2521. Rates: $56 to $95 per night.

Traveling to South Bass Island is relatively easy most of the year, with Miller Boat Line, (419) 285–2421, providing ferry service from the Catawba peninsula to the south end of the island. The company ferries both autos and passengers, though reservations are sometimes required for automobiles. Ferry service to the island is available only from mid-April through mid-November, because the island is iced-in during winter months.

The fastest boats from Port Clinton to downtown Put-in-Bay are Jet Express's hydrojet catamarans, which make the trip in twenty-two minutes. These 3,500-horsepower, super-modern vessels run circles around the older ferry boats as they zip you to and from South Bass Island. For more information call Jet Express at (800) 245–1538.

While some brave (or perhaps foolhardy) travelers drive across the ice to the island in winter, year-round air service is provided by Island Airlines, which bills itself as the "shortest airline in the world." Island Airlines is based at Port Clinton's airport, 3255 East State Road; (419) 734–3149, (419) 285–3371.

The southern tip of Middle Bass Island, which can be reached by ferry from South Bass, is the home of *Lonz Winery,* which first opened in 1863 as Golden Eagle Winery. A German stonecutter named Andrew Wehrle carved a 14-foot-deep wine cellar out of the island's native limestone. Over the cellar he built a dance pavilion that could accommodate hundreds, and by 1875 the Golden Eagle was reputed to be the largest winery in the United States.

A young winemaker named Peter Lonz worked for Wehrle before starting a competing winery. Peter's son and daughter-in-law bought the Golden Eagle during Prohibition and sold grape juice. Following Prohibition's repeal in 1934, the Lonzes built the present castlelike structure over Wehrle's original cellars and got back into wine production.

Today visitors tour the winery and sample its bounty. There are also special events such as a grape-stomping festival, a walleye tournament, and chicken and ribs barbecues. Dockage for 150 boats is available at Lonz Marina.

Lonz Winery is on Middle Bass Island; (419) 285–5411. Open mid-May through late September. Winery tours: $1.50 for adults, 50 cents for children.

The *Island House* in downtown Port Clinton proves that the good life can continue well beyond a hundred years. This restored jewel of a hotel was built in 1886 and has been the focal point of this Lake Erie community for years. But by the early 1980s it had fallen into disrepair.

But James V. Stouffer, Jr., and Associates breathed new life into this magnificent old hotel, purchasing it in 1986 and promptly spending more than $2 million renovating it. This top-to-bottom restoration has been very successful—the result is a thoroughly modern hotel with the ambience of a turn-of-the-century inn. Today, the Island House has plenty of what real estate agents refer to as "curb appeal." It's a substantial three-story brick structure, trimmed in pure white, with outdoor awnings and pleasing landscaping.

Inside, the thirty-seven guest rooms are tastefully decorated and modern. Classy carpeting and wallcoverings, often in stylish grays and mauves, can be found throughout the hotel. A massive oak bar, plenty of natural woodwork, and the original stamped metal ceiling make the Island House tavern a delight.

Chef Kent Kelley, a graduate of the Culinary Institute of America, presides over the kitchen that serves the Victory Dining Room, where fresh Lake Erie perch and pickerel dishes number more than a half dozen. But the menu doesn't end with local fish—steaks, veal, chicken, pork, frog legs, lobster tails, and much more await hungry travelers.

Latest additions to the Island House are the new executive suites, which cater to corporate charter-fishing groups. And the Madison Street Cafe now offers casual dining in a light and informal atmosphere. Sunday brunch is also a favorite here.

The Island House is located at 102 Madison Street, Port Clinton; (419) 734–2166. Rates: $76 to $130 per night for two people, depending on room and season. Visa, MasterCard, and American Express are accepted. Open year-round.

The Lake Erie islands and nearby coastal towns were once the center of champagne production in the United States, and that tradition continues at the historic *Mon Ami Winery,* which also houses a pleasant restaurant. This winery has been in continuous operation since 1870, producing champagne by the old-fashioned "method champenoise," the French technique of fermenting in the bottle.

Constructed of native stone and walnut, the restaurant and winery are surrounded by tall trees and lovely gardens. Old aging barrels are stacked behind the building and are available for sale. Natural woods, exposed stone, classy murals, and intimate spaces dominate the main dining room.

The dinner menu at Mon Ami presents delights such as slow-roasted garlic prime rib, poultry, veal, and fresh pastas. For seafood lovers, a half dozen entrees are offered, including scampi á la pesto; swordfish, salmon, and halibut with black bean sauce; and fresh Lake Erie walleye and perch. After your dinner, the dessert cart will tempt you with sweets: cheesecake topped with chocolate, Amaretto pie, and fresh fruit, to name a few. For lunch at Mon Ami, your choices include homemade soups, fresh salads, a number of sandwiches, and entrees such as salmon patties, seafood pasta, and chicken Parmesan.

Mon Ami offers a complete selection of wines and champagnes, made from Lake Erie island grapes, and a large wine store sells bottles and cases of these wines, as well as the popular champagne–celery seed salad dressing. Tours of the winery are given daily at 2:00 P.M. and 4:00 P.M. (times may change, so call ahead).

Mon Ami Restaurant and Winery is on Catawba Island (which used to be an island but is now a peninsula) at 3845 East Wine Cellar Road, just off Route 53, east of Port Clinton; (419) 797–4445. Open daily, 11:00 A.M.–2:00 A.M. Closed Monday and Tuesday in the winter. MasterCard, Visa, and American Express are accepted.

Not far away is one of the most popular public beaches on Lake Erie—the lengthy stretch of sand at **East Harbor State Park.** Lifeguards watch swimmers during summer months, and there are snack bars and bathhouses (with showers). Unfortunately, a fierce storm in 1972 severely damaged the original beach area, and it is no longer open to swimmers.

In addition to the lakefront beach, the park contains 800 acres of water in three protected harbors. Middle Harbor, with its restriction on motorboats, offers an ideal environment for the thousands of resident and migratory waterfowl attracted to the lush acreage, making bird-watching a favorite pastime. East Harbor State Park is the home of many black-crowned night herons, and a large great blue heron nesting ground is nearby.

Boat launching ramps are in the park, and a park naturalist conducts nature programs during the summer. Winter sports at East Harbor include ice fishing, ice boating, skating, sledding, and snowmobiling.

East Harbor State Park is on Buck Road off Route 269, near the junction of Routes 269 and 163, Marblehead; (419) 734–4424.

The hundred-room **Hotel Lakeside,** a large Victorian structure painted white with black trim, faces Lake Erie on a shady lot at the water's edge. This three-story frame hotel was built in 1875, with additions completed in 1879 and 1890. The hotel is part of the community of Lakeside, a 1-square-mile educational, cultural, recreational, and religious center listed on the National Register of Historic Places. Lakeside consists of hotels, cottages, private homes, shops, restaurants, and recreation facilities, which are used by both guests and residents of this unique village. A modest gate fee is levied during summer months, and with payment of that fee, visitors may use the tennis courts, playgrounds, and volleyball and basketball courts and may swim and fish off the community's pier. A nightly program of lectures, theater, concerts, and movies is offered in Hoover Auditorium during the summer.

At the Hotel Lakeside, a large yet homey structure, guests can enjoy the evening paper on the long screened porch or on the lawn furniture between the hotel and Lake Erie. The spacious lobby is furnished with wicker chairs and couches and a variety of antiques. The guest rooms are gradually being restored with period wallpapers and furnishings such as marble-topped washstands. All have the high ceilings of the era, and many come equipped with ceiling fans. The first-floor dining room serves three meals daily and offers a pleasant view of the lake.

From the pier, visitors and residents of Lakeside enjoy the colorful sunsets, and sailing lessons are available. The shuffleboard and miniature golf areas attract crowds on warm summer evenings in this family-oriented community. Lakeside may not be everyone's ideal vacation or getaway choice—those looking for chic nightclubs will surely be disappointed. But for those who seek a serene and peaceful place to enjoy Lake Erie, Lakeside may be the perfect destination.

The Hotel Lakeside is north of Route 163 on North Shore Boulevard in Lakeside; (419) 798–4461. Since the hotel is not heated (or air-conditioned, for that matter), its season runs only from mid-June through Labor Day. Rates: $65 to $110 per night; the less expensive rooms are not yet restored and share a community bath. MasterCard and Visa are accepted. (Lakeside lodging is available year-round at the community's Fountain Inn.)

Standing guard at what is known as the "roughest point in Lake Erie," the *Marblehead Lighthouse* is the oldest continuously operating lighthouse on the Great Lakes. The shallow water in this part of the lake, along with 200 miles of open water between Buffalo and Marblehead, allow howling northeasters to generate waves 10 to 15 feet tall. The crash of those waves against the rocks around the lighthouse often shoots spray all the way up to the beacon 67 feet above the water. The

Marblehead Lighthouse, built of native limestone in 1821, originally used candles for its light. Oil-burning lamps replaced the candles and were themselves later replaced by an electric light and a 300-millimeter glass lens, which make the beacon visible for 7 miles.

Although rough water often bashes this peninsula in the spring and fall, peaceful days prevail in the summer. Picnic tables near the lighthouse make this an excellent place to stop and relax as you explore the Lake Erie shoreline.

The Marblehead Lighthouse is off Route 163 in Marblehead. Open daylight hours; no admission charge.

Marblehead Lighthouse

One man's love of model trains multiplied by more than forty year's work produced the ***Train-O-Rama***. Max Timmons took up model railroading in 1952, and his family carried on his dream of creating a model train world that would exhilarate model train enthusiasts and charm everyone.

The miniature world created at Train-O-Rama is alive with two dozen operating model trains and some remarkable landscape features, 12,000 pieces of train equipment in all. The display features 0, 0-27 gauges, S-gauge, and HO gauge. Within a few feet you can pass by a whole range of mountains, see rivers and waterfalls, drop by a drive-in movie theater, and go to the circus. The display has more than 1,000 light bulbs, flickering on miniature street lamps or in windows. Along with the trains there are many moving pieces that help the scenes come alive, whether it is a farm field, a ski lodge, or the airport.

Timmons worked for four decades on his trains. His family and the visitors to his dream world keep his love for model training alive.

Judging from the visitor map that the Train-O-Rama keeps, people from around the world share Max's fascination for model trains. Guests from all fifty states and seventy-four foreign countries have all documented their visit to the tiny world of Train-O-Rama.

Visitors can begin or add to their own train sets at the gift shop. Model trains, train supplies, and train-related gift items are for sale.

Train-O-Rama is located 6732 East Harbor Road, Marblehead; (419) 734-5856. Open Monday through Saturday, 11:00 A.M.–5:00 P.M.; Sunday 1:00–5:00 P.M. Extended summer hours: Monday through Saturday, 10:00 A.M.–6:00 P.M.; Sunday 1:00–6:00 P.M. Admission: adults, $4.00; children (4 to 10), $3.00; seniors (60+), $3.50.

Four miles north of Marblehead and 9 miles northwest of Sandusky is Kelleys Island. It was originally called Cunningham Island, named for the island's first white inhabitant, who lived here from 1800 to 1812. But Indians visited the island sometime between A.D. 1200 and 1600 and created the inscriptions (or pictographs) pecked into the 32-by-21-foot flat-topped slab of limestone known as *Inscription Rock.* The rock rests on the water's edge on the south side of the island, and its pictographs have nearly been erased by erosion. Fortunately, a visitor here in 1850, U.S. Army Captain Seth Eastman, made a permanent record of the inscriptions. He carefully measured and drew in detail the pictographs, and, from his drawings, reliefs have been made of the inscriptions. These reliefs, including the one exhibited at Inscription Rock, clearly reveal at least eight human figures wearing headdresses etched in the rock, plus bird and animal figures.

Inscription Rock is near the intersection of Water Street and Addison Road on the south side of Kelleys Island. Open daylight hours; no admission charge.

The quarries on 2,800-acre Kelleys Island once supplied 500 1,000-ton boatloads of limestone annually, and vineyards, wineries, and fruit and vegetable farms flourished. At the turn of the century, the island had a year-round population of 1,700. Today, the quarries have closed and farming activity has declined, but the island, with a year-round population of approximately one hundred, offers restaurants, lodging, bicycle and boat rentals, and tram tours to visitors.

One of the most intriguing lodgings is across the street from Inscription Rock—*Kelley Mansion.* Datus Kelley built this three-story gray stone home as a wedding gift for his son, Addison, in the early 1860s. Datus and his brother Irad, both from the Cleveland area, first visited the island in 1833, and they eventually purchased every acre of it at prices ranging from $1.50 to $5.00 per acre.

Over the years, the mansion has had a number of owners who used it for a variety of purposes, including forty years as a Dominican camp. The Lemley family, William and Garnet and their son Bill, purchased the mansion in 1979 and now rent rooms in the unique structure.

Gray fieldstone forms the exterior walls, which are trimmed in ornate white filigree, and a cupola perches on the rooftop. Tall trees shade the lot, and a knight in armor stands on the front porch, presumably greeting visitors. Across the street is a private sand beach for the mansion's guests.

As you step through the front door, you immediately notice the oak-and-cherry spiral staircase in the center hall. It was built without a single nail, and it seems remarkable that this floating staircase stands, much less that it can actually support any weight. Red Italian glass fills the skylight directly above the stairs.

Other original features of the home include the tulip-and-oak hardwood floors and the Italian marble fireplaces. The Kelley family coat of arms still hangs over the fireplace in the front parlor; guests use this room for reading and relaxing. The mansion has 12-foot ceilings, and the massive 200-pound doors are solid wood and perfectly balanced. Many of the first-floor rooms still have the original shutters, which cleverly fold into a recess in the walls when not in use. The bedrooms are simply but adequately furnished, and guests share a community bath.

Kelley Mansion is at the corner of Lakeshore and Addison roads, Kelleys Island; (419) 746–2273, (304) 525–1919. Open May through October. Rates: $80 per night. Reservations are recommended.

It's a pleasant fifteen-minute bicycle ride to the north side of the island—the site of the *Glacial Grooves.* A glacier moving down from Labrador, Canada, scoured these grooves into the limestone bedrock. The grooved limestone is a trough 400 feet long, 25 to 35 feet wide, and 10 to 15 feet deep, and it's one of the most accessible examples of such grooves in the world.

These grooves were formed at a time when this part of the earth was much colder and wetter than today. Snow and ice would not completely melt during the short summers 30,000 years ago, so an ever-deeper mass of frozen snow accumulated. As the weight of this mass increased, the glacier crept southward at the rate of an inch or two per day, taking

5,000 years to arrive at the site of the Glacial Grooves. The pressure of that mass, which was up to a mile deep, carved the grooves still visible in the island's limestone. Even more spectacular grooves once existed in this area, but they were destroyed by a nearby quarrying operation.

The Glacial Grooves are at the north end of Division Street, Kelleys Island. Open daylight hours; no admission charge.

Just across the road from the Glacial Grooves is Kelleys Island State Park. The park offers campsites (rented on a first-come, first-served basis), a sandy swimming beach, and boat ramps; (419) 746–2546.

The Neuman Boat Line provides daily ferry service between Kelleys Island and Marblehead from April through November, and in July and August service is also provided Monday through Saturday from Sandusky; (419) 626–5557, 746–2261. The Griffing Flying Service provides air transport to the island from the Griffing-Sandusky Airport; (419) 626–5161. Island Airlines, (419) 734–3149, flies between Kelleys Island and the Port Clinton airport.

If you aren't ready to take the last ferry back to the mainland, stay overnight on Kelleys at the *Eagle's Nest Bed & Breakfast*. Three rooms are available in the guest house, which is separate from the owner's, Mark and Robin Volz, residence. The upper unit is a one-bedroom apartment with living room (and queen-size sofa bed), bedroom, small kitchen, private bath, and sundeck. The two downstairs units each have a private bath and plenty of country charm.

Eagle's Nest Bed & Breakfast is at 216 Cameron Road, Kelleys Island; (419) 746–2708 (summer), (419) 625–9635 (winter). Rates: $85 to $95 per night. Visa and MasterCard accepted.

Back on the mainland, amusement park aficionados will definitely want to visit one of Ohio's most popular such parks, *Cedar Point.* Situated at the tip of a long, narrow peninsula jutting out into Lake Erie, this 364-acre park delights guests with a wide assortment of rides, more than one hundred entertainers performing in live shows, and dolphin and sea lion demonstrations. However, it's the park's unmatched collection of roller coasters—a dozen ranging from "junior" coasters to the Magnum XL-200, which drops 195 feet at 72 miles per hour—that attract visitors from all over the country. For those needing accommodations at Cedar Point, the park has its own 400-room Victorian hotel and a modern all-suites hotel, both with a private beach on Lake Erie. The Hotel Breakers was built in 1905 and has rooms and suites ranging in price from $105 to $400 per night. Rates at the Sandcastle Suites Hotel are $125 to $300 per night for up to four people. Both hotels are open from May to early September. Cedar Point also has a large marina on the lake, with slips available for day rental.

Cedar Point is on the Cedar Point Causeway, north of Sandusky; (800) BEST–FUN, (419) 627–2350. Open early May through September.

If you are touring the Lake Erie islands region, you may want to make the **Red Gables Bed and Breakfast** your temporary home. The four guest rooms are in a lovely, old, Tudor-style home in the historic Old Plat district of downtown Sandusky. The home was built just after the turn of the century, around 1907.

Your host, Jo Ellen Cuthbertson, will treat you to a breakfast of home-made muffins, cereal, yogurt, toast, juice, fresh fruit, coffee, or tea in the morning light pouring in from the home's big bay window. The great room features interesting woodwork in light oak, a massive fireplace, and Oriental artifacts. Guests are also welcome to use a refrigerator, coffee maker, and teakettle.

Some of the guest rooms have a private bath and some share. Each is decorated with distinctive one-of-a-kind comforters, slipcovers, and curtains, thanks to the creativity of the innkeeper, who is a semi-retired costume designer.

The Red Gable Bed and Breakfast is located at 421 Wayne Street, Sandusky; (419) 625–1189. Rates: $65 to $95 per night.

In the heart of downtown Sandusky, in a magnificent 1920s neoclassical building that once housed the city's post office, is the unique **Merry-Go-Round Museum.** The centerpiece at the Merry-Go-Round Museum is the fully restored and once again operational Allen Herschell carousel; a ride on this indoor gem is an absolute must. But there is much more to discover in this fabulous structure, now listed on the National Register of Historic Places.

Stop by and watch a nationally known carousel carver at work. He'll explain and show you what it takes to restore neglected pieces, returning them to their full beauty. The museum offers a restoration service for collectors who have significant pieces in need of rejuvenation. Also on display are many examples of classic carousel animals, including those of Gustav Dentzel. A replica of his Philadelphia Caroussell Builder shop, which opened in 1867, is authentic down to the sign over the door, the tools on the wall, the workbenches, and the partially carved animals.

The Merry-Go-Round Museum is at the corner of West Washington and Jackson Streets, Sandusky; (419) 626–6111. Open Wednesday through Saturday, 11:00 A.M.–5:00 P.M.; Sunday, noon–5:00 P.M. Admission: adults, $4.00; children (4 to 14), $2.00.

For tranquil accommodations in the heart of Lake Erie vacation country, try a comfortable Sandusky bed-and-breakfast, **Wagner's 1844 Inn.** This fine old structure features three guest rooms, each with private bath; a Victorian parlor with antique Steinway piano; a living room with wood-burning fireplace; and a screened porch and enclosed courtyard.

Innkeepers Barbara and Walt Wagner decided the time was right for a bed-and-breakfast after their last child moved away from home. Walt continues to work as an attorney, but Barbara gave up her full-time nursing career to operate her own business. As she puts it, "Since I love to cook, entertain, and decorate, a bed-and-breakfast was a logical choice."

Breakfast is served in the formal dining room in the winter and on the porch in summer. A typical morning meal here includes fresh fruit and juice, baked rolls or muffins (perhaps the popular pecan rolls), muesli cereal, or a German pancake. Once the home of grocer and dry goods store owner William Simpson, one of the founders of Sandusky, the 1844 Inn is today loaded with antiques. Its style is Italianate, and it is listed on the National Register of Historic Places.

Wagner's 1844 Inn is at 230 East Washington Street, Sandusky; (419) 626–1726. Rates: $70 to $90 per night, double occupancy, including continental breakfast. Cash, checks, MasterCard, and Visa accepted. Reservations recommended.

In neighboring Huron, take a walking tour of the boardwalk along the Huron River. Many fine pleasure craft dock in the boat basin, and commercial vessels can be seen at the docks.

Not far from the river is the **Wileswood Country Store,** an enjoyable place to browse because of its unusual inventory. Stocked with many items one would find in an old-fashioned general store, Wileswood's merchandise includes fabric, books, wooden toys, Christmas ornaments, and glassware. They stock their own brand of apple butter, honey, and preserves, and fresh popcorn is always available, popped from corn grown at the nearby Wileswood Farm. Other offerings include leather goods, bells of all types, kazoos, inkwells, and quill pens. A "penny" candy counter tempts all ages, and there is a wide selection of teas, herbs, and spices. Upstairs is an impressive collection of Raggedy Ann and Andy dolls; next door is the delightful Marvelous Toy Company.

The Wileswood Country Store is on Route 6, just west of the bridge crossing the Huron River, Huron; (419) 433–4244. Open Monday through Saturday, 10:00 A.M.–6:00 P.M.; Sunday, noon–6:00 P.M.; open daily until 8:00 P.M. in summer.

A bed-and-breakfast with an in-ground swimming pool is hardly typical; *Captain Montague's* offers that and more. A lakefront park, beach, and pier are just 2 blocks away.

Judy and Mike Tann offer accommodations in their Southern Colonial–style home, which is a generous 6,200 square feet. Built in 1876, the home has seven Victorian guest bedrooms, each with private bath.

Captain Montague's is named for ship captain Charles Montague, who made the house famous for its grand parties at the turn of the century. Four of the guest rooms are named in honor of the Captain, his wife Sarah, son Newton, and daughter Edith.

Lake Erie's coastal communities boomed during the early nineteenth century as trade along the lake expanded. Villages located at the mouths of rivers feeding the lake often had natural harbors, and Huron was no exception. Here shipbuilding flourished, including the construction of the mighty steamships—the royalty of lake vessels. The steamer Walk-in-the-Water *kicked off the steamship era on Lake Erie in 1818, but met a tragic end when it went down off Buffalo. Huron's shipbuilding dominance ended with the construction of the canal at nearby Milan.*

The intricately carved solid black walnut front staircase and the parlor and dining room mantles are exquisite. The large gazebo, once a carriage house, offers a relaxing place to enjoy the inviting pool surrounded by begonia-filled hanging baskets and an ivy-covered white lattice fence; the Amish-built, adult-size swing set; and the well-manicured gardens.

Captain Montague's is at 229 Center Street, Huron; (800) 276–4756, (419) 433–4756. Rates: $68 to $135 per night, double occupancy, including breakfast. Visa, MasterCard, and personal checks accepted. Reservations and a deposit required.

The achievements of Ohio-born Thomas Edison are staggering—he invented the phonograph, the incandescent light, the motion picture camera, the fluoroscope, the nickel-iron-alkaline battery. In fact, at the time of his death Edison held 1,093 different American patents.

The *Edison Museum and Birthplace* in Milan provides an opportunity for visitors to learn more about this prolific inventor. Edison's father, Samuel, was involved in the Papineau-Mackenzie Rebellion, an unsuccessful Canadian counterpart to the American Revolution. Samuel migrated to Milan in 1839, attracted by the boom in shipping created there by the canal linking Milan, an inland community, with

Lake Erie. In fact, in the 1840s, Milan was one of the world's major grain ports and shipbuilding centers. For example, in 1847, 918,000 bushels of grain were shipped from Milan, and fourteen warehouses loaded as many as twenty schooners per day—amazing statistics for a town 8 miles from the lakefront! Milan's boom was short-lived, however, for the coming of the railroad and the flood of 1868 ended the town's brief heyday as a port.

The small, redbrick house where Thomas Edison was born on February 11, 1847, is just up the hill from the former location of Milan's warehouses and port. The Edison home and adjacent small museum contain a number of his inventions—an early mimeograph machine (which Edison sold to the A. B. Dick Company in 1887), phonographs, telegraph equipment, dictating machines, motion picture cameras—and a model of Edison's 1893 movie studio, called the "Black Maria," which rotated and had an adjustable opening in the roof to allow sunlight to illuminate the stages.

Pictures of Edison with family and friends like Henry Ford adorn the walls of the home, and Edison's hat, cape, cane, and slippers are displayed, as is an unusual pig-shaped footstool. Edison bought his birthplace from his sister's family in 1906 and was shocked to find on a visit here in 1923 that this house did not yet have electric lights, a situation he quickly remedied.

The Edison Museum and Birthplace is north of Route 113 at 9 North Edison Drive, Milan; (419) 499–2135. Open February through November, Tuesday through Sunday, 1:00–5:00 P.M. (opens at 10:00 A.M. in the summer). Admission: adults, $5.00; children (ages 6 to 12), $2.00.

Two blocks from Edison's birthplace is Milan's central business district, which was built around a 1-square-block park. One-hundred-year-old buildings house many of the town's shops, and the shady park make Milan a pleasant stop.

Vermilion is perhaps Ohio's most picturesque Lake Erie coastal town, with quaint homes set on meandering lagoons, sumptuous sail and power pleasure craft, and fine dining. Vermilion exudes a peaceful and prosperous existenceone of sun, seafood, and recreation.

McGarvey's Riverview Restaurant, located on the Vermilion River not far from the spot where the river spills into Lake Erie, has served outstanding seafood for more than forty years. In the summer, many families arrive by boat and use the private docks. In the spacious bar, standing rigging disappears into the peaked, high ceiling, and blocks and tackle, and ships' lanterns and wheels give the lounge the appearance of the foredeck on an old schooner.

The west wall of the three large dining rooms is glass, so diners watch the busy recreational boat traffic on the river. These three rooms seat 550 customers. The dinner menu offers seafood in every conceivable form and fashion—from the very popular New England clam chowder to the steamed cherrystone clams. Dinner entrees include broiled lobster tails, fried deep sea scallops, and the fresh catch of the day. A half dozen cuts of steak are offered, as are steak and seafood combinations such as scampi 'n' steak. Wednesday night during summer months, McGarvey's offers its "sip, sup, and sail" dinners, which include a cocktail, a choice of four dinners, and a moonlight cruise on Lake Erie aboard McGarvey's own party boat.

McGarvey's Riverview Restaurant is at 5150 Liberty Avenue (Route 6), in Vermilion; (440) 967–8000. Open Sunday through Thursday, 11:30 A.M.–9:00 P.M.; Friday and Saturday, 11:30 A.M.–10:00 P.M. Closed November through March. MasterCard, Visa, and American Express are accepted.

One other Vermilion restaurant warrants special attention—*Old Prague Restaurant.* Set in a delightful cedar structure in the center of Vermilion's shopping district, this distinctive establishment serves both Old World recipes and American favorites. The large, open dining area offers a homey, comfortable setting, and the friendly people at Old Prague make guests feel almost like family.

The specialties at Old Prague are the "Nationality Favorites," which include Hungarian goulash and chicken paprikash (farm-fresh chicken in zesty sour cream sauce). Two other popular entrees are roast duck and roast pork, which are served with sauerkraut. All meals come with traditional egg dumplings.

American dinner entrees include Boston strip steak, ham steak, grilled chicken breast, and roast chicken with stuffing. Those who favor fish can choose from a half dozen dinners such as fresh Lake Erie perch or walleye, broiled salmon steak, or a fisherman's platter. Lunch selections include salads, sandwiches, and entrees—cabbage rolls with dumplings and Wiener schnitzel, for example. Two homemade soups are served daily.

The Old Prague Restaurant is at 5586 Liberty Avenue (Route 6), Vermilion; (440) 967–7182. Open daily June through October, noon–9:00 P.M. (until 10:00 P.M. on Friday and Saturday); November through February,

Friday, Saturday, and Sunday, noon–9:00 P.M.; March through May, Wednesday through Sunday, noon–9:00 P.M. (until 10:00 P.M. Friday and Saturday). MasterCard and Visa are accepted.

Across the street from Old Prague Restaurant is an intriguing shop— the **Musik Box Haus.** Owner Genevieve Smith Clark has collected handcrafted music boxes from all over the world—Steinbachs from Germany, Sorrentos from Italy, and music box movements including Swiss-made Thorens and Reuge. The hundreds of music boxes in stock are constructed of fine woods, metals, and fabrics, in every size and shape conceivable.

Also on display is a true masterpiece—the large Porter Music Box. The mahogany case, inlaid with black ebony, white holly, tulip wood, and burl, is finished with five coats of hand-rubbed lacquer. Constructed in New England, the Porter plays two seventy-eight-note copper discs. And be sure to stop in next door at the Musik Box Doll Haus, filled with collectible dolls and clowns.

The Musik Box Haus is at 5551 Liberty Avenue (Route 6), Vermilion; (440) 967–4744. Open April through December, Monday through Saturday, 10:00 A.M.–6:00 P.M. and Sunday, noon–5:00 P.M.; January through March, Tuesday through Saturday, 10:00 A.M.–5:00 P.M.

The **Inland Seas Maritime Museum,** appropriately located on the Lake Erie shore in picturesque Vermilion, has two floors of marine exhibits, photos, and paintings dedicated to the history and lore of the Great Lakes. Navigation equipment such as ships' telegraphs, compasses, barographs, and a pelorus (bearing finder) are displayed, as are ships' bells, foghorns, and a collection of old nameboards from Great Lakes schooners, freighters, and steamers. The museum also contains the figurehead (or busthead) from an unidentified schooner, circa 1855, which was part of the Cheseborough Lumber Company fleet.

Dozens of old life rings are scattered throughout the museum, including one from the ill-fated *Edmund Fitzgerald,* which went down in Lake Superior on November 10, 1975. The lower level houses a prizewinning wooden 18-foot double-ender, built in 1937, and the complete steam engine from the tug *Roger,* built in 1913. The museum has also acquired several artifacts from the 1813 Battle of Lake Erie, including some old timbers from Commodore Perry's flagship, *Niagara,* plus a grapnel and spike from that vessel, and the telescope used by Perry's staff during the battle.

The pilot house of the 1905 steamer *CANOPUS* is open to visitors. Next to the museum is a full-size replica of the 1877 Vermilion lighthouse.

The Inland Seas Maritime Museum is at 480 Main Street, Vermilion; (440) 967-3467. Open daily 10:00 A.M.–5:00 P.M. Admission: adults, $5.00, children (under age 16), $3.00.

Presidential Path

Rutherford B. Hayes (or "Ruddy" as he was known to his friends) was president of the United States exactly one hundred years before Jimmy Carter. For a glimpse at the politics and lifestyle of that era, visit the **Rutherford B. Hayes Presidential Center** in Fremont. The center, on a lush twenty-five acres known as Spiegel Grove, consists of the stately Victorian mansion built for Hayes by his uncle, Sardis Birchard, the expansive Hayes museum, and a presidential library with more than 60,000 volumes.

The museum contains exhibits from Hayes's early career as a lawyer, first in Fremont (which was then known as Lower Sandusky) and later in Cincinnati. Hayes, in fact, was instrumental in having the name of Lower Sandusky changed to Fremont. With nearby towns named Sandusky, Upper Sandusky, and Middle Sandusky, the residents of Fremont gratefully accepted the change, as did the United States Post Office.

It was in Cincinnati that Hayes became involved in politics, and old party tickets indicate his first race was in 1859 for city solicitor. At the outbreak of the Civil War, Hayes enlisted in the Union army, and a letter from his wife, Lucy Webb Hayes, written to him while he was in the army, is on display. Hayes was wounded several times during the war, seriously at the Battle of South Mountain.

Elected to Congress before the war's conclusion, Hayes refused to leave the army to serve his term until the end of the conflict. After his four years in Congress, he was elected governor of Ohio in 1868 and 1870, and again in 1876. The museum's campaign relics include political cartoons, newspaper clippings, hats, and banners. Hayes's favorite chair, which he used while governor, is also there.

Hayes's election to the presidency also took place in 1876, but a dispute over twenty electoral votes was not resolved until March 2, 1877—three days before the inauguration! By an electoral vote count of 185 to 184, Hayes became the nineteenth president of the United States, defeating

New York governor Samuel Tilden. Photographs of the inauguration of Hayes and tickets to inaugural balls are in the museum, as is the Haviland china used by the Hayes White House. A magnificent sideboard carved by Cincinnatian Henry L. Fry for use in the private White House dining room and the presidential glassware used by presidents from Andrew Jackson through Hayes are displayed.

A short walk from the museum across the shady lawn brings you to the elegant Hayes Mansion. This enormous home has thirty to forty rooms (depending on your precise definition of a "room"), and a large front porch faces the towering trees of Spiegel Grove. Members of the Hayes family lived in the mansion until 1966, when it was opened to the public for guided tours.

President and Mrs. Hayes used all the furnishings now in the home when they returned to Fremont from Washington in 1881. Many of the pieces were gifts from around the world that they received when in the White House. Although each room has lavish appointments, the dining room, with its massive table for twenty-four guests, is exceptional. Fourteen fireplaces warmed the spacious residence, some with mantels of Italian marble, others of hand-carved hardwoods with tile insets. The 14-foot ceilings in the drawing room are just tall enough to accommodate the life-size portrait of Hayes and its ornate frame. Throughout the home are the original gas lighting fixtures, which have been converted to electricity.

The Rutherford B. Hayes Presidential Center is at the corner of Buckland and Hayes Avenues, in Fremont; (800) 600–6919, (419) 332–2081. The museum and residence are open Monday through Saturday, 9:00 A.M.–5:00 P.M.; Sunday and holidays, noon–5:00 P.M. Admission: adults, $5.00 for museum or residence; children (ages 7 to 12), $1.25 for museum or residence. The library is open Monday through Saturday, 9:00 A.M.–5:00 P.M.; no admission charge.

For collectors, the city of Tiffin is well known for its distinctive glass. That legacy continues at *Crystal Traditions of Tiffin*. This glass manufacturing company welcomes visitors to observe glass blowing, glass engraving, sand carving, and acid polishing. The showroom sells both the company's best and seconds, close outs, and discontinued items.

Crystal Traditions of Tiffin is at 145 Madison Street, Tiffin; (419) 448–4286, (888) 298–7236. Open Monday through Friday, 10:00 A.M.–5:00 P.M.; Saturday, 10:00 A.M.–2:00 P.M. No admission charge.

Fort Ball Bed & Breakfast is a fine example of a Queen Anne Revival–style home built at the turn of the century. John King, who also built College Hall at Heidelberg College and the courthouse in Tiffin, built this home. Guests are intrigued by the turret at the front of the home, its wraparound porch, and the lovely details uncovered and refinished during a recent renovation.

It took the innkeeper a year's worth of work to restore the elaborate woodworking in the parlor, the hardwood floors, and the elegant wood paneling to their former elegance. The house now boasts a variety of guest rooms. Some have private baths, others share a bath. Some even come equipped with an in-room whirlpool tub for two. In the morning guests enjoy breakfast in the dining room and set off on a short walk to nearby antiques shops and museums.

Fort Ball Bed & Breakfast is located at 25 Adams Street, Tiffin; (419) 447-0776, (888) 447-0776. Rates: $55 to $110 per night.

The Firelands region of Ohio takes its name from the Revolutionary War period. While the British held New York City, they made frequent raids against the coastal towns in Connecticut, burning homes, barns, and stores. After the conflict, the citizens petitioned the new state of Connecticut for compensation for their losses, and, in 1792, the "fire-sufferers" were awarded land on the western edge of Connecticut's Western Reserve lands in Ohio—the Firelands.

The *Firelands Museum* is operated by the Firelands Historical Society, the second-oldest such society in the state. The museum was described by the society's first members as merely a "cabinet of curios," but today hundreds of items are on display in the two-story Preston-Wickham House, which local newspaper editor Samuel Preston built in 1835 as a wedding present for his daughter, Lucy, and her husband, Frederick Wickham. The extensive gun collection includes dozens of weapons: pistols, rifles, and muskets, some made before the American Revolution, plus military swords and knives. In the Indian exhibit are moccasins, beads, baskets, and tomahawks, as well as ancient points, gouges, and hatchets.

The basement is filled with an impressive group of pioneer tools, such as a 6-foot blacksmith's bellows, a yarn winder and spinning wheel, butter churns, farm implements, and game traps. On the second floor is a marvelous wooden Indian (circa 1860) that once stood in front of a local tobacco shop and the bell clapper from the old Norwalk courthouse that burned down in 1913 (the bell melted in the heat). Period clothing and personal items from early residents of the region are exhibited, as is the first organ manufactured by Norwalk's A. B. Chase Company in the 1870s.

The Firelands Museum is at 4 Case Avenue, Norwalk; (419) 668–6038. Open weekends in April, May, September, October, and November, noon–4:00 P.M. From June through August, open Tuesday through Sunday, noon–5:00 P.M. Admission: adults, $2.00; children (ages 12 to 18), $1.00.

When John Wright arrived in America in 1843, a young man of twenty, he dreamed of one day building a vast estate similar to those in his native England. Forty years later, after acquiring 2,400 acres, he established a sawmill and kiln to prepare lumber and brick for what is today known as *Wright Mansion.*

When listed on the National Register of Historic Places in 1974, the Wright family home was declared significant as "an unusually substantial and stately example of the Second Empire–style mansion found as a relatively isolated farmhouse rather than an urban residence." But for a "farmhouse," Wright's home was constructed with many surprisingly modern conveniences, thanks to his ingenuity. For example, he installed two bathrooms with running water and flush toilets supplied with water pumped by a windmill to a large tank on the third floor. This at a time—the 1880s—when most rural residences still used water pitchers and chamber pots.

Piped natural gas was unheard of in this country setting before 1900, but Wright developed his own gas system, making acetylene in a small brick building at a corner of his front yard and routing it to chandeliers on all three floors of his home. And a central heating plant in the basement sent hot steam to radiators throughout the house.

The Wright Mansion is the centerpiece of *Historic Lyme Village,* a sixteen-structure collection of historic buildings. Tours of Wright Mansion take visitors past magnificent woodwork used throughout this expansive residence: beams and rafters of oak and intricate interior trim of walnut, curly maple, and cherry. After walking past the huge parlor doors, visitors find room after room of period furnishings, including two of Wright's pianos. A graceful staircase ascends to the second floor, which has eight bedrooms. Most of the third floor is a huge ballroom, with a stage set directly under the central tower at the front of the home.

More rustic structures make up the rest of Lyme Village. Ohio settler pieces, such as a rope bed, spinning wheel, and wood cooking stove furnish Annie Brown's log home, built in 1851 in Seneca County. Ms. Brown occupied this modest house from 1869 to 1951.

Spinning and weaving exhibits (and occasional demonstrations) can be found in the Schriner Log House, an 1870-vintage structure that was used as a residence until 1947. Other occasional Lyme Village demonstrations include blacksmithing and woodworking at the North Adams Barn, built more than a century ago.

Antique farm implements fill the Biebricher Centennial Barn (erected in 1876), a Gothic board-and-batten building with unusual louvered windows. The Seymour House, moved to Lyme Vil-

Wright Mansion

lage in 1976 to save it from demolition, is one of the oldest homes in this part of Ohio, and it served as the Seymour family home for more than a century (1836–1948). It likely was a stop on the Underground Railroad. Today it houses country furnishings typical of the early nineteenth century, including a fabulous old pump organ. Other structures of note include the Merry School House, built in the 1860s and used as a school until 1935; the Detterman Church, built in 1848 and believed to be one of only two known remaining original log churches in Ohio; and Schug Hardware, the hardware collection from Bellevue's C.W. Schug Hardware, which was in business from 1927 until the 1980s. The Cooper-Fries General Store, filled with displays and merchandise, is a recent addition.

Lyme Village also includes a unique museum—the Postmark Collectors Club Museum. Formerly housed in private homes, a converted school bus, and in a building that twice served as the Lyme, Ohio, post office, the museum has found a permanent home in the Groton Township Hall. Millions of postmarks—the "cancels" used by postal authorities to show where mail originated and to void stamps—fill the museum, the most extensive such collection in the world.

Historic Lyme Village is just east of Bellevue on Route 113; (419) 483–4949. Tours are given daily except Monday, June through August, 1:00–5:00 P.M. Open Sundays only in May and September. Admission: adults, $5.00; students, $2.50; children under age 12, free.

Railroads buffs, youngsters, and anyone who has ever dreamed of being the engineer on a fast-moving freight as it streaks across the countryside will want to climb aboard the many trains displayed at the **Mad River & NKP Railroad Society Museum.** On self-guided tours of the rail yard, you'll discover a number of intriguing locomotives, passenger cars, and even cabooses. Many of these are open, permitting you virtually to walk through railroad history.

Those who are knowledgeable about trains especially appreciate some of the new Nickel Plate Road additions to the museum's collection, including Alco RSD-12 Diesel and Dynamometer Car X50041. But anyone will enjoy visiting the RPO Post Office Car, complete with mail sacks, sorting bins, and mail crane. Inside the Nickel Plate Box Car and Fruit Growers Refrigerator Car are extensive displays of railroad models, lanterns, locks, timetables, signs, photos, badges, and the like.

And when you climb into the cab of the museum's Wabash F Diesel, you can't help but imagine yourself racing along the main line from New York to Chicago or crossing the Rockies on your way to deliver freight to the West Coast. From the cupola of a caboose, you get a feel for the working environment at the other end of a long freight, while tours of America's first dome car demonstrate how trains treated their passengers in days gone by.

An old section house serves as the gift shop for the museum. It's staffed by volunteers, many of them current and former railroad workers who enjoy answering your questions and explaining life on the rails. Be sure to ask about upcoming railroad excursions on Ohio tracks.

The Mad River & NKP Railroad Society Museum at 253 Southwest Street, just south of U.S. 20, Bellevue; (419) 483–2222. Open daily, 1:00–5:00 P.M., Memorial Day to Labor Day; weekends only in May, September, and October. Admission: adults, $3.00.

Widely known as the "Earth Crack," **Seneca Caverns** was designated a Registered Natural Landmark in 1997. Discovered in 1872, the cave was opened to the public by the Bell family in 1933.

A one-hour tour takes visitors through seven rooms or levels, the deepest 110 feet below the surface to the Ole Mist'ry River. Fossilized fish, shells, and corals are visible throughout the limestone cavern, which remains a cool 54° temperature year-round. Comfortable walking shoes are a must!

Seneca Caverns is 4 miles south of Bellevue on State Route 269; (419) 483–6711. Open daily Memorial Day to Labor Day, 9:00 A.M.–7:00 P.M.; weekends only Labor Day to mid-October, 10:00 A.M.–5:00 P.M. Rates: adults, $8.00; children, $4.00.

PLACES TO STAY IN NORTHWEST OHIO

HURON
Captain Montague's
229 Center Street
(800) 276–4756
or (419) 433–4756

KELLEY'S ISLAND
Eagle's Nest Bed
& Breakfast
216 Cameron Road
(419) 746–2708 (summer),
(419) 625–9635 (winter)

Kelley Mansion
Corner of Lakeshore
and Addison
(419) 746–2273,
(304) 525–1919

LAKESIDE
Hotel Lakeside
North of Route 163 on
North Shore Boulevard
(419) 798–4461

PORT CLINTON
The Island House
102 Madison Street
(419) 734–2166

PUT-IN-BAY
The Stagger Inn
182 Concord Avenue
(419) 285–2521

SANDUSKY
The Red Gable Bed
and Breakfast
421 Wayne Street
(419) 625–1189

Wagner's 1844 Inn
230 East Washington Street
(419) 626–1726

TIFFIN
Fort Ball Bed & Breakfast
25 Adams Street
(888) 447–0776,
(419) 447–0776

PLACES TO EAT IN NORTHWEST OHIO

ARCHBOLD
Barn Restaurant
North of Archbold, ¼ mile
east of State Route 66
(800) 590–9755,
(419) 445–2231

CATAWBA ISLAND
Mon Ami Restaurant
and Winery
3845 East Wine Cellar Road
(419) 797–4445

GRAND RAPIDS
LaRoe's Restaurant
Front Street
(419) 832–3082

TOLEDO
Tony Packo's Café
1902 Front Street
(419) 691–6054

VERMILION
McGarvey's Riverview
Restaurant
5150 Liberty Avenue
(440) 967–8000

Old Prague Restaurant
5586 Liberty Avenue
(440) 967–7182
Seasonal

WATERVILLE
The Columbian House
3 North River Road
(419) 876–3006

Helpful Web Sites

Ohio Division of Travel and Tourism:
www.ohiotourism.com

Toledo Convention and Visitors Bureau:
www.toledocvb.com

Toledo Blade:
www.toledoblade.com

Ottawa County Visitors Bureau:
www.lake-erie.com

Erie County Visitors Bureau
www.buckeynorth.com

Cedar Point:
www.cedarpoint.com

Index

Entries for museums and accommodations appear in the special indexes on pages 214–216.

Special Indexes

Museums

Accommodations

INDEX

About the Authors

George Zimmermann is the Tourism Director for the state of Ohio. Prior to his appointment in October of 1991, he was Bureau Chief for the Ohio Public Radio/Public Television Statehouse Bureau. He worked in broadcasting for twenty years, primarily for public television stations in Texas and Ohio. He spent a year in Los Angeles editing situation comedies, including "The Jeffersons."

Carol and George met when she, too, worked as a statehouse reporter. After ten years in public and then commercial television, Carol Rapp Zimmermann became Communications Chief for the Ohio Department of Youth Services. She was appointed to the post of Assistant Director of the Department in 1992. She and George married in 1989.

An inveterate traveler, George Zimmermann authored two other travel guidebooks: *The Complete Guide to Cabins and Lodges in America's State and National Parks* and *Travel Writers Recommend America's Best Resorts.* He was prompted to write this guide when he moved to Ohio in 1979 and wanted information about Ohio's attractions. He roamed Ohio's back roads for two years researching the points of interest included in the first edition. Together George and Carol add their latest discoveries in subsequent editions. The Zimmermanns live in Columbus with their son, Brian, and Welsh Corgie, Pumpkin.